A Horse-Drawn
Sickle Bar Cutter

— a memoir —

A Horse-Drawn Sickle Bar Cutter

— a memoir —

A life lived, lessons learned. How I was able to
transition from a life of hard work and little money
and emerge into a life of hard work and relative
affluence—my felicity.

ROBERT MERRICK FULLER

A Horse-Drawn Sickle Bar Cutter

Finding My Road to Felicity

By Robert Merrick Fuller

First Edition

Copyright © 2025 by Robert Merrick Fuller

Published by
Munn Avenue Press
300 Main Street, Ste 21
Madison, NJ 07940
MunnAvenuePress.com

Cover art by Gillian Tyler, Thetford, Vermont

This book was written entirely by a human author, without the use of artificial intelligence.

For permission requests, contact MunnAvenuePress.com

Hardcover: 978-1-960299-80-2
Paperback: 978-1-960299-79-6

Printed in the United States of America

*I would like to dedicate this memoir to my parents,
Barbara Lucas Fay, and Douglas Warren Fuller*

*I further dedicate this memoir to my wonderful wife
and the love of my life, the wellspring of my felicity,
Alison Carroll Parker*

Contents

Finding My Road to Felicity

*"Felicity is a state of being happy,
especially in a high degree—i.e., bliss"*

1

Fuller Family Genealogy

"All men whatsoever quality they be, who have done anything...ought if they are persons of truth and honesty, to describe their life with their own hand."

—Benvenuto Cellini (1500-1571)

I am one of approximately 35 million Americans who can trace their ancestry directly to the Pilgrim Fathers who landed in Plymouth, Massachusetts in 1620. Edward Fuller founded the Fuller family in Ludlow, Massachusetts, my hometown. Edward was one of the forty-one signers of the Mayflower Compact.

His story begins in Redenhall, England, a very small hamlet that is part of the small village of Harleston in the county of Norfolk. It was in this hamlet on September 4, 1575, that Edward Fuller, the son of Robert Fuller, was baptized in the Church of the Assumption of the Blessed Virgin Mary. This classic stone church still stands to this day. It was built between the years of 1469 and 1514. It has a beautiful stone tower 106 feet tall.

I know little of Edward's early life in England, but I do know that in 1609, he was part of the English religious refugee movement of about 300 separatists later called Pilgrims, who moved to Leiden in the Netherlands to escape religious persecution from King James I. They referred to themselves as Saints and lived in Leiden for eleven years or more. In 1620 many of these Pilgrims decided to leave for the New World—the Promised Land—because they found Dutch society to be too libertine. They also feared that if they stayed in the Netherlands, they would become Dutch and lose their English identity. Which is what happened to those who stayed. Coit became Koet and McRay became Makreel.

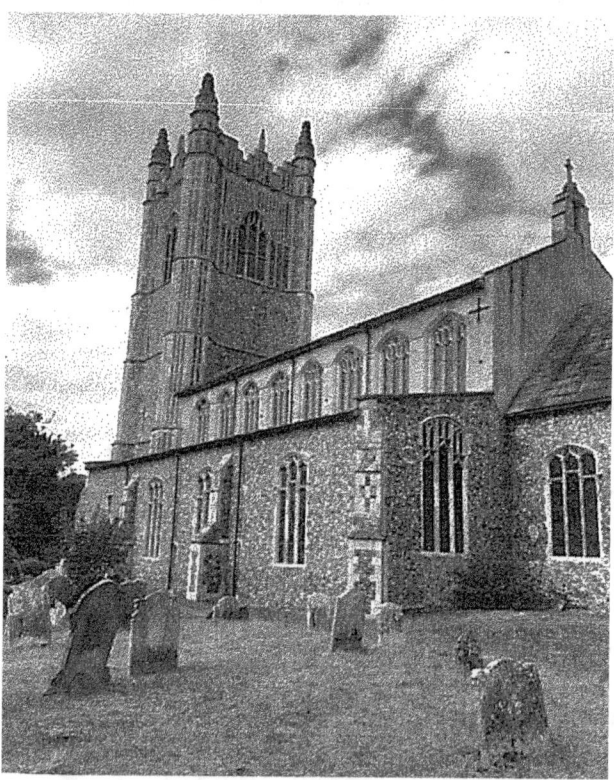

THE CHURCH OF THE ASSUMPTION OF THE BLESSED VIRGIN MARY IN REDENHALL, ENGLAND, WHERE EDWARD FULLER WAS BAPTIZED SEPTEMBER 4, 1575.

On August 1, 1620, the departing Pilgrim Fathers said their last prayers in the Netherlands in a small chapel adjacent to the wharf area called Deltshaven in Rotterdam. A small brass plaque on the chapel adjacent to the wharf commemorates their departure. These faithful Puritan-Protestants, including Edward Fuller, his wife, and their son Samuel, sailed to Plymouth, England from Rotterdam on a ship called the *Speedwell*. In Plymouth, they were to meet up with other Pilgrims and their second ship, the *Mayflower*.

From Plymouth, the Pilgrims set sail on September 6, 1620, for the New World in

 dward Fuller traveled on the *Mayflower* with his wife, (name unknown), and son Samuel. Edward's brother, Samuel Fuller was also a passenger.

Edward was baptized at Redenhall, Norfolk England, 4 September 1575, the son of Robert and Sara (Dunkhorn) Fuller. The date and place of his marriage is unknown.

Edward was a signer of the Mayflower Compact, signed on 11 November 1620, when the ship was at Provincetown, on the tip of Cape Cod.

Both Edward and his wife died during the general sickness the first winter of 1620/21. Twelve-year-old Samuel, now orphaned, was taken in by his uncle, Dr. Samuel Fuller.

Samuel Fuller Jr. received three acres in the 1623 land division, for himself and his parents as passengers on the *Mayflower*. In the 1627 cattle division, he is listed as "Jr." with Samuel Fuller (his uncle).

EDWARD FULLER WAS THE FOUNDER OF THE FULLER FAMILY IN LUDLOW, MASSACHUSETTS. EDWARD WAS ONE OF THE 41 SIGNERS OF THE MAYFLOWER COMPACT ON NOVEMBER 11, 1620 IN PROVINCETOWN, AT THE TIP OF CAPE COD.

their two ships. Unfortunately, the *Speedwell* was leaking badly, forcing them to return twice to make repairs. After two attempts, the *Speedwell* was declared unseaworthy. The Pilgrims made the difficult decision to put as many of the Pilgrims and the other travelers on the *Mayflower* as possible. Fewer than half the passengers that were sailing to the New World were doing so to escape religious persecution. Now down to one ship, there were one hundred and two passengers and twenty-six crew members on a ship 110 feet long and 25 feet wide. They were headed for Northern Virginia which included land up to the Hudson River at that time. They had maps as fishermen and adventurers had been sailing to North America for decades, and they had a patent to establish a colony there.

After sixty-six hard days at sea averaging less than two mph, they made landfall on Cape Cod near what is now Truro, Massachusetts. They knew they were too far north. They tried to sail south toward Virginia but the prevailing winds and currents near the area of Cape Cod, now called Monomoy, made it too difficult. The Pilgrims came to a very treacherous area of bars and currents called the Pollock Rip. It was so full of dangerous shoals and roaring breakers that they were forced to

THE CHAPEL IN ROTTERDAM IN AN AREA CALLED
DELFSHAVEN WHERE THE PILGRIM FATHERS, INCLUDING
EDWARD FULLER, SAID THEIR FINAL PRAYERS BEFORE
SAILING FOR ENGLAND.

turn back north.

Once back at the tip of Cape Cod, the Pilgrims worked their way along the interior arm of the cape looking for a suitable harbor. They were led by Myles Standish and William Bradford. On November 16, 1620, in what is now Truro, they discovered a cache of Indian corn on a hill. They were sure it was God's good providence that they found the corn that they so desperately

THIS PLAQUE COMMEMORATES THE DEPARTURE OF THE PILGRIM FATHERS FROM THE NETHERLANDS ON AUGUST 1, 1620. EDWARD FULLER, HIS WIFE, AND THEIR SON, SAMUEL, WERE ON THIS JOURNEY.

needed. There is a plaque commemorating the spot now called Corn Hill in Truro.

The patent they carried was specifically valid in Virginia, and because they were not landing in Virginia where laws already existed, they decided they would have to formulate some rules or laws to determine how they were going to govern themselves when they landed in this previously uncolonized area. So, while still on the *Mayflower*, the Pilgrims drew up what has become known as the Mayflower Compact. The compact is one paragraph of fairly concise words, to form a 'body politic' saying, any laws or ordinances shall be for the general good and we promise all to submission and obedience.

Of the passengers on the *Mayflower* not all were not Pilgrims.. Many were tradesmen, indentured servants, adventurers and sailors, and as such, they saw no need to make an agreement. However, the Pilgrims differed in their opinion. Of the male passengers on the *Mayflower*, only forty-one were true Pilgrim Fathers. So, it was these forty-one religious Pilgrims, including Edward Fuller, who signed the compact on November

11, 1620, before landing in Plymouth Harbor. The Mayflower Compact is considered to be one of the seeds of American democracy.

The Pilgrims spent their first winter living on the *Mayflower* while trying to get some structures built on land. Conditions were harsh, only about half the passengers and crew survived the first winter. Without the assistance they received from the local natives, they might not have survived at all. They met an Indigenous man named Squanto, also called Tisquantum, who played a pivotal role in their survival because he spoke English and was able to act as their interpreter.

In 1605 Squanto was kidnapped and taken to England by George Weymouth, an English explorer. Nine years later, in 1614, he returned to his homeland with another explorer named John Smith. In his old village, Squanto found that his entire tribe had been wiped out by disease brought from Europe.

But thanks to assistance from the local Indigenous people such as Squanto and Massasoit, the Pilgrims were able to survive and prosper. So much so that over the next seventy years, Plymouth grew to over 3,000 people.

During this period, some of the Fuller family migrated to Connecticut, and then to Ludlow, Massachusetts, about 100 years after arriving at Plymouth Rock. I feel fortunate to have traveled to the Netherlands where I visited the village of Leiden and the Deltshaven Quay in Rotterdam where I photographed the before-mentioned brass plaque.

2

Warren Fuller, Dairy Man

"A man must learn to master his circumstances, or he will be mastered by them."

—Benjamin Franklin

I grew up on a farm owned by my grandfather, Warren Meacham Fuller. He was born February 9, 1886, in Ludlow, Massachusetts. My grandfather's father, Warren Gilbert Fuller, was born on April 17, 1851. My grandfather's grandfather, Gilbert Elijah Fuller, was born January 4, 1818. My grandfather's great-great-grandfather, Elijah Fuller was also born on August 26, 1784. They were all born in Ludlow. Before that, the family lived in Ellington, Connecticut, twenty-five miles south of Ludlow. The farm in Ludlow was located at 333 Fuller Street and was occupied by at least six generations of the Fuller family. I can only assume that my grandfather was born on this farm.

I do not know which one of his predecessors was the first owner of the farm or which family member built or bought the farm. I assume that the Fuller family lived on this farm for at least 150 years. My little family headed by my father Douglas lived on this farm until 1956.

According to online research, the first home milk delivery took place in Vermont in 1785. Originally, people had cows, but as they moved into towns and houses and lived closer together, there wasn't room to keep a cow.

My grandfather was part of a long tradition of milk peddlers. I assume he was born into this profession and then continued it in some similar fashion that had been done for generations. He had a regular route each day so his customers would know when to expect him. In the 1800s and into the 1900s, there were many such delivery services, not only for milk. There was, of course, the iceman, the coal man, and many other people offering goods and services.

For several years before I was born, my grandfather conducted his milk delivery business with an enclosed horse-drawn wagon with step-through doors on either side. There was a windshield in the front with two small holes at the top where the reins went through to the horse. In the rear, there was a section where he carried his milk in cans. My father

THE 150-YEAR-OLD FARMHOUSE, LOCATED AT 333 FULLER STREET IN LUDLOW, MASSACHUSETTS, WHERE I LIVED UNTIL THE AGE OF 10. (ORIGINALLY PUBLISHED BY THE LUDLOW BICENTENNIAL COMMITTEE, LUDLOW, MA, 1978)

told me stories about my family's home-delivery milk business when he was growing up. His father milked his own cows, put the milk in cans, and then drove around ringing a bell. Customers would hail him, and he would ladle his milk from his container into his customers' containers. I assume he was following the example of his forefathers.

In the 1930s, my grandfather, known to all the grandchildren as "Push," decided it was time to upgrade his milk business. In 1929, some communities in Massachusetts were requiring milk to be pasteurized for public safety reasons. He saw the trend and wanted to assure his customers that his milk was safe. So, my grandfather sold his cows and built a small dairy processing plant off the north side of his barn.

A favorite early memory of mine was driving with Grandfather Push in his 1946 Chevrolet pickup truck in the early 1950s, with his English Setter named Jack on the floor between us. Push smoked a pipe, and from time to time, he would strike one of his large wooden matches to relight his pipe. He kept his matches and his pipe in the dashboard ashtray of the truck. Sometimes he would strike a match and just wave it around the cab. I asked him once why he did this. He said it was because his dog liked the strong sulfur smell. After witnessing this behavior a few times, it eventually occurred to me that he wasn't trying to please the dog with the sulfur smell, he was trying to mask the smell of a fart!

I loved these rides with Push. He drove slowly from one small farm to another around the most rural parts of Ludlow. Stopping in the dooryard of these farms, he would spend a few minutes catching up on the latest scuttlebutt with each farmer. Then he and the farmer would unload clean empty cans and load up the truck with cans full of fresh milk. All these farms had between sixteen and twenty milking cows. Normal for the times. After milking, the milk was put in twenty or forty-quart cans and set in a large cold water bath until they were picked up. The cooled cans were then loaded into the back of the truck. After some farewell chitchat, we would continue to the next small farm to repeat the interaction until the back of the truck was full of cans of fresh milk.

I'm sure there was much more complexity to his day than my small mind could fully grasp at the age of five or six. Back at the dairy, the milk was unloaded and poured into a large pasteurization tank where it was heated to 160° and held there for fifteen minutes. After being pasteurized, the milk was rapidly chilled to 39° by running it over a large refrigerated panel that looked like a big washboard. The chilled milk flowed into a large round filling hopper that was constantly turning during the filling process. Clean sanitized glass bottles, moving on a stainless-steel conveyor, went under the filling hopper. There they were mechanically pushed up to the spring-loaded filling valves. As the bottles circled under the hopper like riding on a merry-go-round, they were filled with cold milk. After completing their turn around the carousel, they proceeded to the paper cap machine, and then a transparent cellophane safety seal was applied and held in place by a thin piece of paper tape. The bottles were eventually packed in wooden milk crates by hand. The cases were stacked two by two on a metal dolly equipped with swiveling caster wheels. When the stacks were five cases high, they were pushed and pulled into the walk-in cooler, where they were kept overnight before being delivered to our customers the next day.

Occasionally, we were lucky enough to be in the milk house at the end of the day when everything was being cleaned up. We were lucky because some of the milk always froze to the side of this chiller. When the chiller was shut down, the frozen chunks of milk on the edge of the chiller could be lifted off. If our timing was right, we might get a piece of this iced milk given as a special treat.

It was common in this dairy that if a man had to relieve himself, he stepped outside the back door, and passed the steam boiler to do his peeing in the weeds. My father mentioned to me one day that if I took a

184 A History of Ludlow, Massachusetts, 1774–1974

Warren M. Fuller, Ludlow Dairyman and Owner of Fuller's Dairy.
(Photo around 1920).

MY GRANDFATHER, WARREN FULLER, WITH HIS HORSE-DRAWN
MILK DELIVERY WAGON. HE MILKED HIS OWN COWS AND
THEN LADLED MILK FROM THE WAGON INTO HIS CUSTOMERS'
CONTAINERS. (ORIGINALLY PUBLISHED BY THE LUDLOW
BICENTENNIAL COMMITTEE, LUDLOW, MA, 1978)

half pint of chocolate milk out there with me and drank it as I was peeing it would feel like the chocolate milk was going right through me. I tried it one day and decided he was right. I did feel like it was passing right through me!

The farm I grew up on had not had cows in the barn for decades, only empty stations that sat unused for so long there was no longer any cow smell in the barn. My mother told me that more than once when Push looked at old photographs of his cows in the pasture, he would talk nostalgically about how he missed them. I'm sure he did miss having them. This was a time when farmers had relationships with their small herds of cows, many of whom had unique personalities. Nevertheless, Push was probably better off without them. Keeping a small herd of cows is a lot of work and worry, plus they must be fed and milked twice a day, seven days a week. There are no days off.

My grandfather Push told me stories about socializing in the pre-automobile world he grew up in. Socializing was fit into busy days only after the day's chores were done. This usually happened on the weekend. My grandfather liked to tell a story about when he was courting his first wife Alice. On a Saturday night, he would drive his horse-drawn buggy to her town nearby and they would attend a square dance together. On the way home, which might have been six or seven miles, he would fall asleep. The horse, knowing the way home, would continue until it arrived in the farmyard. After it arrived, the horse would come to an abrupt halt and the jolt would wake up Push! When he realized he was home, he would unharness the horse and head to bed.

Sometime in the 1930s, my grandfather decided to transition from horse-drawn carts to open pickup trucks. The trucks at that time were not especially reliable, especially in the colder months. After two or three years, my grandfather decided he was fed up with these unreliable trucks, and decided to return to good, old reliable horses.

My father told me stories about this going back to the horses experiment. He remembered going into the barn early on winter mornings when it was very cold outside to get the horses harnessed up and ready to work. He said it was clear that the horses did not want to leave the relative warmth of the stable, so in protest, they would start farting. My father said they farted so much the air would turn blue! After about six months of putting up with these reluctant work horses, my grandfather decided it was time to give internal combustion engines another chance, and the horses were sold to a neighbor. Reverting to old methods may have its appeal in memory but in actual application, it may not hold up to expectations.

In the 1950s it was generally accepted that as a result of proper pasteurization and refrigeration, milk could be delivered every other day instead of every day. The routes we had were split up into two groups. Group A would get deliveries on Mondays, Wednesdays, and Fridays and Group B would get their deliveries on Tuesdays, Thursdays, and Saturdays. For the first time ever, everyone on the Fuller farm would get Sundays off. This was a major shift in the way business had been done, and as far as I know, it worked quite well for all concerned.

Also in the 1950s, all farms were being strongly encouraged by the milk haulers to have a refrigerated bulk tank instead of cans to store their milk production. These bulk tanks were very expensive, and as a result, many small farms all over New England simply went out of business because they could not afford this additional expense.

3

My Early Life

My mother and her two sisters grew up as young adults at 12 Rood Street in Ludlow, about a mile from the farm where my father grew up. My father must've known three attractive women were living there. One Saturday, he just walked up and knocked on the front door and asked if there was anyone there who would like to go out on a date. My aunt Caroline answered the door. She already had plans, so she turned to her sister and said, "Hey Barbara, Doug Fuller is here and he's looking for someone who wants to go out on a date. Are you busy?"

I assume they fell in love quickly. My mother was twenty-five years old when she married my father. You can see from some of the early photos I have of her that she was very fashion-conscious. She did tell me at one point that her ideal job would've been as a women's clothing buyer for one of the large department stores in downtown Springfield, like Stiger's or Forbes and Wallace. I think getting married and pregnant very quickly and moving into a 150-year-old farmhouse meant that dream had to be forfeited.

Many years later, I asked my father why he got married when he did. He said, "Well I was twenty-nine years old and I figured if I was going to have a family, I had better get started." When he told me this, it sort

My father, Douglas Fuller sometime around 1940, before meeting my mother. A pretty dashing guy, I would say!

of shattered my Hollywood movie idea of love and romance. It seemed like such a practical and unemotional decision. I had always assumed that you met someone that you fell in love with, and that's why you got married. I think I decided at that moment that if he could wait till he was twenty-nine to get married, so could I.

I guess the stars were in alignment because on February 28, 1943, they were married. They must've gotten busy right away because my brother Douglas was born two months premature on October 28, 1943, while our mother was visiting family friends in Worcester, Massachusetts. I know she was surprised and disappointed that she had to give birth to her first child in a strange town without her immediate family and family doctor close by. My brother also had to spend some time in an incubator at the hospital in Worcester, another situation my mother had not planned. Meanwhile, her husband was sending letters from the South Pacific, where he was stationed during the Second World War. He did not hold his first son until a year and a half later.

I was born on June 8, 1946, at 8:20 a.m., right at the very beginning of the population wave of what would become known as the Baby boom. For me, it was a good time to be born.

My very first memory involved being potty trained. I must've been about two or two and a half years old. My mother had a little potty-training seat that sat on top of the regular toilet. She had to lift me to sit on it. It was a wooden frame with a backrest and armrests. It had a plastic seat with a little, pear-shaped rubber funnel mounted under the front of the seat. Sitting there, looking down, I could watch my pee go into that funnel, swirl around, and then disappear between my legs. I was mesmerized by this swirling—round and around and gone. Consequently, I loved potty training.

When World War II ended, America emerged as an industrial and innovative powerhouse. My life in Ludlow was bucolic, even if it was lower middle class. Much of my early childhood was spent outdoors, exploring and playing. As a very young child, I was allowed to be largely carefree. But my life growing up was like living in two worlds at once. I had one foot in the old farming tradition that had been practiced on this farm for six generations, and the other foot in the rapidly changing post–World War II world.

MY MOTHER, BARBARA LUCAS FAY, AROUND 1940, BEFORE MEETING MY FATHER. YOU CAN SEE SHE WAS VERY FASHION-CONSCIOUS.

The farm I grew up on had been occupied by the Fuller family for 150 years. In fact, many of the buildings on our farm and many similar farms in our area were at least 100 years old. They were built for a type of farming that was quickly disappearing in the mid-twentieth century. The post–World War II world was about to shake the foundations of these century-old buildings. As farming changed, these old farm buildings fell into disuse. Eventually, after years of abandonment, they were dismantled or destroyed. Not one of the barns that I grew up near survived.

Factories that had been making bombs during the war switched to making fertilizers which could dramatically increase farmers' yields. It would be years before people started to worry about the effects of these chemical fertilizers and pesticides on the land, the groundwater, and our long-term health. For hundreds of years before the twentieth century, all farming was organic. It wasn't until people started to become more aware of the negative aspects of artificial fertilizers and pesticides that small-scale farming, in particular, started to turn back to more organic practices.

Bigger tractors and their implements, like high-speed mowers and conditioners, bailing machines, faster milking equipment, and other innovations that came along with them were also completely transforming the farming that had been practiced in my hometown for the previous 200 years. Lucky for me I was able to witness an older type of farming that was still being practiced by the Bator family that lived right across the street.

The farm at 333 Fuller Street was part of the neighborhood where I grew up. It was part of a small cluster of five homes that comprised my world, which was only about three miles from the main downtown area of Ludlow adjacent to the Chicopee River where the remnants of the once mighty Ludlow Manufacturing Company were located and also where most of the commercial activity, the schools, the post office, markets, shops, and banks were located. "Downtown" was an alien world to me. I only went there for school and then back to the "sticks." Downtown was a little frightening for me because most of the kids my age who lived there grew up in a world that was more rough and tumble than the world I grew up in.

For example, when I was about eleven years old, I was outside the local downtown movie theater on Friday night waiting for my parents to pick me up after a movie when a group of town ruffians came by and one of them said he wanted to fight me. I had never been challenged like that before and didn't know what to make of it. When I refused to fight, he punched me in the face. Then he stood there with his three friends behind him, saying, "Come on, fight." I made no attempt to defend myself. So, he and his friends walked off laughing at me. This was a frightening and confusing interaction for me. I couldn't understand why someone would want to fight me for no reason. If I had had three friends standing next to me, perhaps he wouldn't have challenged me. This was not the world I grew up in, and I really didn't know how to react.

Our farm was "in the country." Our country neighborhood was its own little world for me, everything else was "over there."

The house directly across the street was the home of my father's sister, my Aunt Orrice, and her husband, Uncle Jim. There were also three cousins there, Bruce, Priscilla, and Patty. My grandfather Push had given the land to his daughter and son-in-law. They built a beautiful brick house with a one-car garage, a living room with a real fireplace, and a big picture window facing to the east that had a very pleasant view of a beautiful meadow behind the house. The house still stands to this day. The brick that was used to build the house was recycled from the demolition of some unused Ludlow manufacturing buildings. In 1949 the 274-foot brick smokestack was demolished.

My father riding a World War II Indian motorcycle
in Papua New Guinea, 1944.

Another home just to the south of our farm was a single-family home owned by Al and Dot Pobieglo, and their three children Ronnie, Cheryl, and Jeffrey. My neighbor Cheryl and my across-the-street cousin Patty were closest to me in age. As a result, we spent a lot of time together as children. There were several indoor and outdoor games that we created to amuse ourselves. Building forts, picking berries, swinging, swimming, picking flowers, climbing trees. In winter there was always sledding and ice-skating on the small ponds between our homes. When we were hungry, all we had to do was go into one of our three homes where our mothers would make us grilled cheese sandwiches and serve glasses of cold milk or hot chocolate.

Summers were the longest and most fun-filled time of the year, especially when I was very young. There were many favorite summertime activities that I remember fondly. When school let out in mid-June with ten weeks of vacation ahead, in my mind, summer would just stretch on forever.

My favorite spot was a small section of stone-walled field about a quarter of a mile up the slope behind our farm barn, sometimes used for pasture, but mostly unused. It had lots of low-growing juniper bushes and boulders too to move. It was a great place to play hide and seek or tag, and to build forts. We would crouch behind the stone walls pretending to fend off imaginary attackers, imitating what we imagined our father had done during the war.

Sometimes, we would have a picnic lunch there and lie in the warm grass looking for animal shapes in the clouds, soaking up the pure simple joys of childhood. It was a safe pretend place where we were living a kind of great adventure. We called this area Camp Devens after an Army training camp in central Massachusetts established in 1917 as a troop training site for WWI. My father might have done some of his World War II training at the site, which explains why we knew about it and why we used the name.

It was my older cousin Bruce who gave our grandfather the name Push. When Bruce was very young, he was in the dairy with our grandfather who was trying to give him some direction on how to push a dolly of milk. Our grandfather said, "Push, Bruce, push." Bruce couldn't say Warren or Grandpa but he could say push. So, Grandpa became Push. All the younger children followed his example, so Push became his name for all the grandchildren and the other children in the neighborhood.

Bruce was also responsible for the childhood name of our grandmother. Her real name was Ethel, but he had trouble pronouncing her name, so she became "Eshew." All the children knew

MY PARENTS WEDDING PORTRAIT,
FEBRUARY 28, 1943.

her by this name and only this name. My mother and father were called Uncle Doug and Aunt Barbara by all the children in the neighborhood.

Our grandfather Push was a study of the classic old Yankee: a self-reliant, hard-working man who did not suffer fools. He was well-liked, and I'm sure he was proud of his accomplishments. He ran his own business, kept a hunting dog, and was a very avid hockey fan. He was active in the Grange Hall, where he performed in different kinds of theatrical skits, minstrel, or vaudeville shows. He also was a member of the grange baseball team.

One day when I was five or six years old and we were jousting about in the yard, Push said, "I'm going to catch you." I was thinking, he was too old and slow and so I said, "You can't catch me." I started to run away laughing, but I was wrong. He was faster than me and when he did catch me, there was an element of anger in his grip on my arm that scared me just a little bit and made me realize I had hurt his feelings. I felt sorry about that after I had some time to think about it. No one wants to be told they are too old before they have come to the realization for themselves.

My father told me that he and his father used to wrestle on a dairy platform that was used to load milk into the pickup trucks. One day, my father got the best of his father and tossed him off the platform. My father said after that, there was no more wrestling between the two of them.

The early 1950s were a carefree time for me to explore, play, and learn to enjoy the pleasures of a tranquil, secure, domestic farm life. A lot of my time was spent with my next-door neighbor Cheryl, and my cousin from across the street, Patty. We had great fun exploring the old barn behind our house. In the upper reaches of the barn, there were a couple of old horse-drawn wagons and a sleigh that had not been used in decades. There were several wooden trunks containing old vintage clothing and reading glasses. I loved these kinds of discoveries, a little bit like a treasure hunt, and always entertaining. We enjoyed imagining ourselves using these vintage items, for some kind of dress-up event but we never did.

We spent time building hiding places under spruce trees in our yard where we thought no one could see us. We could do imaginary secret things even though we didn't have any secret ideas, these ideas were only make-believe. It was great fun and of course completely harmless. When we got tired or cold, we would go home for a hot meal.

In May and June, I remember picking wild black-capped raspberries that grew along the edges of the farm road we called the "cow path" that led to the more elevated fields at the western edge of our farm. As a child, I picked these black-capped raspberries because they were plentiful and nearby. I thought the big bright red cultivated raspberries for sale in the markets were superior, but they were expensive and the blackcaps were free. To this day, whenever I find a small patch of wild black-capped raspberries—they only grow wild—they bring back these powerful, olfactory childhood memories. There was also one large patch of wild blackberry bushes about half a mile up the cow path. Blackberry bushes are quite tall and have canes and large thorns, making them difficult to pick for a child. Add to that the fact that I didn't really like their taste and their seeds are quite large. As a result, I did not spend a lot of time picking wild blackberries.

In July, we would be sent in groups of three or four to the upper western reaches of the farm to pick wild blueberries. As a young child, this was an arduous task. It was a very long walk—at least it seemed like it—and we were never sure if the blueberries were going to be plentiful or not. These were wild high-bush blueberries, and being a small child at the time made them difficult to reach. Having my older, taller cousin Bruce along made it a little easier. He would pull higher branches down to my level.

My favorite berry-picking container was a Swift's Silverleaf lard can because it had a nice metal hoop handle that made it easy to carry. This was a large can; I don't think I ever got my can much more than half full. Eventually, after some difficult picking, we had to face the long walk home. On this walk, it wasn't uncommon for half the picked blueberries to be eaten before we got home. But there were usually enough left to make some blueberry muffins or pancakes.

I did manage to get into mischief from time to time. There was a time when a neighborhood boy named Billy from the farm next door and I started playing with matches and dry hay. We were in the lower section of the barn behind our house. This low section of the barn was wide open on one side and was used to store old farm equipment. There was maybe half a bale of old dry hay in a wheelbarrow. We started small at first. We would start a small pile of hay on fire and then put it out quickly. Then we started making some bigger piles. Later, we made some little trails

of dry grass, lighting them on fire and watching the fire creep along the trail from one end to the other. Ultimately, we made one of these hay trails go up over the old wheelbarrow. When the flames got to the wheelbarrow, I think we both realized immediately that things were getting out of hand.

We had to take off our coats to beat out the fire. After the fire was out, we were exhausted and frightened by this experience, realizing that we had almost lost control of the situation. We had created quite a bit of smoke and were

My parents with my brother, Douglas, just after my father returned from the South Pacific, around 1945.

very shaken by the experience. After making sure all the fire was extinguished, Billy decided it was time to go home for lunch. I decided it was time to go next door and play with my friend Cheryl.

Cheryl's mother Dot answered the door when I knocked without any noticeable alarm. I asked her if Cheryl was at home and if I could come in and play. She said okay. We were playing for a few minutes when Dot, looking out her kitchen window, commented that there was quite a bit of smoke hovering around the base of our barn, which was about 100 yards away. I pretended to be clueless.

Then she said that she could see my mother and my grandmother investigating the smoke under the barn. I pretended innocence.

After a few more minutes, the phone rang. Dot answered the phone, and I heard her say, "Yes, he is." She looked at me sternly and said, "That was your mother on the phone, and she would like you to come home right now."

I knew the jig was up, but there really wasn't anything else I could do. I went home and my mother and my grandmother questioned me quite thoroughly about the burned hay and smoke in the barn.

I had no alternative but to fess up and admit that Billy and I had been responsible. I said, "I'm sorry," profusely, with little or no effect. My mother and grandmother were upset, of course, explaining to me that I could've burned the entire barn down.

My mother then took me to our apartment upstairs and told me to sit on the couch. A few minutes later, she came out with her favorite disciplinary tool, a large hairbrush. She held me by the arm and started to paddle my behind as hard as she could. I remember it was quite painful, and I cried quite a bit. I promised I would never play with matches again.

She then told me to stay on the couch in the living room until my father got home. It was a long wait. About three hours later, I heard my father come into the kitchen. I heard my mother talking to him, and I heard him raise his voice and say something like "What? He did what?"

My father then came into the living room where I was sitting. I tried my best to look remorseful with the hopes that he would have pity on me. The rage on his face told me otherwise. It was the only time in my life I saw him take off his wide leather belt. I knew I was in for a good whipping. No amount of begging was going to save me. I screamed and begged, and I tried to hide behind the couch to avoid my punishment. All of my tactics were unsuccessful. My father pulled me up by my arm with one hand and pulled my pants down with his other hand. He whipped my behind with his doubled-up belt, the most painful disciplinary action I ever felt, and the longest. Then he told me to sit down, which was difficult because my butt hurt so much. He then lectured me with very stern language about not playing with matches, and if I ever did anything like that again, the punishment I just received would seem minor. I can tell you now that the lesson was well taken, and I most certainly never played with matches again anywhere near a barn. I can't say I never misbehaved again. But I never again had to suffer that kind of disciplinary action.

Our life working a small dairy farm-milk delivery business was an anachronism in the early 1950s. After the war, the pace of change for this type of business was accelerating. Even as a small child, I could sense it. Just like the collapse of the natural ice business in 1920, the home-delivery business for milk and other products was slowly coming to its natural end in the '50s.

It was during this time that Dwight Eisenhower initiated the interstate highway system. The Massachusetts Turnpike, Interstate 90, was built right through the middle of Ludlow in the mid-50s. It was disruptive but also exciting. Soon, we would be able to drive to Boston in one hour instead of three.

Large factories all over the country had converted from wartime

THIS IS THE WAY THE BATOR FAMILY BROUGHT THEIR HAY FROM THE
FIELD BACK TO THEIR BARN. NO BAILED HAY—IT WAS ALL LOOSE.

production to churning out cars, trucks, airplanes, and all kinds of con-
sumer goods at a blistering pace. The world also now had atomic bombs.
In school, we routinely practiced air raid drills where we hid under our
desks pretending to protect ourselves, which, of course, we now know
was ludicrous.

The dairy farm I grew up on, like most of the dairy farms in our
town, was from a previous age, as their roots were still in the nineteenth
century but their branches were waving in the twentieth century. Trying
to preserve these traditions for future generations was like trying to hold
back a river with a snow shovel. They may not have known it then, but
their days were numbered. Within ten years, most would be gone within
fifteen years they were all gone.

By 1970, home milk delivery had become largely a thing of the past;
people bought their milk at supermarkets in plastic gallon jugs. During
this time the economy was prospering, and the country was growing.
There was a palpable sense of relief after so many years of depression,
and the wartime rationing of things like gasoline, flour, and sugar, faded

into the past.

With the end of World War II, the population was generally at ease, and this made life a lot easier to enjoy. Oh yes, there was polio, but we all got vaccinated. The measles vaccine was a reality also, but all these vaccines were welcomed as modern advances in controlling these dreaded childhood diseases. There was the Korean War, from 1950 to 1953 but I heard little about this in my childhood. Yes, the Soviet Union had the bomb, but the Cold War hadn't really started yet, or at least the effects had not reached my little world.

Most Americans were feeling positive about the future. Although it is conjecture on my part, I believe my father was not feeling very positive about his future. Unfortunately, my father did not live long enough for me to find out how he really felt about his future after returning from the war. That's because when he returned, he was expected by his father to resume his position in the family business.

However, he did not relish the idea of going back to the dairy delivery lifestyle of his youth. He was an adult now, with a wife and two young boys. He had seen some of the wider world and the horrors of war. The thought of going back to what he had been doing since childhood did not hold any great charm for him. It felt to him, like a step backward rather than a step forward.

At some level, my father also realized that the future of the home milk delivery business was not especially bright. It was hard to make a profit due to the competitive nature of the business. He told me that during the depression it was common to see people on street corners, trying to sell apples or pencils out of a cup. More than once, he would comment, "I could make more money selling pencils on the street corner."

He needed to change, but he didn't know how. The root of his discontent had to do with feeling obligated to work with or for his father. Yet the milk delivery business was the only thing he had ever known.

It had been good for his father and many generations before him, but the way milk was sold for so many decades was about to disappear. The world was moving in many different directions, and it must've been difficult for him to try to figure out where he might fit in the new order.

In addition, his training by the Army to be an artillery specialist did not translate into civilian employment. My mother told me that when he came back from the war, he felt like he had done his bit for the country, and now the country owed him something for his sacrifice. Unfortunately, he died when I was twelve, I was not able to find out from him how he really felt about these issues.

The Sound of a Horse Drawn Sickle Bar Cutter

The first sensation is not a sound
The first sensation is a vibration in the ground
Like imagining a small, distant earthquake
Draft horses hooves strike the ground and make it shake

1800 pounds times two of living flesh and bone
As they pull, they set their hooves like solid stone
It's by this firm, clumping action
They gain their necessary traction

Percheron or Belgian, leaning as they lunge
Each step forward, looking like a plunge
Lunge, step, lunge, step, hoof plant, pull
Repeating and repeating 'til the field is cut in full

As it draws closer the slicing sickle bar
Can be heard from not so far
There is an oscillation that one hears
A speeding up and slowing down in one's ears

A steady, rhythmic, pulsing like some rains
Like blood pulsing in the veins
The steady blend of horse and machine
Leaning to the task, cutting the field clean

It's the sound of honest work being done
'Til the day ends with the last rays of sun
Birds swoop in, searching for food, then they flutter
All that remains is the memory of a horse drawn sickle bar cutter

4

The Bator Farm

The Bator family lived directly across the street. They were Polish Catholics raising six children. The sight and sound of more modern farm machinery was common in the '50s, but for whatever reason this family preferred not to spend money on machines. They did all their farming with their two horses, Jerry and Kitsa, and their own hands.

As a child, I was drawn to the Bator farm because they had so many animals and there was always something different going on there every day, every season. I didn't realize it at the time, but I was fascinated by all the details of maintaining a vibrant busy life on a small, handmade farm. This was a style of farming that was soon to disappear from our part of the world, and I feel very lucky that I was able to experience their farming style up close. By contrast, the Fuller farm was not a fully functioning farm in a traditional sense. The cows were long gone, and the farm was now a milk processing operation and home-delivery business.

A traditional farm like the Baters' across the street would have many animals that need daily care, feeding, watering, and cleaning up after. Add to that, milking cows twice daily. On the Bators' farm, there was an almost constant number of chores that needed attending. This explains why in the summer I frequently saw mister Bator having a nap on the farmhouse porch, between morning chores and the afternoon chores.

The spring, when the grass started to green up, was an exciting time of year. That first warm day was always a big deal. That's because it was when the Bators' cows were let out of the barn to be taken to the greenest pasture. It was an exciting time for us, but more so for the cows after having been cooped up in the barn all winter eating the previous year's hay. They were very excited to be out of the barn and headed back to green pastures. They would jump and kick up their heels to celebrate their release from all that close confinement in their stanchions.

It was great fun to experience their exuberance, their pure joy of being outdoors after the long winter. Nothing but long summer days lay ahead where they got to eat sweet, moist, green grass, which they loved, and which coincidentally produced higher quality and more abundant milk. They were clearly happy and so was I.

Spring is the perfect word for a new season to spring forth. Cows sprang out of the barn, new grass sprang out of the earth, and leaves sprang out of dormant branches.

With the cows out of the barn, all manners of animal life seemed to spring onto the stage of spring. Birds were always part of the show. My mother always commented that seeing a robin redbreast pulling worms in the yard was a sure sign of spring. Red-winged blackbirds were an early favorite of mine; there were lots of them around, nesting in the cat tails that grew in abundance in the wet areas around the farms. I found them easy to identify and a little later, I also found them easy to draw. Blue jays were another bird I learned to recognize early. My mother told me they had a mean reputation for stealing eggs from other birds' nests. We saw lots of barn swallows too. I recall watching them catch insects on the fly in the late afternoon light of summer. Everything was new, everything was reborn every day and brought new surprises, new flowers, new smells, and new sites to see full of promise, hope, and joy. I was happy.

The lilacs were a very welcome sign of spring. Every farm in our area seemed to have large hedges of lilacs. The Fuller farm had a large hedge between the side yard where the laundry was dried and the milk house to the rear of the main house. The scent of lilacs is still a powerful indicator for me of the welcome change of seasons. My dad was in the habit of putting sprigs of lilac on the dash of our pickup truck in the spring, creating that pleasant olfactory sensation as we were going about our delivery rounds.

My younger years—before helping with the milk delivery—were largely that of a carefree child on a farm. My earliest years are full of days of discovery, and the pure joy of realizing I was alive and the world was mine to explore and enjoy. Of course, this would not last and the reality of life on the farm would become known to me in due time. On good days I was just beginning to realize what a beautiful life I was living.

Most of the Fuller farm acreage was rented to the Bators. It consisted of several smaller fields surrounded by stone walls. My mother often commented on how hard it must've been to clear the land and pile up all those stones so they could then farm the land. The Bators used the lower fields to plant corn, turnips, and rutabagas. The upper fields were used for hay production and pastoring the cows in the summertime.

About a half mile up the cow path, there was a very small watering hole where the cows would drink when they were on summer pasture. In the spring, before the cows were on pasture, this watering hole would be alive with frogs in the mating season. My friend Cheryl's father Al encouraged us to catch some of these frogs so he could make a meal of frog legs. Cheryl's older brother Ronnie and my brother Dougie and I went up to Frog Pond as we called it. I think we caught about eight or ten large bullfrogs. Ronnie's father was quite pleased and showed us how to peel the skin off the legs, dip them in buttermilk, bread them in flour or cornmeal, and fry them in hot oil. Prepared this way—if you were able to forget about the rest of the animal—they really looked and tasted just like chicken wings.

My most cherished farm memory of this '50s era is the sound of a horse-drawn sickle bar cutter. This is something I witnessed many times during the hay harvesting season. It's a sound that is embedded deep in my long-term memory.

As the working draft horses pull, they lunge slightly forward with each step, planting their hooves firmly to get the traction they need when pulling a sickle bar cutter. As the hay is cut, the sound of the sickle bar cutter oscillates as it slides back and forth from side to side with the cadence of the horses' hooves. Fast, slow, fast, slow, a very rhythmic back-and-forth, back-and-forth, back-and-forth. The memory of that sound creates many pleasant images in my mind. Images of warm, sunny, summer days, and all the joys of being a carefree child on a bucolic farm in western Massachusetts. As well as images of animal-shaped clouds, "Oh, that one looks like a rabbit" or "That one looks like a giant bird." "Is that a crocodile?"

After the hay was cut, it was allowed to dry and then it was raked into windrows with a horse-drawn dump rake. When sufficiently dry, it was loaded onto a wagon by men with pitchforks. No bales, just loose hay held high over their heads and tossed onto the pile as high as possible. Eventually, the hay tended to drape off the sides, almost to the ground. From the rear, the hay wagon looked like a large pile of hay

THE BOLETUS EDULIS MUSHROOM, ALSO KNOWN AS A KING BOLETE, WAS THE TYPE OF WILD MUSHROOM THAT I SAW THE BATOR FAMILY COLLECTING WHEN I WAS A CHILD.

teetering down the farm road on its way to the barn.

Arriving at the barn, the wagon was backed up to the barn door. One of the horses was unhitched from the wagon and his harness was connected to a thick hemp rope. As the horse was backed up a large four-prong hayfork would descend into the load of hay. It was a little frightening to me. It looked like a giant four-legged spider. Once this four-legged spider settled on top of the hay wagon, the horse would then be led forward away from the barn. As the horse moved forward, the arms of the hayfork would close and take a huge bite out of the hay pile and ascend straight up. I was mesmerized the first time I saw this. How could this be that the horse walks away from the barn and this big bite of hay is lifted off the wagon and goes straight up? I had to walk to the other side of the wagon and look at the arrangements of pulleys and ropes to figure out how this was happening.

This was perhaps my first physics lesson. The hay fork with its load of hay was pulled into the barn on a horizontal rail. A trip line was then pulled, and the hayfork dropped its load into the hayloft. The person in the hayloft who pulled the trip line was responsible for packing down the hay in the loft with their feet so they could fit as much hay as possible into the loft. This looked like a fun job when I was young, but I found out later it was one of the most disliked jobs during the hay harvest season. It was hot, sweaty work and there was a tremendous amount of hay dust and chaff in the air that would stick to the sweaty arms and face of whoever was in the hay loft.

I have fond memories of the Bator farm. In the early 50s, it was a fully functioning farm with cows, horses, pigs, goats, and chickens. They processed their own animals; I watched them slaughter pigs and chickens. They even had a smokehouse to make their own sausage and other smoked meat products. Kielbasa was always a family favorite.

The Bators were the only people I ever saw who collected wild mushrooms. I did not take any interest in wild mushrooms because I didn't learn to like mushrooms until much later in life. My memory tells me that these mushrooms may have been *Boletus Edulis,* whose common name is King Bolet. This is the same mushroom that the French call cep, the Italians call porcini, and the English call penny bums. In Poland, they are called borowick and are considered the king of wild mushrooms. They are highly prized the world over.

In this era, all the dairy farms in our area were small by today's standards. The Bator farm was normal for the times. They had sixteen milking cows, and all these cows had names and a relationship with the farmers. The farmers knew the cows, and the cows knew the farmers. The Bator farm had one vacuum milker that would be set up on one cow, and then they would strap on their small milking stools that hung low around their butts making it much easier to milk each cow. Mr. and Mrs. Bator would milk one cow each by hand while the vacuum milker was doing its job, enabling them to milk three at a time.

Then they would move to the next three cows, and so on down the line. Each cow had its particular personality and I'm sure the farmers were very sensitive to these traits, knowing which ones were easy to milk, and which ones might be more challenging. All herd animals in the wild as well as domesticated have their unique hierarchy. In the Bators' barn, the alpha cow was always named Bossy. She knew she was the boss, and she expected to be treated accordingly.

5

The Fenney Family

My father's sister Orrice was married to Jim Fenney. Uncle Jimmy and Aunt Orrice were very kind souls who raised three children, Bruce, Priscilla, and Patty. The family was always easy to be around, friendly, loving, and genuinely caring about all the children in the neighborhood. It takes a village.

They built their house at 334 Fuller Street on land that was given to them by Push, directly across from the farmhouse at 333 Fuller Street where Aunt Orrice grew up. Their beautiful house was primarily constructed of recycled bricks from the once mighty Ludlow Manufacturing Company. This house had a large living room in the north side of the house with a real fireplace and an exceptionally large picture window on the east side that looked out on the beautiful meadow behind the house.

Many of the buildings from this factory complex were being dismantled in the 1940s. In 1949, the 274-foot brick smokestack was demolished. But many more of these buildings, including the spectacular clock tower, are still standing to this day, and have been repurposed for other manufacturing uses.

Uncle Jimmy worked at a big Westinghouse plant in Springfield for several years. When they closed that factory, he was offered a job at Westinghouse in Ohio. He did not want to move his family out of Ludlow so It was decided to sell their house and buy a country store and gas station at the corner of Center and Rood Streets in Ludlow just down the hill from 12 Rood Street. Yes, the same 12 Rood Street where my father came-a-courting in 1942.

One of my best memories at the Fenneys' house was celebrating Christmas Eve there. It was so easy to just walk across the street. There was always a big family dinner, after which the children were ushered into one of the bedrooms while Santa had a few minutes to do his magic. We were then released into the living room full of excitement and expectation where we would find the many presents that Santa had left under the tree. Although we knew on some level, that it was best to suspend our rational minds and beliefs and enjoy the spirit of the season.

After that celebration at the Fenneys' home, we would walk back across the street to our home. We would then set up a small table for Santa Claus next to our Christmas tree, where we put out a plate with a donut, a bottle of Coca-Cola, and a bottle opener. We were sure he could use a snack while making his very busy rounds.

MY UNCLE JIM FENNEY AND MY AUNT ORRICE (MY FATHER'S SISTER), AND MY PARENTS LOOKING VERY HAPPY AFTER THE END OF WORLD WAR II.

When we woke on Christmas morning, the first thing we checked was that table. We were always thrilled to see that part of the donut and half of the Coca-Cola had been eaten. "He was here! He was here!" That was all the verification we needed as proof of his existence was a half-eaten snack. We would then run to the Christmas tree to find what gifts awaited us.

Aunt Orrice was a talented piano player and organist. She was the organist in the First Congregational Church where I went as a child to receive my early religious education. The children would sit in the sanctuary for the early service. After the offering was complete, we children would go to the rear of the church for our Sunday school lessons. On the way to these lessons, I could see my aunt sitting down low in her organ pit. She had a big rearview mirror over the keyboard so she could keep track of what was going on behind her and get cues from the choir director. She would wave if she noticed me passing.

CHRISTMAS EVE AT THE FENNEY'S HOUSE, RIGHT ACROSS THE STREET FROM OUR HOUSE AT 334 FULLER STREET IN 1955. LEFT TO RIGHT IT'S ROBBIE, PATTY, DOUGIE, PRISCILLA, AND BRUCE, AND ON THE LOWER RIGHT IT'S LYNN AND MY SISTER, KAREN.

Later in life, my aunt found out I had some interest in classical music, so she asked if I would like to go to a special piano concert with her. The concert was in North Hampton, by the well-known pianist, Van Cliburn. He was an internationally known classical pianist who came to the attention of the world in 1958 when he won the Tchaikovsky Competition in Moscow at the age of twenty-three. I remember his playing was quite spectacular, but honestly a bit over my head at the time. My aunt was thrilled to be able to hear him play. I was thrilled to be there with her and get a vicarious thrill from her obvious love of this music and his impeccably talented playing style.

I love these memories and feel extremely lucky that I still remember them to this day. The warmth and closeness of family celebrating a joyous holiday season and later my aunt sharing the experience of a world-class piano concert by one of the biggest classical piano celebrities of his day. Really, does it get any better?

Neighborhood Sledding 1954

Find the toboggan, walk up the hill
The higher we climb the bigger the thrill
Fresh snow is everywhere as far as we can see
Our world has turned white. We are happy and free.

Pile onto the toboggan, can we all fit?
Scrunch close together as we all try to sit
Dougie the hog upfront getting ready for flight
Patty behind him, squeezed in real tight

There's Robbie in plaid, where are his mittens?
Who cares, he wants his hands to glisten
Bruce is folded up tight a good grip on the rope
Jeffry and Cheryl look ready for the steep slope

Priscilla is kneeling, she may be dragging her toes
She will help with the steering as the toboggan goes

Down the hill we will go as fast as we dare
The faster we go, the more exciting the scare

Snow billows up around us feels cold on our faces
Over bumps and small holes the toboggan flexes and dances
We whoop and we yell what fun it is share
A fast toboggan ride down the hill in cold winter air

As we stop, we roll off both sides onto the snow
We brush ourselves off and laugh at our show
Let's do it again another time up hill from above
Making more sweet memories to cherish and love

6

Life with Mom and Dad

"Keep your face always toward the sunshine.
Shadows will fall behind you."

—Walt Whitman

In 1941 our grandfather Push built a small two-bedroom cottage in South Wellfleet, Massachusetts on Cape Cod for his first wife Alice. My cousin Bruce told me that our grandfather paid $100 for the building lot.

Several times in the early 50s our family would get enough time off from the dairy delivery business to spend a few days in South Wellfleet. These are some of my fondest summer memories because it was just our family—Mom and Dad, my brother, me—and later our baby sister. It was wonderful to be on our own having our private family adventure.

The drive to Cape Cod was an adventure in itself. This was before the turnpike was built, so it took about six and a half hours or more to get to South Wellfleet, a major family car ride in those days. Our route went by Buzzards Bay, a name that always resonated with me because it sounded so exotic. The drive over the Sagamore Bridge to cross the Cape Cod Canal, which had been built in 1934, was always a major milestone on this trip.

A VIEW OF PAINE HOLLOW FROM JUST OUTSIDE THE SEA PINES CABIN, WITH
WELLFLEET BAY IN THE DISTANCE, 1966.

The cabin was named "Sea Pines" and was built on a bluff on the bayside of Cape Cod, overlooking the large Paine Hollow estuary that led into the much larger Wellfleet Harbor. On the west side of Wellfleet Harbor, there is a long spit of sand that from above looks like a giant femur hanging down from Great Island. It was originally known as Billingsgate but on a more modern map, it's called Jeremy Point.

The earliest settlers built fishing houses out there. In the 1950s there were still some remnants of those old buildings. One year my father thought it would be a great adventure if we all got in Push's small fishing boat with its little outboard motor and had a picnic on Billingsgate. This trip is about five miles one way across lots of open water. Needless to say, my mother was very nervous. We had to check the tides carefully. But we made the trip successfully and had our picnic. After our return, my mother made my father promise he wouldn't ask to do it again.

The Paine Hollow estuary was shallow so when the tide went out, it went way out, leaving a large mud flat. A few small boats were left high and dry when the tide was out that would then re-float when the tide returned.

There were also many horseshoe crabs. They looked scary to me with their big wide prehistoric shells, their many legs, and their long spiky tail.

I found out much later that they are older than dinosaurs. They have existed for more than 400 million years.

A few times we would put on rubber boots and go out into the mud flats to dig for Quahogs or hard-shell clams. After collecting a bucket load, we would bring them back to Sea Pines. These clams are hard to open, a stout knife blade and hammer are required to cut the muscle and open the shell. Mom would make chowder with them. The resulting chowder was always a tasty reminder of life on Cape Cod.

The cottage was a very simple rectangle with an exposed stud frame structure that was covered with one layer of horizontal siding. There were two partition walls that separated the bedrooms from the main living area. At night, I slept on a daybed in the living area; it was comforting for me to see the light from my parents' bedroom shining on the roof rafters above their bedroom.

The cottage had an old-fashioned icebox, so the first thing we had to do when we arrived was go to the icehouse nearby and get a block of ice to put in the top of the icebox. The cottage also had an old-fashioned

A PICTURE OUR FATHER TOOK IN 1952 OF MY BROTHER, DOUGIE, ME AND MY MOM WITH OUR SISTER, KAREN, IN UTERO, ON THE SAND BLUFF NEAR A SEA PINES CABIN.

wooden diner-style booth with high-back bench seats on either side.

There was also an old-fashioned toaster that had one element in the middle and a fold-out door on each side. You put your bread in the doors and closed them. When the bread was toasted enough on one side, you opened the doors and turned the bread over to toast the other side. If you didn't watch it closely, you could easily burn the bread. I loved working with this toaster and even more, I love the memory of it. Yes, I burned some toast occasionally.

The sights and sounds in this area of Cape Cod are quite distinctive. The small, stunted sea pines that grew next to the cottage were used to being buffered by winds and they had very stiff needles. When the wind blew, a unique whistling sound was heard. This, mixed with the salt air, the scent of the low scrub bushes, and the other smells off the mud flats that were especially strong at night, created some unique powerful sensory memories for me. So different from life on the farm.

If the weather was promising, after breakfast we would pack up the car, and drive to the beach on the eastern ocean side of the cape at Lecount Hollow Beach and spend most of the day there. These days included lots of swimming, napping, and picnicking, and are among my happiest Cape Cod memories. I loved being in the water, and once I got adjusted to the cold temperature, I would stay in the water for hours until my fingertips looked like wrinkled-up raisins.

One of my father's favorite beach activities was covering my brother and me with sand. Of course, my brother and I begged him to do this. He would dig a small depression, and we would lie down in it with our hands and arms at our sides. He would then build a pile of sand over our bodies, covering everything except our heads. It was fun to be covered, and a little frightening to feel the weight of the sand pressing down on my chest, arms, and legs. When he had built up a small hill over us, my father would say, "Try to move your arms." Even though we did this many times we were always shocked to find it was impossible to move because of the weight of the sand. After some pleading and a little encouragement from our mother, Dad would remove enough of the sand so that we could wiggle out of our temporary tombs. Then we would run into the water to wash off the sand. Late in the day we would gather up some driftwood and build a small fire on the beach to listen to the breaking waves and watch the stars come out. Bliss, pure bliss.

We would usually make one or two trips to Provincetown, so that we could climb up the Pilgrim Monument Tower, at 252 feet, it is the tallest all-granite tower in the US. We would walk around town, buy some saltwater taffy, and look at all the beatniks and other counterculture characters that seemed to flock to Provincetown in the summertime. We would then walk out on the docks to look at the fishing boats bobbing in the bay and eat a fish and chips meal in a wharf-side restaurant. All part of the Provincetown experience.

We would also make a couple of trips into the beautiful village of downtown Wellfleet for grocery shopping, and other errands. In 1954, we went to the local movie theater in Wellfleet to see the movie The Beachcomber, a story based on a W. Somerset Maugham story, "The Vessel of Wrath." I remember a male character in the movie commenting about one of the female characters, saying that she was "well stacked." And I remember my mother being a little shocked, thinking that her young boys should not be subjected to such adult comments. I'm sure my father was quietly amused.

These vacations lasted at most five or six days. After a few days, Dad would start feeling guilty about being away from the farm and worrying about all the work he knew needed to be done every day. He would announce that it was time to head back home. For some reason, it always seemed like we were heading back one day sooner than we had originally planned. These family vacations on Cape Cod were a rare and welcome escape from life on the farm, and I hold them dear to this day.

Our family lived on the second floor of my grandfather's house in three and a half rooms, if you count the unheated glassed-in porch where my brother and I slept. The apartment had an entry hallway that was a combination coat room and pantry that led into our kitchen. In the kitchen was a water heater, a stove, a sink, a small dining table, and a roll-around wringer washing machine. Just off the kitchen was the bathroom. Beyond the kitchen, there was

MY FATHER, DOUGLAS, BURYING ME IN THE SAND ON THE OCEAN SIDE OF CAPE COD IN 1954. I'D HAVE TO BEG HIM TO REMOVE SOME OF THE SAND BEFORE I COULD GET FREE.

a living-dining room from which one could access my parents' bedroom and pass through their room to the unheated porch where my brother and I slept in bunk beds, me on top and my brother on the bottom.

In the winter of 1952, my mother contracted pneumonia. The doctor ordered her confined to bed rest and isolation so my brother and I were required to live with our relatives for a week or two. My brother stayed with the Fennys, across the street. I was sent to stay with the Brennans.

Unfortunately, I had a family secret of my own that I wasn't anxious to share. I was a bedwetter. Being required to stay with the in-laws meant my secret would be out of the bag, so to speak. It was an embarrassment to me and continued to be for many years. My aunt Caroline tried to bribe me with money, saying, "If you don't wet the bed tonight, this nickel on the shelf will be yours." I wanted the money, but this condition was out of my control. I always wet the bed, every night, and then

MY BROTHER AND I AT MCGUIRE BEACH IN 1952. IT'S NOW
CALLED LECOUNT HOLLOW.

was required to change the sheets every morning. For years, an invitation for an overnight stay was a cause for great anxiety. Many times, I simply had to refuse offers to spend the night with friends.

My father had a German friend named Carl who we all called "Heinzie" who named me "Chief Running Water." Shame piled on shame! I was a bedwetter and as far as I knew there was nothing I could do about it. My father said he knew of a plastic sheet that was electrified so if you peed on that you would get a mild shock and wake up. He threatened to buy one, but he never did. I thought it was a good idea—anything to overcome this annoying lack of bladder control. Believe it or not, I continued wetting the bed until the age of fifteen and then one night, mysteriously, my urge to pee woke me up in the middle of the night, and I was able to find my way to the toilet. To break free of that curse, and the stigma that went with it was a watershed—pun intended—moment in my young life.

Sometime in the early 1950s, it was decided to remove one of the interior walls in the house which created a real living room off the dining room on the east side of the house. This dramatically improved our living space.

After the space was set up, our dad came home and announced he had bought a convertible! My brother and I got excited because we thought he was talking about a car. My brother and I immediately had visions of ourselves driving in the backseat of a convertible car with the wind blowing our hair every which way. We ran to the window and looked out at the driveway to see what color it might be. It was not to be. We were disappointed to find out Dad had bought a convertible couch, not a car. My father, the joker. The upside was my brother and I could sleep on the convertible couch in the living room in the winter time where the kerosene space heater provided heat for that section of the apartment. My sister Karen was born on February 20, 1953. For her first three or four years, my sister slept in a crib in our parents' bedroom.

Learning to ride a bike was a major milestone in my life. Initially, my father had tried to teach me to ride a full-size bike. Because I was unable to touch the ground with my feet when I was on the seat starting and stopping, the bike made me very nervous. When he realized I wasn't riding my bike, he decided to cut the frame down with a hacksaw and have it re-braised so that it was a little bit smaller. It was still a challenge for me, and as a result, I was reluctant to ride the chopped bike too. Initially, my brother rode this bike more than I did.

Then one day my cousin Margaret came to visit with her child-size bike. I could sit on this small bike and touch the ground with both feet—my confidence went way up. I practiced all afternoon in the dooryard of the farm, coasting downhill in our backyard and peddling all around the dooryard. I learned about the balance point and got quite excited about the possibility of riding my larger bike. These days, most children learn how to ride by starting on a strider bike. Once I got used to riding the small bike and had gained my balance confidence, I couldn't wait to get on my bike, which my brother had borrowed for the day. Bike riding opened my world to many new adventures. I could ride to my cousins' house a mile away, spend time with them, and then ride back home.

Oh freedom.

It also helped me make my money. In 1953, my brother was given a small paper route of twelve customers by another paperboy who did not want to deliver to these homes because they were disconnected from the main part of his route. At about the same time, two farms on Fuller Street that had grown hay and corn for decades were sold and almost overnight were built into suburban housing developments. My brother's little route grew to forty or fifty customers. I began to help with the daily deliveries and shared the income. Within three years another housing development was built, and my brother had almost 100 customers. We started making a little extra money by also delivering the *TV Guide*, which was a very important publication in its day. The papers were dropped off by bicycle at three in the afternoon on the corner of Fuller and Chapin Streets, about half a mile from our home. Eventually, my brother got a heavy-duty bike with baskets large enough to fit all the papers. The Sunday paper was the bulkiest. Some days in the winter, when it was very cold, our father would help out with the pickup truck. My brother worked at this paper route until 1959. It eventually became too large to be serviced every day by bicycle and our father did not want help every day. The route was sold to our cousins, the Brennans. They made this into a family business. With my uncle Lenny driving our cousins as they delivered these papers from the back of the family station wagon.

Another bicycling adventure was riding to my friend Denny White's house, about a mile up Fuller Street. The ride to his house was mostly uphill, which meant there was a nice, long coasting section on the way home. I enjoyed riding to his house because he was always doing something interesting and unusual. One day I went to visit him, and he showed me a miniature animal cemetery he was making. He cleared a little spot in the woods, made little tombstones out of wood or small flat stones, and put them up where he had buried mice and other small animals. He even made little cardboard coffins for these animals. Denny was also tending a small vegetable garden. I was fascinated by these hobbies. He showed me little miniature homes he was building in the woods around his house too. Denny informed me these were fairy homes. I found his ways of entertaining himself fascinating, always something new and interesting. Later in life, he became a very accomplished beekeeper and organic gardener.

Robbie, Karen (a.k.a. Chicken), and Dougie in front of the Sea Pines cabin, 1954.

I also enjoyed visiting Denny because lunch at his house was always special. His mother served food that I was not used to eating, things like canned ravioli or SpaghettiOs. My mother never served this kind of food. I didn't realize until years later that his mother didn't like to cook and this was why she was serving us canned food. Hot dogs were the high point of her kitchen skills.

Having a bicycle continued to expand my world. Many times, I rode my bike into town to the local movie theater to watch Saturday matinees, usually cartoons and a couple of Westerns. I remember stepping out of the movie theater on a Saturday afternoon, after being inside the darkened theater for two or three hours, and being temporarily blinded by the bright sunlight as I tried to locate my bicycle in the jumble of twenty or thirty bicycles leaned up against the building.

When I was eleven, I convinced a friend of mine to skip school. The two of us rode ten miles to the Forest Park Zoo in Springfield. It is a big park with a zoo that had an indoor/outdoor building called, The Monkey House, that had monkeys of course, but also lions and birds.

There was a polar bear named Snowball that had been given to the zoo after it had been rescued as an abandoned baby by an Arctic explorer. In the '50s, this bear was fully grown. She was kept in a relatively small enclosure. I remember watching her pace back and forth. Many people complained and I think she was eventually moved to a much larger zoo where there were other polar bears to interact with.

In Forest Park, there were many picnic areas, tennis courts, baseball fields, bocce courts, and duck ponds. There were trails that went up and down hills throughout the park. My friend and I had a blast riding on these trails. It was a bit like a bicycle roller coaster. We had a great day together, heightened only slightly by the fact that we knew we were playing hooky. I was proud of myself that I was able to find my way there and back home again and on time.

At dinner that evening, my father started to question me about my day at school. This was not his normal behavior. "What had I done all day?" "What had I learned in class?" "Had I played any baseball?" After a few of these questions, I realized the gig was up. I suspected he knew the answers to all his questions. Eventually, he got me to confess that I had not gone to school. He knew because one of my teachers had seen me and my friend riding our bikes that morning in the opposite direction. She had told my father when he was delivering milk to the school that morning. I was reprimanded but not severely punished for this act of rebellion. My father might have been guilty of similar hijinks when he was growing up. And maybe a little proud of my ability to find my way there and back home. I never did it again without permission, but it was never as much fun as it had been the first time when it was all so naughty.

7

The Brennan Family

Our other family was the Brennan family. They lived at 12 Rood Street. Yes, that house where my father came courting in 1942, about a mile from our home on Fuller Street. They named their home "FayrAcre." My aunt Caroline, my mother's sister, had married her high school sweetheart Leonard Brennan. They had four children, Lenny Junior, Margaret, Maureen, and Michael. Our widowed grandfather, Walter Fay, or Grampa Walter, also lived in the house.

My uncle Lenny had been in the Seabees. The Navy Seabees were officially known as the Naval Construction Force. They specialized in building infrastructure, often in challenging and remote locations, during the Second World War. He had spent some time in the Hawaiian Islands. I remember he had developed fond memories of the taste of fresh pineapples. He mentioned more than once how good they were, and that he was quite disappointed when he returned home and realized freshly picked pineapples simply were not available in our part of the world. I found out much later that pineapples do not ripen after they're picked. In those days they were picked unripe so they could be shipped by boat. By the 1970s, pineapples started to be shipped by air so they could be picked ripe. They were called Jet Pineapples.

MY BRENNAN COUSINS MAUREEN, MARGARET, LENNY, AND
MICHAEL. THE PHOTOS WERE TAKEN 30 YEARS APART, ABOUT
1955 AND 1985.

After the war, Uncle Len went to work at the post office in Ludlow
and worked there until his retirement. Even though there was always
family talk of little money, the Brennans lived a full and creative life.
I loved going to visit them because my aunt Caroline always had some
kind of art project or outdoor activity to keep the family busy.

It seemed to me that every time I went to their house, they were doing
something new and interesting. It started with finger painting. Then it
was drawing, and watercolor painting. My Aunt Caroline, I called her
Aunt KK for many years, was artistic, as her father had been. She painted

almost full-size horse murals on her children's bedroom walls. In the winter she sculpted full-size horses out of snow in their front yard. Many games were played at their house, more than I remember at our house. Checkers, or Chinese checkers, Parcheesi, and chess. Then there were wood-burning images of horses and other animals on pine boards. Then it was making objects out of wood.

In their backyard, they had a great two-story playhouse with a slippery slide from the second floor. They also had the best swing. It was hung from a high, large, horizontal branch on the biggest elm tree I ever saw. The arc of the swing was the longest I have ever swung on.

Aunt KK was also a great cook. Her donuts fried in lard were a favorite of mine, they were warm and wonderful.

She got all her children involved in 4H clubs, so they had sheep to look after. My uncle Leonard made a special grooming bench that the sheep could stand on while their fleece was being cleaned and perfectly manicured before they were taken to a show to be judged.

They kept a small flock of chickens for eggs and an occasional roast chicken for stew. I have a vivid memory of watching Uncle Leonard chop the head off a live chicken and then stick its feet in a chicken wire fence so that it wouldn't run around the yard without a head. My uncle was also an avid gardener, and he always had a large vegetable garden that was able to supply lots of fresh vegetables for the family.

My aunt and uncle were very avid anglers as well. I remember going to a dinner at their house after they both had caught their limit of twelve trout each. I remember the crispy trout being fried in butter and stacked up on two plates like cordwood. The butter-crisped skin on the outside and the sweet white flesh on the inside made the trout very tasty. The only thing that put me off was looking at their heads and eyes. It was the first time I ever ate a fish that had been cooked with its head on.

One of my sweetest and most cherished memories of going to the

Brennans was for their annual Memorial Day picnic. In the early 1950s, with memories of World War II still fresh in everyone's minds, Memorial Day was a big deal. There was a large parade through downtown Ludlow, with marching bands, fire engines, and floats commemorating the veterans. The float I will never forget was a reenactment of the famous Joe Rosenthal photograph of GIs raising the stars and stripes on Mount Suribachi on Iwo Jima in 1945. It was a powerful image. I could not help wondering how the actors were able to hold that pose for the three or four miles on the parade route.

As children, we loved to witness and participate in this parade. We decorated our bicycles with flags on the handlebars and crepe paper streamers in the spokes, and we rode along with the parade as it went through town. After the parade was finished, honor guards went to three different cemeteries in town. Buglers played "Taps," and the honor guard would step forward with rifles raised high and fire a three-shot salute to the fallen. The brass cartridges that came out of these rifles were highly prized by the children, like me, who were in attendance. We would scramble for them in the grass after the honor guard had moved on.

Memorial Day was also the beginning of summer, the summer that was going to last for weeks and weeks, stuffed full of the promise of summer fun. After the parade and military salutes, we would head to the Brennans for their annual picnic. I have clear memories of carloads of families pulling into the driveway and disgorging their children and adults to join in the festivities. Everyone was smiling, and in a good mood, and the children were just running every which way trying to decide what to do first. Getting together, socializing, and getting caught up with people you hadn't seen much during the winter months was a joyous time. Uncle Lenny would labor for hours over the small wood-fired barbecue grill, cooking chicken that he basted with his homemade barbecue sauce. I think now he should've asked other adults to help with this task so he would have more time to participate in socializing.

One of the greatest joys of childhood for me at this picnic was a large galvanized washtub at the base of the giant elm tree. It had a big block of ice in it surrounded by bottles of soda—many, many bottles of soda. Children were allowed to help themselves to whatever they wanted. It felt to me like an incredible cornucopia. I remember looking at it and thinking, "Wow! I can have any one of these sodas I want! Coca-Cola, grape, orange, root beer, 7up, Dr Pepper, Nehi, Moxie, Ginger Ale ... How to decide?" It was my first experience with free choice.

As the day wore on, the crowd started to thin out. As darkness approached, we children liked to play flashlight tag. One person would have a flashlight, and the rest of us would hide in the bushes or behind trees. Once spotted by the flashlight holder's beam we would be considered tagged until we were all captured. The most successful hider would get the flashlight next.

Around eight thirty or nine, the family members that were left would gather in the house and my aunt and uncle would get out their projector and show home movies of trips they had taken with their family. We loved seeing these movies filmed when we were two or three years younger. I remember one clip of me at about six or seven pushing a wheelbarrow full of just-raked leaves. In my mind, it looked like a heavy load when in reality, a wheelbarrow full of leaves is very light. Also, my aunt and uncle had a collection of Laurel and Hardy comedy movies that we never tired of watching. It was a sweet time, a fun time, an innocent time, a lost time. A fond memory to this day.

Swinging

Spring is always the best time to swing
Shorts and a T-shirt, no shoes, just wings
Conditions of winter weather have passed
Days are brimming with green trees and grass

The swing is waiting for us so patient, why?
To lift us briefly from the ground to the sky
To fly through the air, laughing and free
Pumping and pulling for the top of the tree

The higher we fly the more freedom we feel
With maximum effort we laugh and we squeal
At the highest point of the arc the chains go slack
For an instant we are weightless, then we fall back

Exhilarating, thrilling, exciting and scary
Weightless for an instant we wish to tarry
Backward we fall laughing as we plummet
Flying back to earth like a speeding comet

The sensation of weightlessness is fleeting
Swinging like this feels like cheating
To be a child, so carefree and pure
How could we know it would pass in a blur

8

Growing Up, Learning About Work

"The most difficult thing is the decision to act;
the rest is tenacity."

—Amelia Earhart

As a child, my feeling was that most Americans, especially those who had survived the Second World War and had come home in one piece were optimistic about their prospects for the future for themselves and their families. Tom Brokaw's book, *The Greatest Generation* is a good snapshot of what many veterans were able to accomplish after returning to civilian life. They had good benefits from the GI Bill; many of them went to college or other forms of advanced study, and they built the country that we know today.

By the early 1940s, Fuller's Dairy had a fleet of three pickup trucks. My father told me stories of them being difficult to start in cold weather and sometimes they had to use a car or whatever vehicle to push and bump-start the rest of the trucks. Oh, the good old days.

I also remember doing milk deliveries with my father in extremely snowy conditions. So snowy that tire chains had to be attached to the rear wheels, and occasionally one section of the chain would come loose and bang on the inside of the fender with each rotation—*clunk, clunk, clunk, clunk.* Eventually, we would pull over and tie up the loose end of the chain. My hands were always cold in the winter, and I spent a lot of time holding my hands in front of the small cab heater.

We made a lot of deliveries to small, insulated boxes that were outdoors. We worried about the milk freezing in its glass bottles so when the trucks were loaded in winter, one or two forty-quart milk cans of hot water were placed in the center of the load and a heavy insulated blanket covered them. We then tried to take milk from the outside of the load and worked toward the center as we went along. More than once, I remember seeing milk that had frozen in the bottle and had pushed the paper cap off the bottle, the frozen milk rose out of the bottle and bent over like a candy cane.

Delivering milk in the summer was the opposite challenge. We always had to worry about the milk getting too warm. Once the trucks were loaded in the morning, we went to the local icehouse and got a good coating of chipped ice to spread over the load. We then covered the load with that same heavy insulated blanket so that it would help keep the milk cool while we were delivering. This chipped ice was a very popular treat with children in the summertime. When they saw us coming, they would run up to the truck saying, "Can we have some snow, please? Can we have some snow, please?"

My brother, Douggie, who's two and one-third years older than me, started helping my father with the milk deliveries about two years before I did. I was initially jealous, and I remember begging to go on the truck with my father. "Oh, please take me, I want to go really, I do," I'd say. Once I was old enough and started helping out with the deliveries, I found out how much work it was, it wasn't long before I was begging not to go.

Eventually, my brother and I took turns every other day. He would go one day, and I would go the next. After getting up early in the morning, I would help my father load the truck with crates of milk to make our deliveries. When school was in session, I would help with the deliveries until about eight in the morning. Then my dad dropped me off at a city bus stop in Indian Orchard and I would ride the bus back to Ludlow to go to school. One day, my father gave me a dime for the bus. The fair was seven cents. So, the next day when he dropped me off for the bus he said, "Today I only have to give you a nickel because you have the change from the other day." I had to say I didn't have the change.

He said, "What did you do with it?"

I said, "When I crossed the bridge over the river, I threw the pennies in the river."

In a shocked, incredulous tone of disbelief, he said to me, "You threw money away? Do you think money grows on trees?"

I remember a feeling of great shame. To this day, if I see a coin lying on the ground, I always bend over and pick it up. I resolved never to throw money away again.

In the mid-1950s, there were so many Baby Boom children attending school that the schools had to switch to double sessions for two or three years until more classrooms could be built. That meant that about half the students went to morning classes and the other half went to afternoon sessions. When I was entering fifth grade, I was signed up for the morning sessions, which kept me from getting up early to do the milk delivery with my dad. My brother wasn't very happy about this and informed me that I would have to make up this "time off" in subsequent years.

Milk delivery in the spring and fall was generally a very pleasant experience. The weather was not too hot or too cold, and I did enjoy spending time in the pickup with my father, especially in the spring when the maple trees were just budding out. Robert Frost comes to mind:

"Nature's first green is gold,
Her hardest hue to hold.
Her early leaf's a flower;
But only so an hour.
Then leaf subsides to leaf.
So Edan sank to grief,
So dawn goes down to day.
Nothing gold can stay."

As I recall, the first tender leaves on suburban streets in Indian Orchard were the lightest shade of gold-green. Indian Orchard is a suburb of Springfield, but it's actually closer to Ludlow, it's just separated by the Chicopee River. It's made up of mostly residential neighborhoods and one main street with several stores and a few restaurants. It had the first Five and Ten Store I ever went to.

My dad was a practical joker. He had several routines that I was familiar with, but I seemed to fall for them over and over again. When he was lighting his pipe, he would draw my attention to something outside the window and then blow out the match and put the still-hot match on my knee. I would yell, "Ouch! Don't do that." He would laugh.

When the weather was warm and we were driving with the windows down, if he saw young girls on the sidewalk, he would grab the back of my head with his hand and turn it in the direction of the window and yell, "Yo ho!" I lost count of how many times I fell for that trick. Annoying at the time, but now, one of many fond memories.

I knew at certain times of the day he'd be stopping for some special snack. A favorite stop was Al's Lunch, a tiny breakfast and lunch restaurant run by Big Al Johnson. He was not too tall and weighed at least 250 pounds. He and his World War II vet cook named Tom in the back kitchen were all the staff it took to keep things humming. Al worked behind the counter with a white apron tied high up around his ample girth at the back of the dining room with maybe six seats and another five or six tables in front.

There was a small pass-through window behind the counter. Al would pour coffee and call customers' orders through that window to Tom in the back. I used to sit in the kitchen and watch Tom cook and wash the dishes by hand. He almost never spoke, he was just constantly in motion, cooking and cleaning. Watching him wash and wipe spoons and forks mesmerized me. The way he did it, all the flatware would nest up together in neat piles.

A favorite item of mine at Al's was a fried egg sandwich on a kaiser roll. Tom would butter and toast the roll on the hot griddle, put the fried egg in, and wrap it all in white paper. The experience was warm and moist with a powerful olfactory component.

Oatmeal was another common choice; Tom always had a small pot warm and ready to serve in the winter months. I was always told it would stick to my ribs, meaning it would satisfy my hunger for a long time. The little restaurant was small and decidedly not fancy but I think my father was impressed that Al was there six days a week from five thirty in the morning, taking care of his customers, until lunch service was finished around two. He steered his own ship and charted his own course. Coincidentally, he was also able to buy a new Cadillac every other year.

I remember him telling my dad one particularly snowy day he had to walk to work, about a mile, because his Cadillac did not have snow tires. It was quite difficult for him because the snow was deep and he wasn't used to walking to work. But he did it.

The Fuller farm fields were leased to neighbors. I grew up in a 150-year-old two-story farmhouse with a small attached garage for one or two pickup trucks. My grandfather Push and my step-grandmother Eshew lived on the first floor of this farmhouse. Eshew had a unique way

AFTER BEING TOWED IN A SNOWY FIELD ON A TOBOGGAN
BEHIND OUR FATHER'S MOTORCYCLE, MY BROTHER AND I POSED
ON THE MOTORCYCLE AS THOUGH WE WERE RIDING IT. THE
SNOW MUST'VE BEEN QUITE STICKY BECAUSE THERE'S SO
MUCH IN THE SPOKES.

of talking, almost like she had marbles in her cheeks. I remember she had a small collection of carved stone elephants. She told me she was very fond of elephants.

To the rear of the farmhouse, the old farm barn stood guard. It still had the old wooden stanchions that had held the cows for milking and winter feeding. It sat idle and unused for all the years that I was living on the farm. On the north side of the farm barn were the horse stables where my aunt Orrice had kept her horse, Tony. This also sat unused in the 1950s. The corner of the main barn had two additions used to store cars and other vehicles and old unused farm equipment.

The foundation of the main barn was built on a small rise with doors on the east and west sides that allowed horse-drawn wagons to drive in one side and out the other, so they weren't required to back up while loading or unloading. The lower level on the south side was completely open for equipment storage under the barn. There were still a few neglected implements stored there in the 1950s.

There was another addition to the barn where my grandfather kept his car. Push had a passion for Packards, and my father told me that it was his habit in the '50s to get a new Packard every other year. I remember an important lesson my grandfather taught me. He told me that when he drove his new car off the lot it immediately lost $500 in value, a lesson I have never forgotten. I have bought a lot of used things in my life because of this lesson.

I believe the last Packard he bought was a 1956 Clipper. It was much longer than his previous Packard. I have a clear memory of him and a friend of his building an eighteen-inch extension onto the garage so that his new car would fit in the garage with the doors closed. I was extremely impressed watching my grandfather and his friend cut through two-by-twelve planks with hand saws in a matter of minutes. The speed at which they were able to make these cuts amazed me. That's because I had been given an old hand saw to use in my sandbox and I had a couple of small one-by-four pieces of pine board that I wanted to cut. But because the saw that I had was extremely dull, it took me about two days to make one cut in one piece of pine. That left me feeling pretty incompetent.

Winter had plenty of exciting outdoor activities to offer. On the north side of our farmhouse, there was a low basin-shaped area that had been used as an ice pond in the days before mechanical refrigeration. In the 1800s and before, ice was a very valuable commodity. Ice harvest amounts from the Hudson River near Albany were reported in the New York papers. It was not until 1914 that the amount of manufactured ice exceeded the amount of natural ice for the first time. By 1920, the natural ice business collapsed.

There was a small stream that flowed through this low area on the north side of our farmhouse and just before it went under the road, a concrete wall had been built in a way that allowed boards to be laid horizontally into slots in the concrete causing the area to fill with water in the fall and then freeze in the winter. In my memory, this pond was used by the entire neighborhood for ice-skating and playing hockey. One year in the early 1950s, the pond froze over and then somehow the water leaked out or was let out and the flat pond became a giant ice bowl. This created an amazing sledding opportunity, down, one side and up the other, then back again. It was great fun for me on a Flexible Flyer with metal runners. One day I left my sled on the ice and went home for dinner. A few days later I went to retrieve my sled and found the runners had frozen into the ice, making it impossible for me to retrieve. Push showed me how to sprinkle salt around the runners to melt the ice and within an hour or two I was able to pull a sled free.

More traditional sledding was done on the hill behind our neighbors' house.

Once at the local dump, my father spotted a toboggan that someone had discarded. He looked it over and realized that it had been discarded because the bottom was worn enough that some of the screw tips were protruding out of the bottom rendering it not good for sliding. Dad took it home and filed the protruding tips flush with a flat file. We had many wonderful group tobogganing experiences with that reclaimed toboggan.

One winter after the first snowfall, my father tied a long rope to one of his CZ motorcycles and towed my brother and me on the toboggan in the fields behind the barn. It was great fun, but most of what I remember was being sprayed by the snow from the rear wheel of the motorcycle. It was very exciting but also very cold. After this ride, we took a nice picture of my brother and myself sitting on the motorcycle. We thought we were very clever by building a pile of snowballs around the side stand to make it look like we were driving the motorcycle instead of just sitting on it. The snow must've been very wet because of the way it was sticking to the spokes of the motorcycle.

My introduction to skiing involved finding some old WWII wooden skis in the barn and gliding around the small hills behind our house. The skis were primitive by today's standards as they were wood-only, with no metal edges with classic bear trap cable bindings. All I had for boots were my buckle-up galoshes, not even close to a proper ski boot of that era. But it got me interested in the concept and began my fifty-plus-year love affair with cross-country and downhill skiing.

MY GRANDFATHER HAD A PASSION FOR PACKARDS. HIS 1948 PACKARD CUSTOM EIGHT WAS FOLLOWED BY A MUCH LARGER 1956 PACKARD CLIPPER, WHICH REQUIRED AN EXTENSION ON THE GARAGE TO FIT INSIDE.

9

More Life with Mom and Dad

"Life isn't about finding yourself. Life is about creating yourself."

—George Bernard Shaw

Our last vacation on Cape Cod as a family was in August 1955. It turned out to be a tumultuous weather experience. After a dry spring and summer, the remnants of a hurricane came up the East Coast and soaked New England thoroughly. Because the ground was dry and the stream levels were low, the runoff from the first storm was minimal. But two weeks later, another storm dropped a record of over twelve inches of rainfall in Hartford, Connecticut, about thirty miles south of Ludlow. The ground was already saturated by the runoff from the first storm, so the second storm created havoc all over the region. Our family went to Cape Cod on vacation between the two storms.

We didn't spend any time at the beach that year because it was raining and overcast pretty much constantly. After three or four bleak days, we decided to head for home. The normal one-day drive turned into a three-day adventure, prolonged by flooded fields and washed-out bridges. Dad would try one route only to find a bridge so close to being washed away that no cars were allowed to pass over it. I remember we got to a bridge where water was lapping at the bottom of the roadway. So, we turned around to look for another route. We spent two nights in emergency shelters in churches. And when we got back, we found almost every culvert and small bridge in Ludlow had been washed out.

On August 19, while the second storm hit central New England, our grandfather Push and our cousin Bruce were in one of the farm pickup trucks on Fuller Street. They came to the culvert area at Higher Brook and the road was flooded with water running over the road, but the water didn't appear to be too deep. They got about two-thirds of the way across the flooded area with water at about twelve inches deep, when all of sudden a surge of water brought the water level from the

MY GRANDFATHER'S TRUCK GOT STUCK TRYING TO CROSS HIGHER BROOK WHEN THERE WAS A SUDDEN SURGE OF WATER THAT FLOODED THE ENGINE. HE AND MY COUSIN, BRUCE, HAD TO BE RESCUED BY MOTORBOAT AFTER HANGING ON THE TOP OF SOME SMALL TREES.

running boards up to headlight depth and the motor stalled. Push and Bruce then got out of the truck on the downstream side and tried to walk to the closest dry land but they were swept away by the current. Eventually, they were rescued by a neighbor in his motorboat, who retrieved them from the treetops they were clinging to. They were taken to the hospital and deemed to be uninjured. I remember my cousin Bruce telling me how difficult it was to swim with barn boots full of water. I believe Push had quite a bit of wind taken out of his sails by this experience. It is unsettling how someone can appear quite vital at an advanced age and then one stressful incident like this can change the course of their life. It was only about sixteen months later on December 10, 1956, when Push died of pneumonia.

In the mid-50s, I remember riding to a motorcycle racetrack in Stafford Springs, Connecticut, with my dad. This was a half-mile dirt flat track where the riders wore a big metal skid plate on their left foot which they would drag as they were power sliding their way around the turn to the next straight away. Watching the races was not that interesting to me—boring in fact, with lots of noise and dust. The only reason I loved going to these events was because I got to ride behind my father on his motorcycle. It gave me an opportunity to share in his love of motorcycling. I think of it now as a win-win situation. I also would always get a hot dog and a Coke out of the deal. Coke had an advertising slogan at the time: "The pause that refreshes." I remember standing at a large trough-shaped urinal at this track next to my father as we were relieving ourselves, and he said, "This is the pause that refreshes. Not Coke."

These motorcycle trips with my father are among my most cherished memories, and they have carved the deepest, most profound crevices in my brain. They are singularly among the most cherished memories that I still have to this day.

I dreamed I was flying

I dreamed I was flying, wind in my hair
We were slicing easily through the fresh country air
Flying by barns and houses, some red and some white
Sliding through the air of a warm summer night

The pilot, my father, so big, and so strong
Our BSA thumping as we fly, singing its song
How long can this dream last, I wonder, how long
It's pure bliss this flying, it feels exhilarating, so strong

So we fly past the fields and meadows and trees
Gliding down back roads, lost in the breeze
Happy to be sharing this flying machine
I love to hug my dad as into to corners we lean

When flying like this, on the ground, on two wheels
We access a joy together, we both love and can feel
It is the pleasure of the shared experience that bonds
A mutual love of riding, by small streams and by ponds

I dreamed I was flying, just me and my dad
I'm sitting high on my pillion, so happy and glad
Pure bliss is this dream from so long ago
It warms my heart to this day, I won't let it go

10

Life after Push

In the words of Caesar, "Alea iacta est"—the die is cast.

We didn't know it at the time, but our family's life was about to be altered in very profound ways by circumstances beyond our control. Upon Push's death, my father became the sole owner of Fuller's milk delivery business, a business that I believe he did not like very much. Unfortunately, it was the only business he knew. He liked it even less after his father died because of its feeble ability to produce income and the fact that it had a big debt attached to it. He told me that his father had left the farm and the house with all the land, the cottage on Cape Cod, and his 1956 Packard Clipper to his second wife, Ethel, and she didn't even drive!

The summer before Push died, he'd made some major improvements in the dairy. He had three-phase power brought to the site and installed a large, noisy homogenization machine. Customers would now have a choice of regular milk, unhomogenized, which separates into cream and skim milk after sitting, or homogenized milk, which does not separate and is the only kind of milk available these days. But when my father inherited the dairy business, it had $7,000 in debt attached to it as a result of these improvements. My father was not pleased. He couldn't possibly pick up all the milk from the local farms, pasteurize and bottle it, and then deliver it door to door by himself. My father was very disappointed by the situation and expressed his disappointment to me more than once.

Other small dairy delivery farms in our town had gone out of business, mostly because of the bulk tank laws. My father realized he needed to reorganize. He made a deal with the biggest dairy in town, Daylight Dairy. They had a much bigger operation with a large, high-volume bottling plant with several employees. It was the first place I ever saw a bulk tank truck that carried milk. Part of their business was to custom bottle milk for several milk delivery operations similar to ours. My father contracted with them to put our milk in our bottles so that we would then deliver it to our customers. At the end of each delivery day, we would leave our empty bottles and then pick them up the next day full of fresh milk. My father said that this operation could put up our entire load in less than thirty minutes. I have to assume that the profit margin was quite a bit smaller, but the day-to-day work schedule was greatly simplified. Now all he had wass the delivery part of the business. Of course, Dad still had the $7,000 debt. I assume he sold off the equipment from our dairy to get that paid down.

There was another group of milk home-delivery specialists who impressed me and also had their milk custom-bottled at Daylight Dairy. They had three refrigerated trucks, unusual for the time, and they all wore matching uniforms. Their logo, "Hilltop Dairy" was on their trucks and their uniforms. They were definitely looking to the future. I remember being envious of their professionalism. Just the way they moved and talked reminded me of a military operation. They did not have any children in their ranks. I can only assume that if they stayed in business, they transitioned from home delivery to wholesale delivery to stores and supermarkets. As the home-delivery business for milk delivery faded the only future for milk delivery was wholesale delivery to stores, schools, hospitals, and other large-volume customers.

Daylight Dairy is long gone now and so is their dairy bar that was just down the road on East Street called The Double D Dairy Bar. It was a wonderful spot in its day. It had a big parking lot for lots of people and cars to make the scene drinking milkshakes and eating cheeseburgers and french fries and all manner of ice cream sundaes. The banana split was a favorite of mine.

I idolized my father; he was a pillar of strength. He was my example of what a man should be: tall, strong, hard-working, and with a pretty good sense of humor. He was a loving father, who made me feel loved. Like anyone, he had his foibles. He probably had too many beers sometimes. One year on his birthday, we were all having dinner together, and my mother gave him a bottle opener that was in the shape of a donkey's head. He looked at it and said, "You gave me this because you think I'm a jackass." I think now that this was more of a reflection of how he felt about himself. My mother was embarrassed and did her best to explain that she did not think ill of him.

There were other instances when he expressed his unhappiness or dissatisfaction, but they were relatively few and far between. He was not neglectful, but he could have spent more time with the family. There were some times in which my mother would plan a family picnic or some other kind of activity where he had promised to join us, but then for one reason or another, he did not show up. I'm sure he had demons. By and large, he kept them at bay. I wish he had lived long enough that I might have had some substantive conversations with him about these and other issues. Really, I just wanted to get to know him better.

11

A Home of Our Own

Years later, my mother told me that when a woman is setting up a home, she wants it to be her home only and doesn't want to have to share it with another woman. I learned years later that living in the farmhouse with my grandparents was not an arrangement that my mother enjoyed. She felt her mother-in-law was just a little bit too nosy, inclined to ask questions like, "What was in the mail today," or to make comments like, "Oh, that's how you do that?"

I remember my mother as a loving attentive person who was always concerned about other people's happiness before her own. With minimal resources, she did a very good job of creating a wonderful family life for all of us. Her gentle affection for her family was made present every day in her actions, and deeds. She was also active in some women's groups and many church functions.

We lived in the farmhouse on Fuller Street for the first ten years of my life. Around 1956, my mother convinced my dad that we had to have our own home. We went home shopping as a family. The nicest house we saw for sale, near the one that we ended up buying, had a two-car garage, a real fireplace, and a second floor with a total of three bedrooms. But it was deemed too expensive for our budget $12,500.

We ended up buying the cheapest little house in town for $8,000. A two-bedroom raised ranch on a street with eleven other homes that looked exactly the same. My mother was now able to be the matriarch of her own home, and I believe it made her very happy. She also commented to me that my father brightened up with personal pride at having his own home. He began to make improvements, like finishing off the basement, so we could have family gatherings and a children's play area. He skim-coated a concrete block with mortar and then painted it a light yellow color to make the space look larger.

On our first Christmas on Stanley Street, we invited several family members over for dinner. My parents set up some folding banquet tables and card tables and brought down a bunch of folding chairs. We had a Christmas tree in the corner and strung up some lights from the floor joists. And we even had a make-believe fireplace. About as cozy as it could be for a small cellar space, I believe my mother was especially proud of what they had accomplished and all the family members had nothing but kind words to say.

My dad decided to move the gravel driveway because it was too close to the property line on the west side of the house. My father, my brother, and I did this by hand with shovels using our up truck to carry the gravel from the west side to the east side of the house. My dad found a developer just a half mile away who was willing to sell us topsoil for five dollars a pickup truckload. Wanting to get the most topsoil for our dollar, my father, my brother, and I loaded that little half-ton pickup with loam until it was running off all four sides. The rear leaf springs went flat and driving the pickup with that load felt like the front wheels were almost lifting off the ground. We did all this driveway and topsoil moving with three shovels, my dad, my brother, and I. We were able to get a decent layer of topsoil to cover our 100' by 100' house lot and we were able to plant a good-looking grass lawn. My dad also got a friend of his from the highway department to donate four maple tree saplings that he planted in front of the house.

Domestically, things were looking up too. My dad sold the old 1948 Buick and bought a nice 1953 blue and white four-door Chevy Bel Air. Six cylinders with "three on the tree" as we used to call it, a standard three-speed with a hand shifter attached to the steering column. This was the first car I ever drove—only in our little driveway going back and forth about thirty feet with one or two friends in the car with me. It was thrilling and not too dangerous. It was years before I drove a car on public roads.

My brother and I were still sleeping in our bunk beds, me on top and him on the bottom. In retrospect, this makes no sense to me, as a bedwetter I should've been on the bottom bunk. My mother told me once she came into the bedroom in the morning, and I was on my side in the top bunk peeing right out onto the floor! Very embarrassing to think about now.

In our new area, there were lots of new forests to explore with forts to be built with our new neighborhood friends, streams to fish in, and trees to climb or chop down. I had a hatchet and I loved to chop down small trees and yell "Timber!"

The land nearby was being cleared for more development. Watching men and machines has always fascinated me. One year, a crew came through clearing land nearby for a new powerline. My young friends and I were amazed at how they would clear wide swaths of wild forest and trees mostly by hand. The larger logs were then hauled away and the slash was piled up and burned. The Massachusetts Turnpike was being constructed around the same time right through the middle of Ludlow. Bridges were being built, and some roads were being rerouted. It was the first time I ever saw pile drivers that were being used to create solid footing for bridges. The turnpike was built in sections that were later joined together to make up the entire network.

I have pleasant memories of riding incomplete sections of the turn-pike with my father on his motorcycle late in the day after the workers had left the job site—sections that were completely built but were not yet open to the public. We might ride for five or six miles to the west until we came to an incomplete section—either not paved, or waiting for a bridge to be installed—and then we would turn around and ride back. It was quite amazing to me to be on this big, flat, wide road with no other traffic, just me and my dad. Riding like this on warm summer evenings with my father is among my most cherished memories. Just the two of us wearing our dungarees, white T-shirts, and our plastic bubble goggles to keep bugs out of our eyes.

On country roads, I would look over his shoulder, holding onto his belt loops, and watch the beam from the headlight bounce down the road ahead of us. I can't pretend to explain, or totally understand it, it's just to say these early motorcycle experiences with my dad are cemented in my brain. I loved motorcycling then and I love it still to this day. There is, of course, an exhilarating sense of freedom, of being exposed to the elements, and able to smell whatever fragrances nature has to offer—pleasant and offensive. Of course, there is also an element of danger. If something goes wrong, it's likely to go very wrong. There is no external protection that one might feel driving inside an automobile. There is unmistakably a heightened contact with the natural world and a sense of excitement that cannot be duplicated by other modes of transportation. Save, perhaps riding a horse at full gallop.

I didn't know it until it happened. But something was about to go wrong, very wrong.

12

My World Gets Turned Upside Down

"We tend to think of life as an inexhaustible well. As though we have always been alive and we will always be alive, but in fact, it's a very finite experience... How many times will you see a full moon rise? How many times will you hear a baby laugh?"

—Paul Bowles

The die had been cast in 1956 when my grandfather died. Further tragedy with profound implications for me and the rest of our little family came two and half years later on Saturday, May 30, 1959.

On this date, at approximately two in the morning, I was awakened in my bedroom by Uncle Jimmy. My first thought was what are you doing in my bedroom in the middle of the night?

He said, "Robbie, you have to get up, we're going to the hospital. Your father has been in an accident and we're going to see him."

With those words, my world, the world I had known for twelve years—the safe, predictable world of my bucolic childhood life came crashing down. It was about to be profoundly altered in ways that would cling to me for years to come and over which I had no control.

We all got a car and drove to the hospital in Holyoke. When we arrived at the hospital, we pulled up by the front door. Everything was dark, very dark, except for the long, brightly lit hallway that led to the interior of the hospital. It was decided that our mother would go in and my uncle would wait in the car with me, my brother, and my sister. I have a clear memory of watching my mother walk through the front door and slowly disappear down that long, brightly lit hallway to where I could no longer see her. Almost as if she were walking into that famous white light that people talk about who have had a near-death experience. She just disappeared into the bright white light and vanished. As a child, I wondered if she had been swallowed up by the white light. The experience was otherworldly.

After quite a long time, I probably had fallen asleep, perhaps an hour or more, our mother returned. She reported to us that our father was still alive, but he had a very serious head injury. She and my uncle decided that she would stay at the hospital with my father, while he would take us back to Aunt Caroline and Uncle Lenny's house in Ludlow.

The next day when she got home, of course, I wanted her to report on our father's condition. She said he was still alive and they were hoping for the best. "Hoping for the best." I can't tell you how tightly I held onto that thought. Very, very tightly.

This was now Sunday, there was no milk to be delivered on Sunday, but we had to make a plan for the next day. Somehow it was arranged that our Air Force neighbor on Stanley Street, Don Higgins, would drive the delivery truck on Monday. My brother and I had the routes memorized so we could tell him which way to go. So, with the help of our neighbor, we were able to make our milk deliveries that Monday, June 1. I recall many people asking me about my father's welfare, and I recall quite clearly my standard answer was, "He is seriously injured, but he's very strong. I'm sure he will pull through." Of course, I really believed this. I had no way of knowing how seriously he was injured, or that his chances of surviving this injury were minimal at best. I know now that he had a fractured skull and there were no CT scanners in 1959. The first CT scanners were not used until 1971. The protocol at the hospital was to watch, wait, and hope. I could not let the idea that this accident might end his life. It never entered my mind. This simply was not possible.

Coincidently, in 1987 I fell off a bicycle and hit my head really hard. I was taken to the medical center in Burlington, Vermont. A CT scan showed the doctors that I had blood accumulating on the right side of my skull as a result of a subdural hematoma—a broken blood vessel inside my skull. They were able to drill into my skull, draw out the blood that accumulated, and cauterize the leaking capillaries. Ten days later, I walked out of the hospital and I've never had any side effects from this life-threatening condition. The female surgeon who did the operation told me that I was their favorite kind of patient. Someone who comes into the hospital with a serious life-threatening condition that they can treat successfully and send that person back out into the world to resume their normal life.

My mother spent most of that Monday at the hospital with my father. She came back to the Brennans late that night after all the children had gone to bed.

I was waiting for her Tuesday morning when she came down the stairs from sleeping and I ran up to her saying, "How's Dad? How's Dad?"

She looked down at me, close to tears, and said, "I'm very sorry, but he died last night."

"What!? What did you say?"

My mind exploded with grief. I couldn't understand what she was saying. I didn't want to believe what she was saying. I could not completely comprehend what she had said. It was such a shock to me, and so completely unexpected. I couldn't imagine how I could go on without him. He'd been such a rock in my life, such a stabilizing force.

I tried to run away from the pain. I recall running into one of the bedrooms and throwing myself on the bed and crying uncontrollably. This unbelievable grief gushed out of me, and I didn't know what to do with it. I didn't know how to process it. I didn't want to believe it. I wanted my father back. I wanted him the way he had always been.

I was quite literally unconsolable for several days. There was about a week that was a complete blank in my memory for many years. I was sleepwalking through the experience, wishing and hoping that it wasn't true. That my big, strong father, the joker, would jump out from behind the door or out of a closet and say, "Haha! I was just fooling around." I could not, I would not let my mind go to such a sad and horrible place.

Then I blamed myself for his death. I told my mother that it was my fault he had died. Just a day before his accident, my father and I argued about french fries. He told me I couldn't have any because of some lapse in my work attitude that day. I remember sitting in the truck by myself fuming and angry saying to myself, "I wish you were dead! I wish you were dead." I said it several times. I confessed this to my mother, I told her it was my fault, because I had wished him dead, and now he was. Of course, she told me this couldn't possibly be true, and I should not blame myself. But still, I felt incredibly guilty, and somehow complicit in his death. A terrible added burden that I carried for some time.

In hindsight, it took me about seven years to come fully to grips with the fact that he was really dead and gone, and he was never going to come back. This was a painful period for me in many ways, good and bad. After psychoanalyzing myself for years, one of my takeaways was to be personally responsible for my actions and behave in a way that would not jeopardize the safety and security of those who are relying on me. If you have a wife and three children at home, you should not be out at a bar drinking and then joyriding on your motorcycle. You should be at home with your family.

Life as I had known it up to this point was about to change in many ways. I was also going through puberty at this time, and I don't recall getting any accurate or responsible information about what was happening to me. A few weeks before my father died, I had visited a friend nearby. He was a year and a half older than me, and I considered him smarter, more mature, and more worldly-wise than I was. During our visit, he said, "I have something to tell you about, it's a really big deal."

"What are you talking about?"

He told me his cousin had visited him the previous weekend and he had shown him how to jerk off. I didn't know what he was talking about. He explained to me what his cousin had demonstrated for him. He told me how his cousin had jerked his stiff penis until some sort of thick white stuff—he called it jizz—came out and dribbled down the side of his penis!

"What!? What are you talking about?"

I didn't have a clue, I had never heard of anything like this.

He said, "If you want to, we could try it?"

Not knowing what he was talking about I said, "OK, sure."

So we went into the woods, found a quiet spot, and we both pulled our pants down. He looked at my crotch and said, "Wow! You already have hair down there!" He did not. That was the first time I realized that I had pubic hair, just a few wispy curls. I had not noticed this before he pointed it out. Then we laid down and played with our little erections for a while, but nothing happened. We eventually gave up and went home to eat dinner.

About a week later, I was at the local swimming beach, Haviland Pond, late in the day with my mother. I was in the water by myself. There weren't any other swimmers nearby, so I started to play with myself. I found this very stimulating. I slipped my bathing suit off which aroused me even more; I just had my suit around one ankle. I started to play with myself a little bit more. I was startled by how really good this felt, an experience I never had before, a kind of pleasant rippling in my groin. My knees and thighs started to tense up and tingle, I didn't know what was happening, but it felt amazing and I did not want to stop. I looked around to make sure no one could see me and what I was doing. I kept playing with myself. It felt so good...I thought I should stop, but I found that I could not, it felt so good... almost too good ...Then all of a sudden, I had what I now know was my first orgasm. That incredible release of tension and pleasure! I looked down into the water and saw my semen squirting out of the end of my penis in a long, sinewy strand. I was shocked, and I was embarrassed and hoped no one had seen me. I looked around. No one seemed to be noticing me thankfully. I quickly pulled up my swim trunks and tried to pretend nothing had happened, but that feeling stayed with me for some time and the memory of it was extremely pleasurable and also shocking. This was the beginning of a long love affair with my sexuality.

13

Moving to Grandpa's House

*"Real change, enduring change, happens
one step at a time."*

—Ruth Bader Ginsburg

In 1961, the Brennans, who had been living with our grandfather, bought a farmhouse with eighteen acres of land at 392 Fuller Street. In 1962, my mother sold the house at 42 Stanley Street and we moved in with my grandfather at 12 Rood Street.

We settled into our new home quite easily. I think our grandfather was happy to have someone in the house for company and to help with things like mowing the grass and shoveling snow. He had his dog and his hunting and fishing interests, but he did not want to live alone. His professional career had been at the Springfield Armory as a gunsmith, retiring after twenty-five years with a gold watch. He maintained a small shop in the cellar. His hobby business involved doing modifications on double-barrel shotguns, modifying them in such a way that both barrels could be operated with one trigger instead of two.

My mother eventually sold the milk delivery routes to Daylight Dairy

MY MOTHER'S FATHER, WALTER, AND HIS FRIEND, JACK
BRADSHAW, RIDING ARROW MOTORCYCLES IN CHICOPEE FALLS,
MASSACHUSETTS IN 1915. NOTE THE SINGLE-SPEED BELT DRIVE.

and she went to nursing school, graduating on December 19, 1965. She started working as a licensed nurse at the Springfield Memorial Hospital where she worked for over ten years.

As I got older, my relationship with my brother Douglas was not especially close. Even though he was only two and one-third years older than me, I felt like he was from a different generation. He was from the '50s and I was from the '60s. We got along fine, and I respected him but we did not share a lot of common interests. After high school, he went to a junior college and got interested in computers, an exercise of the mind that he enjoyed. I was much more interested in hands-on interests, making stuff with my hands which eventually led me to a cooking career. We became much closer later in life, spending more time together and sharing some common interests.

Douglas had graduated from high school and enlisted in the Army to avoid being drafted. He went to Vietnam where he was a radio operator and nothing bad happened to him. He came home and settled in

Arizona with his new wife, but that relationship did not last. When he was discharged from the Army, he was in Seattle, Washington. My mother paid for me to fly out there and drive back with him. Six days on the road together was a good bonding experience for both of us.

By this time, I was glad to be done with the milk delivery business. I was ready for something different. While I was still in high school, I got my first food service job. I learned how to make donuts at a Polish bakery called Chmura's in Indian Orchard. It is still there to this day. A great place to work, always busy. It was a nice cooperative environment where everyone chipped in when needed to get the work done that needed to be done.

Besides making donuts, I learned how to form dough into bread loaves by hand, and how to peel loaves in and out of the hot oven. The rye bread always got a wash of cornstarch and water on the way into the oven and then on the way out to make up a nice chewy crust.

All the guys I worked with were extremely hard-working and friendly. They called me, "Bobby." "Hey Bobby, how you doing today?" "Hey Bobby, can you give me a hand with this?"

I stumbled on with my education. I think I went through a standard adolescent phase of narcissism which distracted me from my studies, so I managed to fail seventh grade. The second major failure in my life. Laziness was my Achilles' heel. I can't really explain where my mind was at this time. I definitely was not focused on my studies.

I also have wondered more than once why my mother didn't intervene more. I assume she thought I was still suffering from the loss of my father. Maybe I was.

I remember for the longest time I teased and pestered my younger sister Karen mercilessly. I remember her asking our mother, "Why is he so mean to me?" I'm not proud of it now. I wish I hadn't done it, but I did eventually change. And what changed me in that regard was my first love interest. Unfortunately, she was also the love interest of a good friend of mine. Slowly, over a period of years, I developed quite a bit of affection for this young woman. When I confided in one of my teachers about this budding relationship, she said, "Don't do it. If she'll do it to him, she'll do it to you." But I went ahead anyway. The positive effect of this love interest was that I stopped teasing my sister and I began to get much better grades in school. Almost overnight, as if a switch had been flipped. This was as much a mystery to my sister as my meanness had been. I remember listening to her talking to our mother after the change of attitude, saying, "What's happened to him?" I knew what was happening, but I didn't want to talk to anyone else about it. Things definitely became easier for my sister Karen.

It took three attempts to get my driver's license. On the first attempt, I was making a three-point turn in a residential neighborhood and while I was backing up, waiting for the rear wheels to touch the curb, there unfortunately was a fire hydrant next to the curb. I didn't see the fire hydrant and bumped it with the bumper. The instructor said, "That could've been a small child." Failure number one.

On my second test, in another residential neighborhood, the instructor told me to take a left at the intersection. I looked both ways and started through the intersection, but it was too late before I realized that I had missed the stop sign. Failure number two!

On my third—and final attempt—I messed up one of my answers on the oral exam. But I think the instructor felt sorry for me because he knew it was my third try so he gave me a pass.

The first time I drove down the street by myself in one of our old trucks was thrilling. I couldn't believe how much fun it was. I kept thinking to myself, "I can go anywhere I want." Of course, I now had the responsibility to not run into any other cars or go into a ditch. I fell in love with driving. I still love to drive to this day.

Even though my father died riding a motorcycle, I have never lost my love for these machines. They speak to me, talk to my inner self. When I was seventeen or eighteen, someone set up a motorbike rental business in our town. A friend and I would go there and rent these small motorcycles on an hourly basis. I was a little afraid of upsetting my mother, so I didn't ride where I thought she might see me or others might see me and tell her that I had been riding a motorcycle. This love affair with these machines continued unabated.

In 1966, when I was nineteen years old, I told my mother I wanted to buy a motorcycle. I tried to make the argument that if my father died driving in a car no one would expect me not to drive a car. A weak argument obviously, but it was the only one I had. After a brief discussion she agreed, and she took me to a brand new motorcycle shop in Springfield. I think this was the first year Suzuki imported motorcycles from Japan. Their slogan in the magazines was "Suzuki are here!" They were the first production motorcycles with a six-speed gearbox. I was fascinated by that feature, so with my mother's help, I bought myself a brand new 1966 Suzuki X6 Hustler for $625. And a helmet, of course.

At that time I was working at Chmura's Bakery just over the bridge from Ludlow. The first day I drove the motorcycle to work, I parked it behind the bakery. I was going about my job as everyone was when it occurred to me that no one was talking to me and I thought it was because they saw my motorcycle and they didn't approve. I had some guilt attached to this purchase

My grandfather, Walter Fay, reading the morning newspaper, about 1960.

because of how my father had died.

After about two hours, one of the other workers came in from outside and said, "Hey, whose motorcycle is that out there?"

I said sheepishly, "Oh, it's mine."

They all started congratulating me and we all went outside to look at it. It turned out my guilt was misplaced. The fact was, they were all happy for me, which of course made me feel much better. They told me they were excited for me.

Instead of going straight home that night, I went for a long ride through Belchertown and Amherst, about forty miles. The feeling was euphoric. I remember looking down at the motorcycle as I was riding it thinking how thrilling, how exciting. I loved it. I also had some thoughts of my father's feelings when he was out joyriding on his motorcycle in 1959. But I had not been to a bar, and I did not have a wife and children at home, and I was

MY BRAND NEW 1966 SUZUKI X6 HUSTLER. THE FIRST PRODUCTION SIX-SPEED GEARBOX THAT I KNOW OF. IT COST $625. YOU CAN PAY MORE THAN THAT FOR A GOOD HELMET THESE DAYS!

wearing a helmet. Of course, I had a mother and sister at home but I did not feel irresponsible. I felt happy and free. I still love it, I can't help myself. I can't adequately explain it except to say it's in my blood.

In June 1966 I graduated from Ludlow High School. Our class was the first one to graduate after four years in the new high school that had opened in 1963. My high school experience overall was very positive despite my slow start. Thanks to some excellent teachers and the encouragement of friends I was able to develop a lifelong love of learning. After graduating, I took some evening college courses at American International College, but courses like Sociology 101, did not have any relevance for me.

I took a job working in a paper tube factory in Ludlow and rode my motorcycle. I drove that motorcycle to work five days a week every month of the year. At the end of the year, the odometer read 13,000 miles. I had ridden to Cape Cod and up to Laconia, New Hampshire, for bike week in early June. The ride to Laconia was a trip down memory lane for me. In 1955 and 1956, our father took the entire family to Laconia, so that he could watch the motorcycle races there at Belknap Park. In 1966 the races were at Bryar Motorsports Park.

I loved these trips because we were all together as a family. My father would go to the races and mom and the children would go to Weirs Beach to spend a day swimming and picnicking. We also would get to take a ride in a big mahogany cruising boat on Lake Winnipesaukee, maybe it was a Chris-Craft, or a Hacker-Craft—either way, it was always a special treat.

One year I begged my dad to take me to the races, a request I lived to regret. All I remember is sitting under a pine tree in the hot sun watching motorcycles zoom by thinking to myself I had made a big mistake. But I had no one to blame but myself. I could've been spending the whole day at the beach, which would have been much more enjoyable for me.

14

My Public Education

*"Success is not final, failure is not fatal.
It is the courage to continue that counts."*

—Winston Churchill

When I look back on my public education, I think it's a small miracle I've been able to achieve what I eventually achieved in the way of personal success. I enjoyed going to school but I did not enjoy doing school work. I was a lazy, lackluster student for most of my schooling. Despite the fact that I stayed back twice and most of my grades were dismal until my last two and a half years, it never occurred to me to drop out. I knew I needed to get a high school diploma and possibly additional education to be able to make it successfully through life.

Did I mention I failed second grade? Nobody fails second grade, but I did. It was only because I was lazy, not because I couldn't do the work. I remember handing in assignments with my name on a blank piece of paper. My mother arranged for me to go to summer school working with a teacher at her home two hours a day, three days a week. I don't recall getting much out of the sessions, probably because I wasn't putting much effort in. I learned much later in life that in schooling, as in so many other things, the result is directly proportional to the effort.

Teachers also played a very important role in my success or lack of success. I repeated second grade with a different teacher, who I liked more than my first second-grade teacher and I did better.

Third grade was no problem, I loved that teacher, Miss Gary. At the end of the year she announced that she was going to go to Europe that summer, and if anyone would like to get a postcard, they could put their name and address on the paper she passed around. She sent me a beautiful postcard of a castle in Denmark, commenting, "Oh Robert, what fun you would've had exploring all the little stairways and passageways in this castle." She was right, I still love exploring the passageways in old forts and churches when in Europe.

In fourth grade, I had my first male teacher, Mr. Weaver, which was unusual at the time. I did well.

I did OK in fifth grade with Mrs. Hill and in sixth grade.

Junior high school was a different story. I managed to fail seventh grade mostly because of a lack of effort. In eighth grade, we were asked to fill out what track we wanted in high school. I signed up for the college prep track because it seemed like the logical thing to do. Anyone who wanted to become someone had to go to college.

In my eighth-grade math class one day, our teacher, Mr. Robert Steele, called me out in front of the entire class saying, "And then there's Robert Fuller. He's got a lot of nerve signing up for college prep when he can't even do the simple geometry we're working on here."

Of course, I was embarrassed, hurt, and angry. But rather than being crushed by him, I decided I would show him. I might have been a late bloomer, but once I woke up, my results started to improve. Perhaps Mr. Steele did me a favor by embarrassing me out of my indolence.

Every person needs to find something that they are good at and once they can get that fire lit, they can get much better results in other studies also. It took me some time to figure this out.

In my freshman year of high school, I went out for the football team. I'd never played football before, but I weighed 250 pounds so I made a pretty decent tackle. There were some other large players on our team also, so we went undefeated in our first season. Being part of a successful football team made me quite proud of myself. But not proud enough to work hard at my studies.

My first semester of my sophomore year in high school I flunked off the football team. Out of five subjects I got three F's on my report card. I went to the locker room and the coach said, "Hand in your gear. You're done." I was shocked by what he said. He said, "You heard me. You can't fail three courses and play football. You need to buckle down on your studies and not be distracted by football."

This was like the glass of cold water my father had thrown in my face many years before. Football was the only thing I cared about, or certainly the thing I cared most about. So I resolved to do better in the future and I began to apply myself more fully to my studies. Little by little I made progress by doing more of my homework and engaging more in my daily class time. Achieving better results—i.e. better grades—gave me an improved image of myself and my confidence level rose, leading to even better results.

This cycle of self-improvement became addictive. Doing better made me feel better about myself, and as I had more confidence in my ability to achieve things that I had previously thought were beyond my ability, I realized I could do even better. It might sound trite but I began to realize that the result is directly proportional to the effort.

I didn't know it at the time but this was perhaps where I took my first steps on my road to felicity. My yellow brick road, if you will.

Each semester, there was an honors assembly in the school auditorium at which students who had made honors were mentioned and congratulated. There were minimum honors, general honors, and maximum honors. Names were called by year and by level of achievement.

As the names were called for freshman minimum honors, each student would stand up, and when all the names for that class had been called, there was a round of applause. This format would be repeated for each grade level. High honors students were called up on the stage one at a time, given a certificate of achievement, and applauded one by one.

The first time I made minimum honors the entire auditorium burst into a spontaneous round of applause the moment my name was called. I stood up and looked down at the floor, it appeared to me to be at least ten feet away. I had never felt anything like it before. It was the first time I actually felt proud of myself, and realized that I really could do better than I had done previously. Just because I had a lackluster record at that point didn't mean that I couldn't do better. I began to realize that if I made goals for myself, and worked toward them, I might be able to make some of these achievements that had previously eluded me. A good lesson to carry forward in my life.

I found this sense of achievement to be quite addictive. The better I did, the better I wanted to do. I became more interested in learning, and the pure love of learning became a source of joy for me, an experience that was new to me. I had some really good teachers that I liked and it gave me great pleasure to please them.

I would like to think that as my results improved they realized their efforts to be good teachers were working. I hope they felt good about their important profession. I hope they realized that their good work was the root of my success. I now believe that the education of young people is one of the highest callings.

In my senior year, I decided to run for class president. I had no experience in politics of any kind but I set this as a goal for myself just to see if I could do it.

With the help of a few friends, a couple of good speeches that I wrote myself, and quite a few humorous campaign posters, I mounted my campaign.

Elephant jokes were popular at the time: "How do you know an elephant has been in your refrigerator? You see their footprints in the butter." I used these kinds of silly jokes to draw attention to my campaign posters. I was running against two other candidates who intellectually were much more highly qualified than I was. One of these students went on to Brown University, and the other one went on to Bryn Mawr.

Part of the process of running for president was to attend a general assembly where each of the candidates stood on stage to face the rest of the student body and give a short speech about why they should be elected.

I wrote my speech. The week before the speech presentation was due our student newspaper had a heading that said, "Vote intelligently in our class election." I used that headline as the theme for my speech. I had never spoken in front of a large group before; I wasn't sure I could do it.

The day before the assembly, I went to the auditorium by myself, stood behind the lectern, and practiced my speech to an empty auditorium. This turned out to be a very good idea. I practiced my speech three or four times that day.

The next day when it was time for me to give my speech, I got to the lectern and because of nerves, I had trouble getting started. I just stood there for a moment or two. I'm sure some people were starting to wonder if I was going to say anything at all, but then I found my footing, my voice. I gave my speech and I got a nice round of applause.

After I had given my speech a couple of students came up and complimented me on the quality of my speech. They wanted to know who helped me write it. I was proud to tell them I had written it myself without assistance from anyone, and that what I had said were my true thoughts. They had trouble processing that information which made me realize that there were probably a lot of people in my school who thought they knew what my capabilities were. Of course, this added to my self-confidence.

I guess I impressed enough people in the audience because when the votes were counted, I had won. This was another feather in my cap of achievement. Another thing that added to my belief in myself and my possibilities for achievement.

On the other hand, my dating life in high school was a pretty dismal story. At one time I remember telling a friend, "I've had more broken dates than completed dates." I was not especially outgoing at the time and I did not feel good about my appearance. The idea of approaching a young woman and asking if she'd like to go out with me was frightening. What if she said no? As it turned out, there were several times when a girl who had agreed to go somewhere with me called me later and told me that she couldn't go for some reason. Hence more broken dates than completed dates. I was so inept at this process, I actually asked a girl if she would go out with me even though I knew she was already going out with someone else.

She looked at me befuddled and said, "You know I am going out with Pete right?"

I went, "Oh...yeah, I just thought...ha...I'm sorry. That was pretty dumb of me, wasn't it?"

I mean it doesn't get much weaker than that. It was a painful process. But little by little, I learned. I realized that women have similar feelings. It's an awkward time for all concerned.

15

My First True Love Interest

First love often doesn't last, but its effects can cling to the psyche for life.

My first real lasting love interest was Sally, whom I met as a child in eighth grade. She had a profound impact on my development, my learning, my self-esteem, and so many other personal successes that I've been able to experience in my life. Our relationship was platonic for many years. We had mutual respect and curiosity about things like music, poetry, and classic literature. She was very smart and I was thrilled that she enjoyed talking with me. We shared many common interests even though we operated at different levels academically. Our friendship continues to this day.

We've had many peaks and valleys along the way, but she is the only person I know outside my family members who has kept in touch with me all these years. She was one of the students at the honor assembly who got called up on the stage because she always got straight A's on her report card.

One of our earliest common interests was the poetry of E.E. Cummings. We read many of his poems together. Anyone familiar with his poetry knows he was particularly adept at the subject of love, with lines like:

"consider O, woman this, my body. for it has, lain, with empty arms, upon the giddy hills, to dream of you."

Or "your little voice, Over the wires came leaping, and I felt suddenly, dizzy."

Or "when i have thought of you somewhat too, much and am become perfectly, and simply Lustful."

Or "somewhere I have never traveled, gladly beyond, any experience, your eyes have their silence: in your most frail gesture are things which enclose me, or which i cannot touch because they are too near... (i do not know what is about you the closes, and opens; only something in me understands, the voice of your eyes is deeper than all the roses) nobody, not even the rain, has such small hands."

Or "love is a place & through this place of, love move, (with brightness of peace), all places, yes is a world & in this world of, yes live, (skillfully curled), all worlds."

Or "i thank You God for most this amazing day: for the leaping greenly spirits of trees and the blue true dream of the sky; and for everything which is natural which is infinite which is yes, now the ears of my ears are awake now the eyes of my eyes are opened."

These lines and many others touched us then, and still touch me to this day. Making these discoveries with this very special friend, heightened my love and appreciation of all things beautiful and ethereal. My sensitivity, appreciation, and aesthetic values began to blossom in the heart of this beautiful friendship.

Sally was very intelligent and gentle-natured and she had high ethical standards, and she also liked a good joke. "I just heard that it is national sex week, so don't let your meat loaf." This was long before our relationship became more intimate.

Slowly, over a long period of time, the relationship developed into something more. In high school, we would go for long drives in her car stopping at different romantic spots, talking, and eventually kissing and hugging and touching, making out, and fogging up the windows. For me, it was a very exciting time of discovery. I can remember those feelings still, the sense of the new, the realization that I was finding out what love feels like, feelings I had never felt before. I really couldn't believe what we were doing. I'm sure this road of romantic discovery happens to everyone at some point but this was my own personal road of discovery and I was loving it. This friendship continued through high school, college, and continues, despite long stretches of radio silence. Sally was a significant influence, who affected my development as a thinking and feeling being.

After high school, Sally went to Smith College in Northampton. During this time, I was often away on one of my many different adventures. We continued to correspond by letter and postcard. When I was back home I would go to visit her. She was my only love interest for many years. I wanted her all to myself. But when she made it clear to me that I was not her only love interest, that she was a free person who could be with whomever she wanted, I understood her feelings and could not disagree. I was hurt, but I didn't allow it to diminish my desire.

About 1965 the first contraceptive pills became widely available. It also coincided with the beginning of the women's liberation movement. Mores and attitudes about sex and a woman's place in the world were changing rapidly. It's hardly surprising that Sally was swept up in the times.

In the fall of Sally's sophomore year, we would go for rides on my motorcycle. On one of these rides, we went to visit a waterfall in the Berkshires. We arrived late in the day and there were no other people around. It was quite a romantic spot as I recall, especially when we had it to ourselves. Sitting on the grass next to the waterfall, we started a predictable sequence of kissing, touching, and rubbing our bodies together,

SALLY, MY FIRST TRUE LOVE.

something we had done many times before. It typically would continue for some time until we had exhausted our passions, or had absorbed all the sexual frustration we could hold. Then we would pull apart and profess our love for each other and move on to other activities.

But this time was different, very different. I didn't realize it until it was happening, but it was going to be a very profound shift in our relationship's behavior. We were lying in the grass kissing and bumping and grinding. I'm sure she knew I was quite aroused, hugging and kissing most passionately, as we had done many times before. But this time she whispered in my ear, "I want to feel you inside me."

I thought to myself, "What? What did she say? Now? Here?"

I had to ask her with my eyes to make sure I had heard her correctly.

"Yes," she said, "yes," like Molly Bloom in Ulysses.

My heart was racing like mad.

With her eyes, "She said yes, a thousand times yes. The answer is yes! Yes, right now!"

I really never expected such a request. I was caught off guard.

Of course, I wanted to please her. But was I ready? We had had many make-out sessions in the past, but I never dared or expected them to culminate in actual sexual intercourse. I was both surprised and pleased. I think this was the first time I realized that women are capable of having strong sexual desires, similar to but different from those of men.

Before this time I assumed sex was all male-driven. To realize that a woman actually wanted me in that way was a revelation, an entirely unexpected and unanticipated turn of events. A pleasant turn.

I never was taught anything about this aspect of being human. I had virtually no sex education when I was growing up. The only fractured information I had was the sort of stuff you learn about by talking with friends, most of it not very reliable information.

To realize I was lying in the grass with a real live willing sexual being was exciting and a little terrifying. What if I did something wrong? What if I did something that was not pleasurable? But I went ahead anyway... blindly, and the memory of it is still a sweet spot in my extra special memory book.

16

Leaving Home for the First Time

"Every path but your own is the path of fate. Keep on your own track, then."

—Henry David Thoreau, *Walden*

In May 1967 I decided to go to Montreal by motorcycle to see Expo '67. This was one of the most successful World's Fairs ever. They had sixty-two nations participating between April and October and over 54 million visitors. I wanted to see the American Pavilion with its large geodesic dome designed by Buckminster Fuller. I rode on the monorail and spent two days visiting many of the other pavilions and exhibits.

The ride home was not pleasant, it rained most of the way. I went down the west side of Lake Champlain through Plattsburgh and across the Champlain Bridge picking up Route 125 east which brought me through Middlebury, Vermont to Route 7 south, which took me to Rutland and finally, back to Massachusetts.

It was about 325 miles of rainy riding. One of the few things that stuck in my mind on the whole ride was a vision of the Middlebury College campus. In particular, a building called the Château. It looked like it had been transported from the Loire Valley in France. I made a mental note to go back and visit this town sometime in the future when the weather was better.

My first major motorcycle adventure happened the year after graduating from high school. In June 1967, my friend Howard and I decided we'd like to take a cross-country trip. Howard had a cousin in Laguna Beach, California.

We purchased a 1950 Ford sedan that had been partially customized. It had a V-8 flathead motor with two deuces—two twin-barrel carburetors. It also had a Hurst shifter on the floor. It had two bucket seats up front and no seat in the rear. A pretty hot setup for its day.

The person we bought it from had been rebuilding and customizing it. He had stripped off the original paint and painted it a flat gray primer. He lost interest in the project and sold it to us for $125. Both Howard and I had motorcycles which we wanted to take with us on this trip. Howard had a 305 Yamaha Big Bear Scrambler and I had a 1966 Triumph TR6R, a 650 with a single carburetor. So, we bought a homemade trailer for thirty-five dollars.

While we were making our plans to carry our bikes with us to Laguna, our friend Jack, who also had a Yamaha Big Bear 305 Scrambler, caught wind of our plans and said, "Hey, I want to go too." Jack had already done his freshman year at the University of Massachusetts, Amherst. He was excited about having a summer adventure.

Jack, Howard, and I were well acquainted, as we were all good friends all through high school. We had played on the football team together and graduated from Ludlow High School the same year. But Howard had signed up for the Navy and was scheduled to report to basic training in August.

We loaded the three motorcycles on the trailer and one of the bike tires went through a rotten spot in the trailer. Not to be discouraged, we inspected the rest of the trailer and put a small piece of plywood over the rotten section, reloaded the motorcycles, and went for a test drive on the Massachusetts Turnpike to see how the car would handle the extra load.

Howard and I sat in the bucket seats and Jack was in the back on some wadded-up sleeping bags. All was going pretty well until we got to one of the long uphills and we noticed the needle in the temperature gauge was in the red zone, a bad sign. These cars had a very simple radiator cap. It had a large tension spring to hold a gasket in place and keep the water in the radiator. If the engine got too hot, the spring would flex under the heat and pressure and allow water and pressure to escape out of a metal overflow tube on the side of the radiator.

We pulled into the breakdown lane, lifted the hood, and noticed that water was squirting out of the overflow pipe on the side of the radiator. After studying the situation for a few minutes, we decided to wait for the engine to cool down some. Eventually, we took the radiator cap off and added a little more cool water that we were carrying with us.

The ultimate solution we came up with for this overflow problem was to jam a piece of wood into the bottom of the overflow pipe so the hot water could not escape. Not the smartest solution, but it's the one we decided to try. We continued our test ride, keeping a close eye on the temperature gauge. When we went downhill, the temperature would go down. When we went uphill, the temperature would go up. But as long as it didn't get to the red line, we knew that the water that was in the radiator couldn't get out. We figured we had it all sorted out. Within a week our plan to drive to Laguna was ready to hatch.

Jack did not want to tell his parents that he was going to spend the summer driving to California with Howard and me, as he was afraid they would forbid it. So, instead of confronting them he just left them a note:

"I've been kidnapped by Robert and Howard, they are taking me to California to visit with Howard's cousin in Laguna Beach. We're going to spend the next six or seven weeks driving there and then back to Massachusetts. I'll be back in time to go back to college. Love, Jack."

This was the summer of 1967, what became known in California as the Summer of Love. We knew nothing about this at the time, we were just going to visit Howard's cousin. Just before we pulled onto the Massachusetts Turnpike to head west we rechecked our load. We had two spare tires for the car, one for the trailer, a five-gallon jerry can of water, and a few extra quarts of oil.

We were on the road! All were excited—no cell phones, no credit cards, and very little cash. I think I had about $250, and Jack and Howard had about $150 each. We had not spent any time obsessing about budgeting for this trip, it was more like a blind expectation that everything would work as we hoped.

We agreed that if we could at least make it as far as Lake George, New York, about 100 miles west, we would spend the summer there. That would be our point of no return. Several people knew we were going on this trip and we didn't want to be seen as quitters or failures. I'm happy to say we passed Lake George with flying colors and continued west across New York State. Howard had a friend in Cincinnati, so that was our first destination.

We had mostly fast food on the interstate rest areas and slept in the car or on the ground next to the car. I don't believe we had a tent with us. This was the first time in my life I had been on a trip where it took more than one day to get to a destination. I remember feeling in awe of how big the country was and how much there was to see.

We made it to Cincinnati on the second day. From there, we drove toward Indianapolis, Indiana. Late in the day we just happened to go right by the entrance to the famous Indianapolis Motor Speedway. I insisted that we stop and look around. The gates were closed but easy to climb over. Which is what we did. The place was completely empty. I decided I just had to walk around the track, all two and a half miles of it. I loved looking at the braided skid marks on the asphalt where cars had gone around and around and around before hitting the wall and leaving huge black smudges on the wall where the tires had impacted. It was fascinating to me to think of all the racing that had gone on there over the years. The first race was held in 1909. The track was paved in 1910 with 320,000 paving bricks. The first 500-mile race was in 1911. So much racing history.

When I got around to the start/finish line, there was still a small section of the original brick that gave this racetrack the nickname, "The Brickyard." A little past the start/finish line was an area of the track that had been dug up for repairs. The asphalt had been stripped away and some of the original bricks were exposed while some had been dug up and were sitting there in a little pile. I thought, wow, what a perfect souvenir from this storied racetrack. So, I picked one up one of the bricks and I started heading for the exit where Jack and Howard were waiting for me. A security man came along in a pickup truck and asked me what I was doing. I told him how we were driving cross-country and I just wanted to look at the track. He noticed a brick in my hand and said, "You better just leave that here." Then he took me back to the gate where Howard and Jack were waiting just outside. He then told us to remain a little longer and that he'd be right back. After about ten minutes, I realized he was allowing me to climb back over the fencing and be on my way. Which is what I did. I'm still sorry I don't have that brick.

The next milestone I remember was St. Louis. The stainless-steel Gateway Arch had just been completed. I remember being quite impressed with the quality of the welding on the outside of the arch. It was so new that the observation train that ran inside it was not functioning yet. We walked around, looking at the arch and Busch Stadium. And I think we probably went on a tour of the Anheuser Busch Brewery.

We continued west toward Denver and veered south to Colorado Springs. We were surprised to find out that it was legal for eighteen-year-olds to drink 3.2 percent beer. I'd never been to a bar where we could get served legally.

The next day we decided to unload the motorcycles and ride up Pikes Peak—nineteen miles and about 4,000 vertical feet up to the 14,000-foot summit—quite a thrill. I'd never seen anything like it before. It was the biggest mountain I'd ever seen. It was a whole new world, a whole new expansion of my life, and my world view.

In 1967 most cars and motorcycles had drum brakes. Drum brakes are subject to overheating on long downhill roads like the one coming off Pikes Peak. As the drums heat up, they are distorted, so that less of the brake shoe touches the drum. They become much less effective. It's called brake fade. So there was a checkpoint about halfway down the nineteen-mile road where cars were required to stop and their brakes were checked for overheating. If they were found to be too hot, they had to wait there until the brakes were cool enough so that they could descend the next nine miles safely.

We decided it would be fun to just coast on our motorcycles for the entire nineteen miles. It was a blast! When we got to the checkpoint we didn't stop, we just kept coasting right on by the park rangers who were waving at us. A ways farther down we were finally flagged to a stop by an irate park ranger.

He said, in a very agitated voice, "What do you think you're doing?"

I remember saying, "Having fun...This is so cool..."

He was very mad. He said, "Do you think dying is cool?"

I apologized.

He looked at our brakes, detained us for a while, and then let us go with a promise to not misbehave again.

"Yes sir, I promise."

I was still amazed that we could drive all day and not reach our destinations but after a while, we sort of settled into the rhythm of being on the road, wondering what we would see that day.

From Colorado Springs we headed south to Pueblo and then turned into the mountains. Our first big test for the car was to get over Wolf Creek Pass. On our way up the pass, we kept a close eye on its temperature gauge. When it got into the red zone we would stop at a rest area and let the engine cool down. With the help of a heavy glove, we would release the radiator cap, which was usually accompanied by a small gusher of hot water and steam. Having lost two or three quarts of hot water, we would refill the radiator with some of our cool water and then continue to the top of the pass.

One stop per pass for cool water was usually adequate. By the time we were at the top of the pass, the temperature gauge would be in the red zone but as soon as we started to go downhill, the strain on the engine was much less and it started to cool off. Our plan was working quite well, and we were pleased with ourselves.

We had not done a whole lot of trip planning so I'm sure there are many places that we would have found interesting but we were too focused on getting to the West Coast. Our next target was the Grand Canyon. We went through Flagstaff, Arizona, and then headed northwest, toward the canyon. We viewed the canyon from Mather Point on the south rim, where the north rim is about ten miles away.

Once we had filled up our senses there, we headed for Las Vegas. On route, we drove over Hoover Dam. In 1967 the East–West Highway went across the top of the dam. You can still drive on top of the dam, but only to get to the parking lot on the southside. The main highway now crosses over the Colorado River on the Mike O'Callaghan-Pat Tillman Memorial Bridge, a very long, beautiful concrete arch bridge just down the river from the dam outside Boulder City, Nevada.

We happened to cross the dam late at night. There was very little traffic, so we stopped halfway across and looked over both sides. Wow, we were awestruck. Pikes Peak, Wolf Creek Pass, the Grand Canyon, Hoover Dam, holy cow, it's one thing to read about them and look at their pictures. It's quite another to have an up-close experience. This was just the beginning of my love affair with travel.

We arrived in Las Vegas around eleven or midnight, even then it was a city that never sleeps. We went right downtown to look at famous casinos such as Golden Nugget, Pioneer Club, Horseshoe, and Mint.

EILER LARSON, THE OFFICIAL LAGUNA GREETER, WHO WAS
STILL VERY ACTIVE WHEN I FIRST WENT TO LAGUNA IN 1967.
WE WOULD SEE HIM ON THE SIDE OF THE COAST HIGHWAY
ALMOST EVERY DAY.

We noticed that in casinos there are no clocks anywhere to be seen. We stopped at a bar called Whiskey A Go Go to watch a topless dancer. I recall having a sad feeling of sympathy for the dancer. It did not look like she was enjoying herself and consequently was not very enjoyable to watch. We went to one of the many casinos to try our luck at the slot machines, a.k.a., one-arm bandits.

I was playing a nickel machine when I surprisingly hit a jackpot! While I was waiting for a bunch of coins to spill out of the machine, an attendant came over and gave me two dollars and sixty cents in nickels and then informed me that I had to put at least one more nickel in the machine to clear it before I could leave. I remember thinking that was so cheap. I mean, I'd already given that slot machine five or six bucks and they had to get one more nickel out of me. Fortunately, I've never been addicted to gambling of any kind.

From Las Vegas, it's pretty much a straight shot across the Mojave Desert through Barstow to Newport Beach and then a little bit south to Laguna Beach. I think the whole trip across the country took us about seven days, plus or minus.

Howard's cousin was deeply involved in the surfing scene. He was happy to see us because he had a 1950 Ford Woody Wagon, the ultimate surfer vehicle of the era. Unfortunately, his car had a blown engine. So we made a deal. We could stay in his apartment for a couple of weeks if we gave him our car. Maybe some money changed hands, I don't remember. But we checked out the Laguna Beach scene and swam in the ocean as we tried to figure out what to do next.

We were quite amused when we saw a unique Laguna personality—Eiler Larsen, a.k.a., "The Greeter." He was a well-known fixture in Laguna by that time. He had been living there for over twenty years. He would stand on the Pacific Coast Highway by the main beach and wave to every car, pointing his wooden cane, and shouting his catchphrase,

"Hellooo! Delighted to see you. Are you alive?"

He was a Danish vagabond who had traveled to many places around the world, but he had been in Laguna since the 1940s, and there is still a statue of him there in Laguna Beach. He was sometimes referred to as Laguna's first hippy because of his long hair and beard. He ended up being adopted by the town. People gave him a free place to stay and free meals. He was proclaimed Laguna's official greeter by the mayor in 1964. He continued his waving ways until 1975 when died at the age of 84.

After a couple of weeks, we found a room for rent in an old motel on the Pacific Coast Highway in Corona Del Mar, a few miles north of Laguna; a suburb of Newport Beach. And right across the street from the motel was a big Denny's restaurant. I went there a few times for breakfast. I thought they had great pancakes. I was very impressed with the Denny's because it was so big and flashy.

I was also very impressed when I went to the crosswalk on the Coast Highway, a very busy highway. The traffic would stop and allow me to cross. This is a law in California that was strictly enforced and it was new to me. On the East Coast, I would expect to have had to wait for a break in the traffic and then dart across the road as fast as possible.

It was July now, and Howard was making plans to sell his motorcycle and report to the Great Lakes naval station training center north of Chicago. I'm not sure when he left but once he was gone, it was just Jack and me in the motel room. Money was running low and I was having trouble finding a job. In desperation, I went to an employment agency and they found me a job at a small factory in Anaheim called Simco Silicone. I didn't even know what silicone was at the time, but I was desperate. The job was a second shift, from four to midnight, six days a week, and paid overtime over forty hours. I don't remember what the rate was but, it wasn't much.

My job involved running a heated press. I had a set of molds. I was to put slabs of raw silicone into a mold and then put it in the heated press, pull a lever, and watch the pressure in the press. When it reached the correct pressure, I would release the lever and pull out the mold wearing a pair of thick leather gloves. The press was very hot. I would pry apart the mold and blow the cored silicone pieces out with an air hose.

I was making little round tube-shaped insulators for a toy called a VAC-U-FORM to be used in a Mattel toy. Each one of these toys had four of these insulators on the heating pad. Simco had been making these heating pad insulators for years. I was amazed to think of how many VAC-U-FORM toys there must be out in the world.

I had to keep track of my production on a worksheet. I think each mold had about one hundred of these small silicone cylinders per mold and I probably processed one mold every five or six minutes. It was a hot, mind-numbingly boring job. Perhaps the worst job I ever had.

Years later a friend said, "Sometimes it's easier to decide what you don't want to do, so by a process of elimination you can get to what you do want." One thing I knew for sure, I didn't want to work at a job like that for an extended period, it was just too boring. I spent a lot of time staring at the concrete block wall next to my hot press wondering what kind of summer adventures my friends back in Massachusetts were having.

One of the odd memories I have about riding to my job there in Anaheim at three thirty in the afternoon was going right by Disneyland. It was just off the freeway. I'd never been to Disneyland, and now it was right there. I mean I could see Magic Mountain. But I was not going there, I was going to work at this terrible Simco Silicone job instead.

While living in Corona Del Mar, I read a copy of *The Wizard of Loneliness* by John Nichols. I was attracted to the title because I was feeling a little lonely after being away from home for several weeks. Coincidentally, this novel was made into a movie that was filmed in

Bristol, Vermont, in 1988. Several local people, mostly children, appeared in the film. A friend of mine was paid to let his 1937 Chevy be parked on Main Street during the filming because the story was set in that era.

The book had a positive effect on me, as I identified a little bit with the main character. I remember there was a funny sequence in which two boys had a skunk by the tail—if you hold a skunk by the tail, it can't spray. Their goal was to toss it down a neighbor's cellar hatchway. They lifted the hatchway door and swung the skunk by its tail as they counted, "One, two, oh shit! I dropped the skunk!" I found the telling of this prank quite amusing, I remember laughing out loud.

The book had a pleasant ending, where the two main characters were married, and spent their honeymoon in a small cottage in the Champlain Islands of northern Vermont. I recall feeling warm and heartened by the story and hoping that some version of it would become my life someday.

I've driven through the Champlain Islands many times since moving to Vermont, and there are still some of those small cabins on the islands. When I see them it reminds me of this book and how my life has become a pleasant version of it. How lucky I am.

Another cherished memory from this time was when I went to see the movie *Walkabout* subtitled, "An Aborigine and a girl, 30,000 years apart, together." The story, as I remember it, is about a young girl who is a nanny to an even younger boy. They are taken into the Outback of Australia by the boy's father. While they are picnicking, the father sets the car on fire and shoots himself, thereby abandoning these two young children. They are completely unprepared to live in the Outback. They find a small watering hole where they drink and decide to sleep for the night. When they wake up in the morning, the watering hole has gone completely dry.

They're quite confused and don't know what to do next. Then out of the heat waves on the horizon comes a mostly naked Aborigine boy running in their direction, chasing a lizard with a wooden spear. When he gets close to them, he stops, and there's a beautiful and brutal close-up of a bunch of dead lizard heads, hanging out of his waistband with flies buzzing around their heads. He looks at these two White children briefly and starts to walk off. They call to him for help. He realizes their water source has gone dry. So he shows them how to break off a hollow reed and push it down into the sand enabling them to suck up water that is just below the surface.

Satisfied that he has done all he can for them, he turns away to continue on his walkabout. The young girl yells, "Stop, stop, we must come with you."

This young Aborigine is on his walkabout, a rite of passage for young males who leave their tribe and live by themselves relying on their wits for a year before returning to their tribe.

He tolerates them tagging along. The three of them have several adventures filmed in a way that makes this way of life look quite natural and beautiful—hunting and cooking your own food and swimming in beautiful natural quarries.

The young girl and boy eventually find their way back to civilization which almost immediately looks less civilized than the wild world they have been traveling in. The first person they encounter is quite rude to them, asking them not to walk on the grass or something similarly banal.

At the close of the movie this young girl, now grown, has become a married adult. She's living in a high-rise apartment in Sydney or Brisbane. Her husband comes home from the office and starts talking about some office politics, who might get promoted or fired for some infraction or another. She then has a flashback. Her mind wanders back to her time in the Outback with the young Aborigine—30,000 years ago swimming in a natural quarry in a little piece of paradise where all the gifts of creation are at your fingertips if you just know how to look for them. This film taught me that it's not how much you have but how well you can man-age what you do have that contributes to building a happy life.

17

A Long & Wild Ride Home

*On a motorcycle you are completely immersed in the
environment, not merely riding through it.
You feel and smell everything.*

On a Saturday afternoon in the third week of August 1967, I was sitting
in my room with my roommate Jack. Howard had already flown back to
enter the Navy. I was thinking about going to this job I didn't want to go
to. Then out of the blue, Jack says, "Let's ride to San Francisco tonight. If
we don't do it now, we won't have time."

We didn't have any maps, we didn't have the vaguest idea of how
far it was or how long it would take. I was due to be at my job at four
that afternoon, but the idea of riding to San Francisco was much more
appealing than going to work. Plus, I had an ulterior motive. My friend
Sally had been to San Francisco and when she found out I was going
to California she said, "If you go to San Francisco, go to Market Street
to the London Fog store and buy me a scarf." So, that was my mission.
Simco Silicone be damned.

Jack and I got on our motorcycles and headed north. We did virtually no preparation for this ride. I think Jack was wearing sandals because

if you want to be cool in Southern California you don't wear leather boots, you wear sandals. We had to ride up through all the suburbs of Los Angeles and Los Angeles proper. Somewhere near Los Angeles, at around seven o'clock, just as it was starting to get cool, we went by a big sign that said San Francisco 405 miles. Yikes, we had no idea it was that far away.

Jack pulled over to the side of the road, looked at me, and said, "I don't think I can do that. I'm heading back."

I informed him I was committed to going without telling him why. I know it wasn't a good idea but I was on a mission. I had to buy a scarf.

"OK, I'm gonna keep going." And I did keep going, all night. Riding behind big trucks on the freeway in a dense fog all night, I could hardly see. When it started to get light I pulled into a rest area. My hands were freezing, my whole body was freezing. I went into a restroom at a truck stop to put my hands in a basin of hot water. Looking at myself in the mirror was pretty horrifying. My face was completely covered with grime and dirt from following those trucks in heavy fog for hours. But I was within striking distance of San Francisco and I wasn't about to turn around now. So, after I don't know how many hours, maybe fifteen in the saddle, I pulled onto Market Street in San Francisco and parked my motorcycle in front of the London Fog store.

They weren't open yet, so I went to the cable car turnaround at Powell Street. I rode the cable car to Fisherman's Wharf and had an early lunch. I have to say riding those cable cars was quite a thrill. I loved watching the cable car operators start and stop the cars. Oh, the way they pulled those big levers to grab the constantly moving cable and then to release it and pull on the brake lever when they let people on or off. I also loved the way they rang out tunes with their warning bells.

It was a beautiful morning and I was thrilled to be in the city by the bay, "where little cable cars climb halfway to the stars..." Fortunately or unfortunately, I did not know of the Summer of Love. I didn't hear about Haight-Ashbury until I was back in Southern California and told someone I had been to San Francisco. They couldn't believe I went all the way to San Francisco and did not go to Haight-Ashbury to experience the Summer of Love.

I went back to the London Fog store and bought a scarf for Sally. Then I got back on my motorcycle and started to head south. By about four in the afternoon, I was feeling pretty tired so I pulled over to the side of the freeway, laid down in a grove of pine trees, and immediately fell asleep.

Sometime later, a truck went by and blew his horn, and woke me up. Good thing or I might've slept there for hours. I got back on my motorcycle and continued my journey south. As I was passing through Los Angeles, I knew I was getting close. But I could hear my rear drive chain slapping around inside the chain guard. It was probably almost worn out so I decided I would just go real easy on the throttle. I made it to the Newport Beach exit in Orange County.

I got off the exit with about ten miles to go. I was shifting up very gently but the drive chain just let go and rolled off the sprockets onto the ground. I could see the lights from the Orange County Airport about three miles away. I thought about pushing my motorcycle there, but I was just too tired. So I pushed it off the road into some tall weeds and started walking.

It was dark by now and I was very tired. I was walking very slowly. Very, very slowly. I was spotted by a couple of highway patrolmen. They pulled up behind me and asked me what I was doing and why was I walking so slowly. I think they thought I was high on drugs; they shined a flashlight in my eyes. I explained to them what I had just done and where I was trying to get to.

They said, "OK get in the back of the car." They took me back to where my motorcycle was stashed in the weeds to verify my story. Then they offered me a ride back to Corona Del Mar. I thanked them profusely.

In trying to be friendly and make conversation so I said, "Are you guys friends with Broderick Crawford?"

He was a television actor who played a detective on a highway patrol series on television that I remembered.

"Hell no," they said. "That guy is a drunk, he's been arrested for drunk driving several times. He's not a friend of ours, he gives us a bad name."

I apologized and they took me to my motel room. I think I got there at about ten at night. Jack was a little surprised and happy to see me and I was pretty happy to see my bed. Jack couldn't believe it.

"Really! You rode all the way to San Francisco and back."

"Yes," I said, and I showed him the scarf that I had purchased to prove it. I told him about my broken chain, and how I had stashed my Triumph in the weeds. Then I fell asleep.

On Monday morning there was a knock on our motel room door—unusual. I opened the door and the guy said, "Are you Robert Fuller?"

"Yes."

"I'm from Western Union, this telegram is for you."

I thought, who could be sending a telegram to me? Had some relatives of mine died? I opened it up and it said:

"This is to inform you of your termination of employment."

It was from the manager of Simco Silicone. Wow, these guys were tough. Miss one overtime shift and you are out on your ass. That was fine with me. I was ready to be done with that job.

I was able to purchase a new chain for my motorcycle, and Jack gave me a ride up to where I had stashed my motorcycle in the weeds. After putting on the new chain, I rode up to Simco Silicone, collected my final pay check, and started making preparations for our trip back to

Massachusetts.

We decided we needed to get tanned before we went home so it would look like we had spent all summer at the beach, which we had not. So a few days before leaving, we spent most of one day at the beach and promptly got badly sunburned. On our way off the beach, someone even commented to me, "You've got a pretty bad sunburn there, buddy." It was a big mistake: that sunburn haunted me for days afterward.

Jack decided that we should also lighten our hair so it would look like we had spent a lot of time in the California sun like all the surfers we saw on the beach. We bought some hair coloring at a drugstore. That didn't work so well either, it looked like a really bad dye job.

In less than a week, Jack had sold his motorcycle and sent the money back to the University of Massachusetts, Amherst. We made our plan to ride back to Massachusetts on one motorcycle. We packed up what little gear we had in one backpack which Jack wore on his back. We didn't have a lot of money. So, we planned to sleep on the side of the road because we didn't have enough money to rent motel rooms. We would eat as cheaply as possible and hope for the best.

Now this motorcycle we were riding was my 1967 Triumph TR6R. It had a three-gallon gas tank and a long flat uncomfortable seat. With two people on the bike, there's nowhere to move around, you just sit and ride. This proved to be quite uncomfortable. The longer we rode the more uncomfortable it became. Riding two-up we got about 125 miles per tank of gas before I had to put the bike on reserve and then look for a gas station. I got to where I could hardly wait for that bike to go on reserve so I could get off the seat and rest my butt in a less painful position.

We rode out through Barstow and then veered to the right onto the famous Route 66, "The Mother Road." We stopped in the towns of Ludlow and Amboy to get gas. As I recall, it was about 112° when we stopped for gas in Amboy. I asked the young attendant if he liked living there because it was so hot.

He said, "Oh, it's not that hot today. Yesterday it was about 118."

I asked, "Do you really like living here?"

He said, "Oh, I don't live here. I live in Barstow. I came out here for the summer to get away from it all."

I guess everybody has their own idea of paradise. For me, a ride across the Mojave Desert in late August on a motorcycle felt like riding in an oven. At one point, we saw a sign on the side of the road advertising the restaurant up ahead that said it was "water-cooled." So, we stopped to take a break from the heat. Well, water-cooled is not air-conditioned, so we went from 112° and zero humidity outside into a restaurant that was about 85° and about 80 percent humidity. It didn't seem like such a good trade to me, we immediately started to sweat profusely. We ordered a couple of cokes and were on our way. We were out for an adventure and we were getting one.

By about eight thirty, we pulled into a gas station on the Arizona border in the town of Needles. We sat there drinking a couple of sodas. We had driven about 300 miles, but it felt like 500. I don't know what Jack was thinking but I was thinking this is gonna be one hell of a long, uncomfortable ride. Are we really going to sleep on the side of the road in the desert?

Then a guy came through the parking lot on a pristine Triumph Bonneville, all black and chrome. He was wearing black jeans and a white T-shirt, and he had a full head of red hair that was swept back. He circled a second time to where we were sitting, butt-ass tired and sweaty, and asked, "Where are you guys headed?"

"We're riding to Massachusetts," I said.

He said, "I'm riding to Detroit. Maybe we should ride together."

It immediately sounded like a good idea to us. It would be good to have some company, especially if there was a mechanical breakdown.

He asked, "Where are you staying?"

We said, "We don't have a clue."

"Well, I've got an air-conditioned room over here," he replied. "If you don't mind sleeping on the floor, you could spend the night with me."

We told him we didn't have a lot of money.

He said, "Well here's what we'll do. I'll pay for what it costs for a single room," which was about twelve dollars a night those days, "and you guys chip in what it costs extra for a double, which is like another three dollars."

Sounded like a pretty sweet deal to us. Air conditioning and shower for a dollar-fifty each. What's not to like? That was the deal we struck.

His name was Rusty, of course, and riding with him was an education in itself.

Rusty wanted to see the Grand Canyon. We'd already seen it once and didn't care to see it again but were happy to tag along with him because of our arrangement.

When we got to the south rim and were all standing there looking out over the canyon, Rusty said, "He's out his ever-loving fucking mind."

We said, "Who?"

"Evel Knievel. He's been telling people he's going to jump the Grand Canyon on a motorcycle! There's no fucking way he's gonna jump this. He's done some pretty crazy shit in his day, but this is impossible."

We had never heard of Evel Knievel until that moment. So, Rusty explained to us a little bit about Evel Knievel and how he had been a regular customer at the motorcycle shop of Bud Ekins in North Hollywood, where Rusty had worked for a couple of years.

On December 31, 1967, Evel Knievel did his famous jump over the Caesar's Palace fountain in Las Vegas. It was the longest jump he ever attempted, 140 feet. He had a terrible crash at the end of it, which resulted in multiple broken bones, and he was in the hospital in a coma for twenty-eight days.

September 8, 1974, Evel Knievel attempted unsuccessfully to jump the Snake River Canyon in Idaho. His parachute opened prematurely and he survived with minor injuries. He performed more than seventy-five ramp-to-ramp motorcycle jumps in his career. He died on November 30, 2007, in Clearwater, Florida.

Later in the trip, Rusty told us about a lot of well-known people who rode motorcycles like Steve McQueen, Paul Newman, and Clint Eastwood, who were regular customers at the shop where Rusty had worked as a mechanic. They would just show up with one or two motorcycles in the back of a pickup truck and leave them there for service. The shop he described was pretty fancy compared to the shops I had been in. It was complete with walls of tools and hydraulic lifts to hoist the bikes and make them easier to work on. It was a celebrity bike shop in its day.

Bud Ekins was a professional racer and stunt rider. He was Steve McQueen's stunt double for the famous jump in the film *The Great Escape* because the directors did not want to take a chance on their star being injured. Bud Ekins was the person who introduced Steve McQueen to desert racing which became a passion of his. Steve McQueen was quoted as saying, "Racing is life. Anything before or after is just waiting."

Leaving the Grand Canyon, we went up through the Rocky Mountains and headed toward Denver. At one of our gas stops, Rusty said he thought there was something wrong with his clutch. In Denver on a Saturday afternoon, he got in touch with a bike shop in Boulder that said they would let him use their tools. One of the employees was going to be there late working on his own bike. So we took a left turn and headed up to Boulder.

In the shop, I watched Rusty take the primary case off the side of his engine, take his clutch out, and dismantle it to make some adjustments. I was impressed because I had never done any deep adjustments like that on my own bike. In fact, the internal workings of a motorcycle engine were a complete mystery to me at the time. The idea of taking one partially apart while on a cross-country motorcycle ride was also frightening. What if I couldn't put it back together again? Then what would I do? Watching Rusty work on his bike, I realized it is possible to work on your own bike. I had never considered it before because I didn't have any experience, and no one had ever tried to teach me.

When Rusty was done working on his clutch, he went for a little test ride and was satisfied with the results so we mounted up and headed east into the night. We stopped at a low-class motel in a small town in eastern Colorado, maybe Firestone or Fort Lupton to spend the night.

The next day we were hell-bent on putting on some serious mileage. So we rode east onto the Front Range riding across eastern Colorado into Kansas, and then into Iowa, stopping only for gas and to get a bite to eat. We went through Omaha and were headed to Des Moines. As day turned to night, we started seeing signs saying Des Moines 60 miles, then Des Moines 50 miles, then Des Moines 40 miles, etc. Every time we saw one of those signs, we leaned a little more forward to cut our wind resistance while twisting on the throttle a bit more. By the time we got to Des Moines 30 miles, we were going flat out, as fast as my single carb 650 could go, about seventy-five or eighty miles per hour, side-by-side, slicing through the night air with one thought: let's get to Des Moines as fast as possible and find a place to sleep. We were ready to find our motel for the night.

We had just passed the Des Moines 10 miles sign when all of a sudden without warning my rear tire blew out! Completely out! The first thing I heard was the sound of metal and asphalt. I thought we had thrown the chain, but it was the metal rim scraping on the asphalt! The bike started to wobble, violently. I let off the throttle and I put my feet out as though I might have had a chance in hell of bracing the bike if it decided to go down. I didn't dare touch the front brake for fear that that would definitely lead to a catastrophe.

When Rusty realized what was happening, he went to the left-hand side of the road and tried to stay out of the way. We went from one side of our lane to the other, we went into the breakdown lane, we went back into the travel lane, and all this time my friend Jack had a death grip around my chest. It's fair to say we were petrified—scared stiff! By the time we slowed down to about thirty miles an hour, I began to think, we might actually come to a stop without going down, which is what we did. I think we all considered it a minor miracle. So, there we were on the side of the freeway, ten miles outside of Des Moines, Iowa, with a blown-out rear tire in the dark. Now, what the hell are we gonna do? We all discussed our situation. Rusty also thought it was a small miracle that we had not crashed, and we should be thankful for that.

Without a lot of options, once again, I pushed the bike off the road into some tall weeds. We had enough tools that we were able to take the rear wheel off. Jack and I successfully hitchhiked with the rear wheel to the Des Moines exit and the friendly driver who picked us up drove us to the nearest motel. We rented a room and we fell into our beds.

The next day, Rusty and I rode into downtown Des Moines with my rear wheel to find a motorcycle shop. I couldn't afford a new tire so I bought a used Avon tire. Same size but a different brand. I had a Dunlop tire on the bike up until that point. We got the tire installed and Rusty gave me a ride back out to my motorcycle in the weeds. I reinstalled the wheel and we headed to the motel to pick up Jack and the rest of our gear.

When I stopped at the top of the exit ramp while exiting the freeway, I smelled burning rubber. I turned the bike off and put it on the stand.

I looked down at my new/used Avon tire and couldn't believe my eyes. The side of the tire had been rubbing on the chain guard. The Avon tire was slightly wider than the stock Dunlop tire. The rubber side wall had rubbed off the side of the tire, exposing the interior fabric! This was a major low point of the trip. I remember being close to tears. I remember thinking, "I'm halfway across the country, I just spent forty dollars on a used tire that now appears to be ruined, and I only have about forty dollars left to make it the rest of the way to Massachusetts." At first glance, the situation looked pretty hopeless. We readjusted the rear wheel, so it was no longer rubbing on the chain guard and rode the rest of the way back to the motel.

We discussed the situation. Rusty said, "Well, it's still holding air. I'll tell you what. Jack can ride on the back of my bike to take some of the weight off your tire and we'll see how far we can get." So that's what we did.

To save money, we rode all day and all night from Des Moines to Detroit, about 600 miles. I don't remember what time we started, but I do remember passing the turn-off to Kalamazoo, Michigan, at about three in the morning. Sometime in the middle of the night, we were riding in a heavy fog and I was following the white line on the side of the road. Half asleep, I followed the white line right up an exit ramp! Rusty was riding on my left. He almost missed the exit ramp. After that close call, we found an all-night restaurant and drank some coffee, a lot of coffee.

We got into Detroit later that morning at ten or eleven. I could hardly believe it: I had ridden 600 miles with a tire that looked like it could burst at any moment. But we did it, thanks to our lucky stars. Rusty's parents were friendly and accommodating. They gave us a place to sleep and fed us a meal.

The next day, Rusty said, "Tell you what, I'm going to give you the rear Dunlop tire off my bike. I was going to buy a new one anyway. The Dunlop I have is in better shape than that beat-up Avon tire." I don't know what we would've done without his help. After we got the tires changed, Rusty took the throttle grip off his bike and pulled a stash of pot out of the inside of the handlebar. We toked up a little bit to celebrate the end of our time with him.

For the ride home, Jack and I put on our cheap plastic rain gear because it was drizzling when we left Detroit. It drizzled all day. We rode 730 rainy miles back to Ludlow, Massachusetts in one day—one very long day.

Somewhere in western Massachusetts, on the turnpike in the dark, we were pulled over by a state trooper because my rear tail light was not working. He followed us to the next service area on the turnpike and we were able to ascertain the problem. The wire to the rear tail light runs up inside the fender and the extra weight of a rider with a backpack had caused the rear tire to wear away the wire. We rerouted the wire to the outside of the fender and the trooper allowed us to continue on our way without a citation. I'm sure he felt a little sorry for us, riding all day in the rain and all.

We got to the Ludlow exit at about eleven at night. We did not have the money to pay the toll, probably about thirty-five cents. Hard to believe now, that we were that close to the edge. We literally did not have thirty-five cents between us. But we did know where there was a gap in the fence in Ludlow. A gap we had used many times in the past to enter and exit the turnpike. Oh, what a wild bunch of lawbreakers we were.

To get to the gap we had to turn left across the grass median separating the east/west travel lanes and cross the oncoming westbound lane—traffic was nonexistent at that time of night—then cross a small one-hundred-yard field and up a five-foot hill and through the gap in the fence. The whole time we were making this a dangerous and illegal maneuver I was thinking, "I hope they haven't fixed that fence yet." The gap was still there. Yay! We were elated. We were back home.

Despite all our challenges and our lack of money, we successfully crossed the continent by motorcycle. We rode to Jack's house. I said, "I'll see you in a couple of days. I've got to get some sleep."

Well, when I had time to reflect I was pretty happy with myself. We had set a goal for ourselves to drive to the West Coast, and then to drive back, and we had accomplished our goal, albeit by the skin of our teeth. I also proved to myself that I could do what needed to be done and that I could make such dreams come true.

It was a good feeling and one that I have carried with me all these years—to believe in myself, and my abilities. Of course, one has to be careful not to become too overconfident and to carefully assess your abilities. In the words of Clint Eastwood, a.k.a. Dirty Harry, "A man has to know his limitations."

I also slowly formulated the philosophy that everyone starts life with a blank sheet. Whatever they became they had to learn how to master certain skills to achieve their goals. I am fond of saying, "If you have the interest, you will develop the skill." I certainly have made some mistakes along the way, but I have not had any major disasters, except one. More on that later.

In recent years I wondered whatever became of Jack and Howard. When I attended my fiftieth high school reunion in 2006 I was hoping to see them there. Unfortunately, they are both dead. Jack had died in 1996 and was buried in the same cemetery as my mother and father in Ludlow. I was told Howard had been living on Sanibel Island, Florida.

I'm sure they would have held on to different memories of this coming-of-age adventure than I have and it would have been interesting to cross braid these memories and have a few good laughs.

After I regained my equilibrium, I went to Smith College to deliver that scarf that I had put so much effort into procuring. I believe Sally was pleased, but I don't think she could really appreciate what I had been through to get it for her. But I was in love and would have done it again if she asked me.

The funny thing I still couldn't figure out was why would a very bright, young woman like Sally be in love with a working-class guy like me. I can only say that her affection for me greatly improved my sense of self-worth. If this smart high achiever thought I was worth spending time with then, of course, I felt better about my capabilities and that made me want to please her. I learned to build on these good feelings and slowly, little by little, I built up the confidence I needed to become a high achiever or at least a higher achiever. Over time our relationship blossomed into a full-blown love affair with all the accompanying mix of emotions and activities. The ups and downs, the joyful times, and the painful times. You can use your own imagination.

18

Leaving Home for the Second Time

Goodbye home, hello adventure.

After my first return to Ludlow, I found a job with an overhead door company. I was attracted to it because it involved working with my hands outdoors, something I generally feel confident doing. Jack went back to the University of Massachusetts. Howard was at the Great Lakes Naval Training Center north of Chicago.

After his basic training, Howard came home on leave to visit his family and pick up his 1957 Chevy. He invited me to drive back with him to Chicago, which I was only too happy to do. We decided not to take the New York State Thruway, but rather its precursor, Route 20. It's a much nicer, slower drive through places like Cherry Valley, skimming just over the top of the Finger Lakes, to stop in towns like Skaneateles, Auburn, Seneca Falls, Geneva, and Canandaigua. And a lot less traffic.

As I recall, it took us two days to get to Chicago. Howard introduced me to some of the local sites like the observation deck in the Hancock tower. The Navy pier on the waterfront. We went to the charming Old Town Neighborhood, which was having some kind of street fair when we were there, very lively. He took me to my first Burger King. Home of the Whopper. I'd never seen one before. We spent a couple of days together.

Howard took me to the hospital, where he was in training to be a medic. Turns out when he got to basic training and was given some tests he did quite well so one of his instructors called him aside and said, "You're a pretty smart kid, you should put in to become a medic," which is what he did. He was still in training when I visited him there. He explained to me that a lot of the patients in this hospital were just in from Vietnam.

"You know, it's so weird. One day they're walking around the rice paddy and boom! A few days later they wake up here," said Howard.

They ask, "Where the hell am I? and How did I get here?"

I realized right then and there that I did not want to go to Vietnam.

While I was in Chicago, I visited the offices of the National Restaurant Association on Lakeshore Drive. I had already decided that I might want to pursue a cooking career. I had read in a magazine that the National Restaurant Association would have information there about cooking schools around the country. They were a little flummoxed by my request but eventually, a woman came out from the back office and told me about the Culinary Institute of America in New Haven, Connecticut, which she described as "the college for cooks." I knew right away that's where I wanted to go. I wanted to have a profession that would make me marketable. I wanted to have a credential that certified me as a professional. I wanted to travel, and I was sure that if I had a solid, certified profession I would be able to find a good job anywhere. Unlike the experience I had in Southern California.

I flew back to Massachusetts and immersed myself in my new job installing overhead doors. One of the side skills I liked best was learning how to weld with an arc welder, what's known today as stick welding. It's a pretty rough kind of welding but very useful if you're trying to build something sturdy like a bracket to hold up an overhead door.

Then I received my first draft notice. I had six weeks to report. My plan was to fail by being overweight. In six weeks, I gained almost twenty pounds and I was already overweight. When I went to the draft board, everyone had to strip down to their underwear. The guy who was measuring my height was pretty short, so he stood next to me in a chair. I stood with my head bent down, and he said, "Stand up straight." So, I bent my head up, and I bent my knees down. He measured me at 6' 2½". My real height at the time was 6' 4". When I got on the scale I weighed 292 pounds. I was forty-eight pounds overweight. I was informed that I would be getting a 1-Y, which was a temporary deferment. People I knew who were not in college were getting drafted left and right.

I had another motorcycle friend, Dennis, who was not in college and hadn't been drafted yet. We started to formulate a plan for another road trip, this time to Florida. He was working an overnight shift as a shelf stocker at a large supermarket.

We bought a 1954 Chevy panel truck, the precursor to the van. We rigged the truck with a big piece of plywood on top of a bunch of milk crates and other boxes, which we eventually filled with dented cans of food that Denny got from his job at a deep discount. Some of them may have been "accidentally" dented. I was able to "procure" some angle iron from my job and weld it onto our utility trailer frame forming two rails where our motorcycle tires would go. I also welded a trailer hitch directly onto the heavy-duty bumper of our panel truck.

We planned to leave in late February 1968, after the Daytona 500. We didn't even know about Bike Week at the time, which was not as big an event as it is now. We packed up our rig with food and other gear and a couple of sleeping bags on top of the plywood and headed off down Route 91.

We didn't even make it to Hartford before we had our first flat tire on the trailer. We didn't have a spare tire so we parked in a breakdown lane, took off the flat tire, and disconnected the trailer. Dennis stayed with the trailer and I went off looking for a junkyard and bought a used tire and got it put on. We put everything back together and continued down to the Connecticut Turnpike. Then somewhere between New Haven and Bridgeport, we started having transmission trouble. The transmission would not stay in high gear. It kept jumping out of gear and going into neutral. We tried holding down the shift lever, but that didn't work. We continued in second gear to Bridgeport, Connecticut, where we pulled off the highway and went looking for a transmission shop. It was late on our first day, but we found an AAMCO transmission shop. They were closed for the day so we parked in their parking lot and that's where we spent our first night on the road—in the back of our panel truck in our sleeping bags, eating green beans and corn out of dented cans.

We were relieved when the workers showed up the next morning. However, they informed us that they only worked on automatic trans-missions. They referred us to another shop in town that could help us out. Amazingly when we got there with no reservation or other advance notice they said, let's put it up on the lift and have a look. They pulled the gearbox out, put it in the back of a pickup truck, and drove us to a large junkyard a few towns to the east that they had called. They had one of these gearboxes on the shelf ready to sell for thirty-five dollars. So we paid for it, went back to the shop, and they installed the gearbox—a stroke of luck for us.

As I was backing out of their parking lot's driveway onto the street, there was a deep rain gutter at the edge of the lot. As the rear wheels went into this rain gutter, the trailer hitch hit the roadway surface pretty hard and cracked one of the welds on the hitch. I pulled back into the yard gingerly. We looked it over and one of the guys at the shop kicked it a little bit with his foot and said, "That looks OK." It didn't look OK

A POSTCARD OF A RESTAURANT THAT NO LONGER EXISTS, RIGHT ON
ROUTE A1A IN ORMOND BEACH, FLORIDA, IN 1968. THIS IS WHERE MY
COOKING CAREER BEGAN, MY VERY FIRST COOKING JOB. I LOVE THE
SLOGAN, "YOU'LL BE GLAD YOU STOPPED."

to me, but they had already helped us with our gearbox. I didn't want to
press for more favors.

So we hooked up the trailer and down the turnpike we went. As
we were pulling away from the toll booth in Norwalk, Connecticut,
the trailer hitch succumbed to its injury and fell off the bumper. I had
installed safety chains so the trailer didn't scuttle off by itself; we dragged
it to the side of the road. The weather was fair, but my mood was pretty
pessimistic. I left Dennis on the side of the road with the trailer and the
motorcycles, and I went into Norwalk looking for a phone booth so I
could consult the Yellow Pages to find a welding shop.

Yet another incredible stroke of luck: I found a shop and got directions to it. I pulled up in front of this welding shop with a yard full
of mismatched parts and other junk surrounding a rough-looking shop
building. There was a big Black man sleeping in his car in front of the
shop. It was Saturday morning, and I surmised later that he didn't want

to go to work but he couldn't stay home, so that's why he was there sleeping out front. Another incredible stroke of luck: He woke up and asked me what he could do for me. I was holding what was left of my homemade trailer hitch and I said I was hoping you could weld it back on my bumper.

He was a remarkably friendly and helpful guy. He took one look at my homemade welding job and said, "Who the hell did that for you, man? You're lucky the cops didn't spot you! You could've got arrested."

I said, "Well, I did it myself and as you can tell my skills in welding are minimal." He shook his head a bit and said, "I'll see what I can do."

He went into his yard and got some very heavy-duty C-channel and cut three pieces, two short vertical pieces about six inches long, and one horizontal piece about twenty-four inches long. He welded the short vertical pieces to the long horizontal piece and then welded the two vertical pieces onto the frame of the truck, not on the bumper but right onto the frame. I think it's fair to say when he got done you could've lifted the entire truck from that trailer hitch, it was that sturdy looking. He charged me twenty dollars.

I thanked him profusely and went back to pick up my friend Dennis. By the time I got back to Dennis, I was pretty discouraged.

He said, "Hey what's the problem?"

I said, "Look, we've only made it to Norwalk, Connecticut, and between the flat tire, the gearbox, and a trailer hitch we've already spent almost half our budget. Maybe we should just go home."

I was ready to bag out, but Dennis was very upbeat and gung ho to continue. I let him talk me out of quitting. Thank you, Dennis. The rest of the trip went pretty smoothly.

It took us six days to get to Florida; we were on secondary roads, not I-95. We had a flat tire every day. The tires on that panel truck were seventeen inches which was an unusual size at that time. Nobody had the right size tubes for them, so we just had to put in fifteen-inch tubes and hope for the best. We didn't have a spare tire so every time we got a flat, we had to stop and take off the wheel and roll it to the nearest gas station. All gas stations fixed flats in those days. We would get it fixed and then roll it back, put it back on, and trundle off down the highway. Because we were traveling on smaller roads it wasn't a serious problem. Nonetheless, I learned an important lesson about persevering in the face of adversity.

I remember distinctly getting to the Florida State Visitor Center and getting a free cup of orange juice. It was something my mother had told me about experiencing when she went to Florida during the war to meet up with my father before he shipped overseas, and I was looking forward to it. I was glad they were still carrying on the tradition.

We drove past Jacksonville to St. Augustine, stopping to look at the oldest fort in the US and then down Route A1A, right along the coast till we got to Ormond Beach just north of Daytona Beach. We found our way to Tomoka River State Park. At the campground, we signed up for one week at three dollars a night, a total of twenty-one dollars. After we paid our fee, and I remember this quite distinctly, I had six dollars left in my pocket.

I was going to need to find a job. I spent two days checking with places like car washes, but they were not hiring. On the third day, I went to a restaurant called The Quick and Tasty, right on A1A in Ormond-by-the-Sea. The building was all white, with big red letters, proclaiming the name and their slogan, "You'll be glad you stopped."

I went to the back door and spoke with the chef, Ralph Sawer, trying not to look too desperate. He said, "Yes, we have a job washing dishes." He paused "It pays one dollar an hour."

I think he expected me to turn around and walk out. The federal minimum wage at the time was one dollar and sixty cents, but only if you produced products that went out of state. There was no minimum wage in the state of Florida in 1968.

I said, "When do you want me to start?"

He said, "You can start this afternoon at four."

"OK, great. I'll be here."

I remember thinking at the end of my six-hour shift, I now have twice as much money as I had when I started my shift. I had also gotten something to eat which was a nice bonus.

I'm pretty sure now this dishwashing position for a dollar an hour was a pretty hard position to fill, but I was happy to have it. I was trying very hard to make a good impression because I needed the income, so I tried to make myself the best dollar-an-hour dishwasher they ever had.

Payday was every Sunday night. Gloria who owned the place had everyone line up at the cash register after the restaurant closed, and she paid the entire week's payroll in cash out of one day's receipts. The Quick and Tasty was closed on Mondays.

After a week or so Gloria started complimenting me, telling me, "You're a really good worker. I bet you'd be a good cook. It's too bad we just hired a cook two weeks ago."

I think she was just brushing up my ego because she wanted me to continue doing a good job washing dishes. Well, a week later the new cook quit. So I went to her and said, "I'm interested in that cooking job."

There was a long pause and she said, "Well, I'll have to discuss it with Ralph the chef."

As far as I could tell, Ralph had been some kind of rough street kid when he was younger and he'd been taken in by this couple and trained to run the kitchen at The Quick and Tasty.

Ralph had been trained by Gloria's husband Clem who had died. Gloria continued to run the restaurant with Ralph, in charge of the kitchen. As far as I could tell, Ralph was completely devoted to the restaurant and Gloria. I'm sure he would've rather hired someone who was already a trained cook. He did not want to train a cook from scratch. But there was no one else around, so I was promoted to cook.

My very first cooking job! I was basically thrown into the fire with little or no preparation, broiling snapper cheeks and other fish, and making some simple spaghetti and meatball entrées. It was the first time I ever worked with a microwave, which was called a Radarange by Amana. That's how we would heat our spaghetti before we put the sauce and meatballs on it. We also used the Radarange to poach eggs in monkey dishes. If you left the eggs in the microwave too long, they would start to explode, making a mess inside the microwave.

This cooking job was a salary position at eighty-five dollars a week. That was for twelve hours a day, six days a week from ten to ten with a short break in the afternoon to have a meal. On Sunday night, after withholding, I would be handed seventy-one dollars and fifty cents in cash. I was still working for a dollar an hour.

Ralph was a hard worker but not a great communicator. He expected me to know things that I did not know. More than once he would say something like, "You don't even know how to poach eggs?" And then he would show me what he wanted.

Over time I learned quite a few basic cooking techniques such as how to broil fish properly and how to sauté dishes like shrimp scampi and chicken piccata. Ralph's primary job was to run the fryolators—four of them. The majority of the food at The Quick and Tasty was deep-fried.

Ralph was a rough, hard-working man who didn't waste a lot of words—he only spoke when absolutely necessary. One day by accident he dropped a meat grinder on my foot. Even though I limped around the kitchen for five days afterward, he never bothered to apologize. A negative role model.

There were three or four prep people in the kitchen, mostly

semi-retirees, working for what they called "their rocking chair money." They would work just enough for part of the year so that they could get unemployment money for the rest of the year.

The Quick and Tasty was a very hot kitchen. Every worker there had a personal fan blowing on them to make it tolerable. One afternoon the power went out for about two hours. The dining room had lots of picture windows, so we just kept cooking and sweating. We were all very grateful when the power was restored.

Every night after the last meals were served, Ralph would sit down on the milk crate at the edge of the hotline and pour two bottles of Budweiser into a large milkshake glass. After drinking the beer, he'd get up and start cleaning up, straining and filtering the fryolators.

The thing was, I had the confidence that this cooking thing was something I could learn to master. This is way before the age of the celebrity chef. Way before I had heard names like Paul Bocuse, Ferdinand Point, or James Beard. I wasn't looking for stardom, I was looking for a respectable job where I could earn a living. I worked at Quick and Tasty for five months.

In July, I got a notice from the draft board ordering me to report for my second physical in Jacksonville. I did not pass the physical. I tried to pass because I was pretty lonely at the time and I had the ridiculous thought maybe I should go into the military. That maybe it would give my life some structure. So, I stood up very tall and was measured at 6' 5". At 268 pounds, I was only ten pounds overweight, but I also had high blood pressure. I received another temporary 1-Y deferment.

But I had had it with this lonely cooking job at Quick and Tasty. I'd been living alone for the last two months because my friend Denny had returned to Massachusetts in May. So when I went back to the restaurant and told Gloria that I had passed the physical and I was probably going to get a draft notice within six weeks, I had to give my two-week notice. She was not very sympathetic, maybe even a little bitter. She wasn't happy that I was leaving in the middle of the summer season. But of course, there wasn't much she could do. She was a bit of a negative role model.

I packed up my gear in a duffel bag, strapped it to the back of my motorcycle, and rode back to Massachusetts by myself.

19

Beginning My Cooking Life

I love creating meals, to please people working with many ingredients and create something that wasn't there before. Bread is my favorite example.

After returning to Massachusetts, I got a job working in a mall at a restaurant called The Flaming Pit. It had a live charcoal fire for grilling steaks. It turned out to not be a very good job and it only lasted about two weeks.

Several times when I went to work, one of the managers would say, "Oh sorry, but the dishwasher didn't show up today, would you mind filling in for the day?" After this happened three or four times, I quit the job because it appeared to me that they didn't really need a cook, they needed a dishwasher. I thought I had risen above this level of employment.

There were still one or two dairies in Ludlow that were doing home delivery. I took a job working for Miller's Dairy. I didn't tell them, but I knew I was only going to do that job until I could go to the Culinary Institute of America in September 1969.

I had been exchanging letters with my friend Sally, but when I returned to Massachusetts I found out that she had another boyfriend.

It was the first time I really felt heartbroken. We agreed to remain friends and I would visit her from time to time when she was in college, but our relationship had changed and would continue to devolve, something I regretted because she had been so instrumental in waking me up to the finer things in life. No other person had that much effect on my aesthetic sensibilities. Of course, it was a period in my life that I'm sure many young people go through, a time of discovery while trying to develop into a well-rounded, educated, sensitive human being. We communicated less and less, and eventually the light all but went out. At least for a while.

In the spring of 1969, I went for my third and final draft board physical. I had spent the previous six weeks gorging at McDonald's. My friend Denny and I would go frequently, our standard order was three cheeseburgers, two fries, and a Coke. Then we'd go to a Dairy Queen for some kind of ice cream treat. Disgusting to me now, but that was then.

The doctor at the draft board looked at my chart, and without even taking my clothes off or checking my height, asked me to step on the scale. He set the balance beam to 300 and when I got on it, it sprang up. He said, "You are out of here." A few weeks later, I got my official 4-F designation, meaning I was unfit for military service, and I would not be called again for a draft physical. I now no longer had an excuse for being fat.

20

Attending Culinary School

I applied to the Culinary Institute of America and went for a site visit sometime in early 1969. The Culinary Institute had been started by two women, Frances Roth and Katharine Angel, in a storefront in downtown New Haven, Connecticut, in 1946, specifically to take advantage of the GI Bill. They reasoned that not all the GIs who came back from the war were going to use their benefits to go to college. So, why not create a school for cooks?

By the time I went there, it was a compact campus on Prospect Hill next to the Yale Divinity School. The campus was a collection of old mansions and other buildings that had been repurposed into classrooms and practical kitchens. There was one new dormitory and one of the carriage buildings had been converted into a bake shop and teaching production facility.

The school had also built one large demonstration kitchen where a very talented, entertaining chef, named Mr. G, would demonstrate how to produce the next day's menu. After watching the menu being produced, the students would go into smaller practical kitchens and repeat the lessons they had learned from Mr. G.

They could not house all the students on this little campus, so they had contracts with two old hotels in downtown New Haven, the Taft and the Adams hotels at the corner of College and Chapel Streets adjacent to The Green and the old campus of Yale. The hotels were about a mile from the main Culinary Institute campus.

I was accepted for the class of 1969. It was a regular scholastic schedule at that time, running from September to early June. Students were expected to get a job in the food service business during the summer break. My first year I roomed in the Adams Hotel. My room was on the second floor directly across College Street from the Sherman Theatre.

In September 1969, the movie Butch Cassidy and the Sundance Kid was released. Paul Newman had attended the Yale Drama School, so he arranged for the premiere of the movie to be screened at the Sherman Theatre. I was able to watch the action from my second-floor window right across the street.

They had big spotlights set up in the street and velvet ropes in front of the theater to try to hold back the crowd. It was quite a spectacle when the limousines pulled up with the big movie stars—Paul Newman, Robert Redford, Katharine Ross, and others. The whole scene turned into a bit of pandemonium. I heard later that Paul Newman had to punch someone just to get into the lobby. This was a very interesting introduction for me to my life in New Haven.

I, of course, went to the Sherman a few days later to watch the movie along with several other avant-garde films at the time, like Allen Funt's *What Do You Say to a Naked Lady?* and Andy Warhol's *Trash*.

The educational possibilities at the Culinary Institute of America when I went there were vast and varied. Many of the instructors were Europeans—French, German, Italian, English, and Swiss. My knowledge of food and cooking was extremely limited. As an example, my first week there I went out to dinner with a new friend-classmate Phil, and he ordered lasagna. I said, "What's that?" I had never heard of lasagna.

I SPENT THE SUMMER OF 1970 ON
MINNESOTA KEY, A LITTLE BIT SOUTH
OF SARASOTA, FLORIDA. I WENT
FISHING ALMOST EVERY MORNING
AND ALWAYS CAUGHT SOMETHING
DIFFERENT.

He said, "You don't know what lasagna is? You'll love it."

In one of the classrooms, I remember seeing a picture from *New York Times Magazine* of a Greek moussaka that had been made in a bowl with the dark, oily eggplant skin on the outside and then turned out of the bowl onto a serving platter. This dark, shiny dome had a wedge-shaped piece cut out to expose the layers inside. I thought it was the most exotic food I'd ever seen.

Learning about cooking and how to cook was like traveling around the world and having a multitude of new food experiences. I found it all fascinating. Honestly, I wish I had applied myself a little more seriously, but I did get a very good foundation of education there that has served me well in my professional career.

While I was a student in my first year, I worked nights right across the street from my room in a not-very-good fast-food franchise called The Smorgasbord. The best part of that job was the night manager Joe who became a good friend and helped me improve my self-worth by complimenting me and encouraging me to think better of myself. I was still quite overweight at the time. He was a good role model, trim, educated, and outgoing. I have tried to emulate his style.

Joe was highly educated and had only taken this night manager job because his wife was doing graduate studies at Yale University. They had one of those old, two-cycle Saab cars where you had to add oil to the gas tank every time you did a fill-up. These cars had an odd, freewheeling aspect to the transmission. When you let off the gas, the transmission would disengage, otherwise, the engine might suck too much gas-oil mixture into the cylinders and foul the spark plugs. I thought that was fascinating. I'd never heard of anything like it before.

They invited me over to their apartment a couple of times for dinner and drinks. Jane was studying cultural anthropology, she was a big fan of Margaret Mead. She told me interesting stories about Margaret Mead's studies in American Samoa. All new to me at the time. Getting to know this couple who were a little older and obviously highly educated, and who wanted to engage me in conversation, improved again my sense of self-worth.

My two years in New Haven were an important learning and growth period in my life. I knew I was embarking on a new path that was not the dairy business. Charting a new course for myself by myself. I'll list just a few things I learned in culinary school.

I learned a tremendous amount not just about cooking but about the restaurant business. I was exposed to multiple international types of food and cooking techniques. Of all the types of cooking, I was drawn like a moth to a flame, to French cuisine; it seemed so sophisticated and refined. Learning about Auguste Escoffier and Marie-Antoine Careme and the roots of haute cuisine fascinated me.

Learning the five mother sauces and their many daughter sauces, was an epiphany for me. Before culinary school, the only sauce I had ever heard of was not called sauce it was called gravy, most commonly turkey gravy. I bought a copy of *The Saucier's Apprentice* by Raymound Sokolov and studied it obsessively.

The culinary school's bake shop was also a favorite of mine and consequently where I did some of my best work. My earliest successes in the kitchen as a child were at my mother's elbow baking Duncan Hines cakes and learning how to make frosting, later called icing. So, learning some of the finer aspects of baking bread, pastries, and cakes was fascinating.

There are a lot more details that I would like to tell about my cooking career, but I think that'll be in a second book.

I also found facilities planning very interesting, where we learned the nuts and bolts of planning, starting, and or improving a restaurant.

Many of the students were ex-military who had been trained to cook military food and they knew they wanted to learn some of the finer points of cuisine. Working and learning with them broadened my view of the world too.

During my first year in culinary school, I didn't lose any weight, but I certainly did eat a lot of good food.

In the summer of 1970, between my two years at culinary school, I took a summer job as an assistant pastry chef at the Irving Hotel in Southampton on Long Island. This was a staid old hotel that no longer exists. It had a large complement of European staff, including the chef who was from Provence. He was a very nice man who was near the end of his professional career. I remember asking him if he was married. He said "I've been married twice, and both times I came home in the evening from work and found my wife in bed with another man. A danger of the profession I suppose. I will not marry again, but I do have a very nice friend now."

The head pastry chef was a much younger man, also from France. He worked with me in the bake shop during the day and as a waiter in the dining room at night. He taught me quite a bit about the art of making finer desserts. I still have the notebook I kept while I was working with him.

There were also lots of young American staff. We always had a break between lunch and dinner service when we would go to the beach. At the beach, I became increasingly aware of my weight problem. Back at the hotel, I got on the shipping scale and measured my weight at 315 pounds! My all-time high.

I decided to take drastic action. I decided to stop eating solid food for a day. After I did one day, I decided to go for two days, and then three days. After three days not eating solid food became easier. I was able to complete seven days without eating any solid food, only water. I had never done anything like this or even thought about doing it. I fasted completely taking nothing but water for seven days.

I made several interesting discoveries about food, appetite, and myself during this time. After about three days, my craving for food dissipated to almost zero. When I started thinking about eating again, I had a long serious conversation with myself about what I would eat first after not tasting any solid food for so long.

I considered many options. I decided I would break my fast with a leaf of iceberg lettuce, just one leaf, it was a good choice. I discovered how really good, flavorful, sweet, and moist a leaf of iceberg lettuce can taste—a food that I had previously considered to be bland and uninteresting. This was a major discovery. This made me realize that you can change your behavior. It is possible, and if you do adjust your habits, other positive changes may follow. What else can you do if you want to effect change in other aspects of your life?

You have to take the bull by the horns, you have to become the change. I know it sounds trite now but it was new to me at the time. It was a major course correction for me. I knew when I started to eat solid food again, I would regain my appetite. I was not sure I would be able to control my reentry. I made a list of foods that I would no longer eat, things that I knew were high calorie and high fat. What I found out was that after a week or two my craving for things like cheeseburgers, french fries, and ice cream just went away. As the craving dissipated, it became much easier not to eat these foods and to seek out healthier, lower-calorie alternatives. Through force of will, positive thinking, and momentum I started to lose weight seriously for the first time in my life and proved to myself I could do something that I had previously thought of as out of my control.

I started to see positive results, like putting on my pants—they weren't so tight anymore. Knowing that I had the power to control my behavior also made me feel good about myself. Later in my life, I would read books on the subject of fasting. It's just one of many disciplines like yoga, tai chi, or silent meditation, among other forms of disciplined physical exercise. I began to realize that I could control my behavior. I could take control of my life and I could become the person I would like to be. Just like my eventual success in high school, I became addicted to this feeling of self-control. To actually have control of my mind through the power of positive thinking, the ability to direct my life in whatever direction I wanted it to go. This was not a perfectly straight road. There were zigs and zags, ups and downs along the way, but I found out how satisfying perseverance can be.

The job at the Irving Hotel did not last. They were having a very slow season. I believe the entire operation shut down two years later. It was a type of vacationing that had gone out of fashion. In early July, several people were laid off, including me. I did not want to go back to my hometown for the summer. I was away, and I wanted to stay away. So, I called up a culinary school friend, Phil in Florida, to ask if I could spend the balance of the summer with him. He enthusiastically said yes. I packed up my gear in a duffel bag, strapped it to my Triumph TR6C motorcycle, and headed for Manasota Key in Englewood, Florida, a little south of Sarasota.

PERHAPS MY FAVORITE MOTORCYCLE OF ALL TIME. I BOUGHT
THIS BIKE BRAND NEW FOR $1,150. IT'S A 650-CC WITH A SINGLE
CARB. I REALLY LOVED THE UPSWEPT EXHAUST.

I got a job at Smitty's Beef Room in Venice Beach. I Rented a room
in Englewood just south of Venice Beach. My friend Phil was living with
his parents for the summer on Manasota Key. We spent a lot of our spare
time riding around in his brand new MG Midget sports car. If you've
never been in one of these cars, I can tell you it's kind of like driving a
go-cart with fenders. Very low to the ground, has very quick handling,
and is beaucoup fun.

Almost every morning, I would go to Phil's parents' house, and we
would fish off the beach in front of the house, catching something different every day. I spent many hours walking up and down the beach
looking for shells and fossilized shark teeth. These teeth are dark gray
and are said to be 50,000,000 years old.

There was a shell shop in Venice that advertised that Venice was the
shark tooth capital of the world. I still have a coffee can half full of them
on my workbench. Phil had a job at a private club and I had my job

at Smitty's, but we spent all the time we could together exploring the region. This area of Florida was new to him also because he had grown up on the East Coast but his parents had moved to Manasota Key on the west coast of the state seeking a less hectic lifestyle at about the same time he went off to culinary school.

We visited places like the beautiful Ringling Museum of Art in Sarasota. We took a tour of the Van Wezel Performing Arts Hall designed by a student of Frank Lloyd Wright. It looked to me like a giant purple clam.

We went to Lakeland, Florida, to see Florida Southern College designed by Frank Loyd Wright. It is the largest concentration of his work in one place.

We went bird watching in Myakka State Forest.

We drove down to Sanibel Island because we had read that it was the best place on the west coast of Florida to look for seashells. When we got there, we were told it might be true, but only in the wintertime after a storm. There weren't very many seashells there when we were there.

We did get to drive down Palm Beach Boulevard in Fort Myers lined with beautiful majestic Royal Palm trees.

We got to take a tour of Thomas Edison's winter home, which was quite fascinating. We learned about his famous insomnia and saw the small daybed in his lab, where he would take short cat naps averaging about four to five hours a day total. We learned that he didn't like the smell of food being cooked, so they had a separate building for the kitchen. We also toured his arboretum, the first place I ever saw a banyan tree. Fascinating and beautiful.

Phil and a friend of his were experienced scuba divers. So one weekend, the three of us drove up to Crystal River north of Tampa. We rented a small boat and some scuba gear and went out into this crystal-clear river. The river is mostly very shallow, and we had to keep an eye out for manatees. There are hundreds of these freshwater rivers in northern Florida are fed by underwater springs.

When we got to the source of the river, there was a large funnel-shaped hole about sixty feet deep as I recall. We anchored the boat on the edge and put on the scuba gear. I had never done this before. I got a little instruction from Phil, and down we went. It was completely clear from top to bottom. There was a small cave at the bottom and I remember Phil shined a light in the cave. It was full of large catfish, which looked very spooky to me with their long whiskers. I remember looking up from the depths watching the bubbles rising from my tank thinking to myself, stay calm, stay calm. We ascended slowly; the whole dive went beautifully.

Phil and his friend had done this type of diving many times before and decided they'd had enough. So when my air was used up I put on one of their tanks and continued to swim mostly in the shallows. It was fantastic, otherworldly, nothing else like it in my previous experience, and all completely natural. I couldn't get enough. What a gift, a really beautiful gift. Thank you, Phil.

Before we finished out our summer, we worked up an even more adventurous plan. The three of us drove to Key West and stayed in the campground there for two nights. We went to a dive shop and rented a sixteen-foot boat with a fifty-horse motor and some scuba gear and headed out to a little spit of land called Sand Key about eleven miles south of Key West and very near the edge of the continental shelf.

On the way out, we were passed by a submarine coming out of the base there that had two mini subs mounted on the deck. I think in retrospect that was the best part of the whole trip because the ocean was not calm. I'd always thought it would be fun to ride up and over small swells in a small boat but after a few miles of this, I realized it's not much fun at all. And you can't speed up unless you want to be pounded silly.

We made it to Sand Key and anchored in about twenty feet of water on the southeast side of the Key. The only thing there, literally, was a patch of sand maybe a quarter-mile long and a small metal lighthouse to warn off approaching boats. Sometimes you might say getting there is half the fun; for this adventure getting there was pretty much all the fun. We got our gear on and jumped in. The visibility was not good, maybe twenty feet or less. The water had been stirred up by the rough action of the waves. As soon as I got down about twenty feet, it became harder and harder to get a breath of air out of my tank. I motioned to Phil that I was going to the surface.

He came up with me and said, "What's up?"

I said, "I'm having trouble sucking air out of this tank."

He said, "Well, try pulling a reserve."

I pulled a reserve and got a nice burst of fresh air. We headed back down but within five minutes the same problem happened again because I had used up the reserve air and the tank was empty. So I went back to the surface and found out how hard it was to get back into a small boat while it was pitching around in rough water. Apparently, we had rented a tank that had not been refilled. Getting back in the boat was not easy, I drank a fair amount of saltwater in the process.

It was doubly disappointing, low visibility, and nothing interesting to see there, except a few sea fans. In retrospect, we should've stopped at the John Pennekamp Coral Reef State Park just off Key Largo. But we wanted more adventure than that. Our reasoning turned out to be misguided at best. Live and learn right?

After a brief lapse in losing weight after getting to Florida, I recommitted to restricting my caloric intake and made critical decisions about what and what not to put in my mouth. For starters, no more cheeseburgers, no more french fries, no more milkshakes, and no more ice cream. I had a major revelation like the one I had in Southampton. After two weeks of not eating those very high-calorie foods, my cravings for them went away again, and my taste buds recalibrated. Powerful, profound, and useful information.

Fresh ripe tomatoes with a sprinkle of kosher salt became my favorite snack food. Walking for miles up and down the beach looking for shark teeth helped also. By the end of the summer, I had lost fifty pounds and I was feeling like a new person, reborn and feeling pretty darn good about myself, and my self-image had improved dramatically.

One of the oddest things I noticed as I was losing weight was there was more space between my toes. My feet have never looked like this before. I know now when you have confidence in your abilities, your chances of achieving your goals increase dramatically. The idea that I was in control of my destiny was becoming more firmly anchored in my mind. Realizing that I have the ability to control some of my behavior was empowering. This led me to many successes, large, and small. I'm sure most successful people come to these realizations way before I did. I will always consider myself a late bloomer.

As the end of August approached, we made plans to leave. We were going to drive together in Phil's MG Midget and tow my motorcycle with his car. We took the small chrome bumpers off the back and replaced them with four large eyelets. I bought a one-inch-wide steel bar, that was four feet long, took the front wheel off my motorcycle, and slid the steel bar through the eyelets at the bottom of the front forks of the motorcycle. We strapped the front motorcycle wheel to the handlebars. I also took the final drive chain off to reduce drag and wear. I built a small luggage rack out of wood that we strapped to the rear trunk for additional storage. Remember, this car is very small. As improbable as it all sounds, it worked quite well.

We decided to avoid the interstate as much as possible on our way north back to Connecticut. We aimed to see some of the country. We wanted to extend our summer of adventure. We planned on a five- or six-day trip.

Our first big attraction was Stone Mountain, Georgia, a 1,600-foot-high stone monolith that has a huge relief sculpture depicting Civil War confederates Stonewall Jackson, Robert E. Lee, and Jefferson Davis carved into its side. We rode the cable car to the summit to take in the view.

Our next stop was Asheville, North Carolina, the site of the largest private home ever built in America—the Biltmore Estate. Constructed between 1889 and 1895, it contains at least 250 rooms with more than four acres of indoor floor space, including thirty-five bedrooms, forty-three bathrooms, and sixty-five fireplaces. I'd read about this house and really wanted to see it. When Phil and I went there in late August of 1970, we were virtually the only people there. We drove right up in front of this magnificent monument to capitalism and took a picture of our little traveling rig with the motorcycle by the front door.

We went inside and did a small self-guided tour viewing, among

AUGUST 1970, ALL PACKED UP AND READY TO HEAD BACK TO
CONNECTICUT FROM FLORIDA WITH MY FRIEND PHIL IN HIS NEW
MG MIDGET TOWING MY TRIUMPH BEHIND. WE HAD A GREAT TRIP!

other marvels, a remarkable Renoir portrait, *Child with an Orange*. The child had very dark, black hair. I remember staring at the painting for a few minutes and realizing that this amazing head of hair seemed to contain little specks of every color in the rainbow. Remarkable. Much later, someone told me that black reflects all light and that's why there was so much color in this child's hair.

The Biltmore was originally a 30,000-acre estate. Today it is a major tourist destination. The last time I was there, I was with Alison, and there were hundreds, if not thousands, of visitors. We had to make a reservation for a house tour, but it was much more informative. I learned a lot more about the house and…I got to see the kitchens, something I'm always interested in. The gardens were much better tended than they had been in 1970.

We drove into downtown Washington, DC, and drove around the mall, just looking at the buildings like the Lincoln and Jefferson Memorials without going inside anything. We then drove into Philadelphia to look at the Liberty Bell and Constitution Hall.

We made it back to Connecticut without any major issues. Phil had arranged for an apartment for his second year of culinary school. So we went there and unloaded everything. I then put my motorcycle back together.

We decided we had a little extra time, so we drove to Portland, Maine, to visit another student friend of ours, Edward. He showed us around Portland and introduced us to his absolutely beautiful, new girlfriend, Lauren. A real goddess in the flesh. When we met her, after we got control of our slack jaws, Phil and I looked at each other and winked. We thought wow, what a beauty. I assumed Edward spent his summer break wrapped up in romance. Phil and I had not spent any time on a summer romance with all our rambling. Oh, we talked about women, and we thought about women, and we fantasized about women. But we didn't do anything with women.

Like the old joke:

A crusty old cowboy goes into a bar and orders whiskey.

A woman comes in and sits down next to him. She looks him up and down and says, "Are you a real cowboy?"

He says, "Well, I spend most of my day, mending fences, herding cattle. Yeah, I guess I'm a real cowboy."

He looks at her and says, "What do you do all day?"

She says, "Well, I'm a lesbian so I think about women all day, morning, noon, and night."

He absorbs that and takes another sip of his whiskey.

A couple comes in and sits on the other side of him and asks, "Wow, are you a real cowboy?"

He thinks for a minute, and says, "Well, I thought I was, but I just found out I'm a lesbian."

There's a vibrant waterfront in Portland now, but in 1970 it was not what it is today. It did have the beautiful Harbor Fish Market that is still there. There was a large loft-like multi-use building/music venue and an interesting antique bottle shop, otherwise, it was fairly derelict with lots of unoccupied buildings. Now, it has a thriving commercial district along the waterfront with many shops, restaurants, and brew pubs.

Phil and I drove to Boothbay Harbor to experience the rocky shoreline of Maine and then back to Connecticut. Afterward, I picked up my motorcycle and rode to Ludlow. Summer was over and it was time to go back to culinary school for our second year.

Before returning to New Haven, I went to North Hampton to visit Sally. We swapped stories. Her summer had been much less adventuresome than mine so I think she got a vicarious thrill when I told her about all my motorcycle and sports car driving up and down the East Coast and some of the things I had seen and done. And I think she was impressed with my weight loss, which, of course, buttressed my personal feelings about myself. It's wonderful to get confirmation and praise from someone you love.

Sally then took me to a music room at the college and played a piano for me. She played quite beautifully, quite skillfully, and with love, perhaps my favorite bit of Beethoven, the second movement of Sonata in C Minor, opus 13, no. 8, "Pathetique." I believe the theme of this piece of music is unrequited love, not an uncommon theme in literature and music.

It would come back later to bite me. She had first played this movement for me when we were in high school. The melody is permanently imprinted, tattooed if you will, into folds of my brain; it speaks to me in a way very few other pieces of music can. I suppose it's the combination of the sounds, and the fact that it has been played for me by the one person whom to this day I consider to be my first true love.

First true love only happens once. Subsequent experiences are just that. Like losing your virginity. There's only one first time for true love. I believe if it's real it stays with you for life. Sally is a very large thread in the tapestry of my life and I'm eternally grateful that it is so. She introduced me to the finer side of life and over the years I have built much of my foundations upon these early experiences. I know certainly that many others more talented than me have written about love and the lovely aspects of first love, but this is my story, and this is how I express my feelings as I understand them.

Overall it had been a very good summer of self-discovery and adventure. I learned again I could navigate my way in the world safely. I also learned that I could control my lust for food. I was beginning to get my feet under me and improving my self-confidence. And I had gotten to see a large swath of America. I was happy, very happy.

21

My Second Year at the CIA

During my second year at the culinary institute, I took an apartment even farther away from campus with two classmates. I also took an after-school job at Yale's Berkeley College's dining hall. The best thing I learned there was how to be a good boss. The head chef was an African American man named Willy. I really enjoyed going to work there because every time I walked in the door he would look up and say, in a genuine, friendly tone, "Hey Robert, how are you doing, man? It's good to see you," which made me feel very welcomed and appreciated. And he didn't do this with just me, he did it with everyone, a very positive role model. And he always made me smile when somebody was leaving, he would say, "Bye now, you be good. If you can't be good, be careful." He was a great guy, and he showed me how important it is to be a positive, friendly force when you are in a position of leadership and responsibility. I tried to carry that example with me as I worked my way through forty years in the restaurant business.

While I was working my part-time job at Yale, I enjoyed talking with the assistant managers, they were seniors on work-study. Being able to have meaningful conversations with them made me realize they were not that much different from me, even though they were students at a prestigious college. I had an interesting talk with one of these seniors about the value of a college education. He made a very interesting statement: "The point of college is of course education, but more importantly it is to get well-rounded and exposed to many different ideas. Your real education happens after college when you are out in the world." This was a novel idea for me at the time but over the years as I traveled along my personal journey, I realized he was right. I did learn a boatload of stuff in culinary school but I know now I was just laying the foundation for my lifetime of learning.

Later in my career, I continued to carry Willy's example with me. One of my seasoned managers commented, "You're the only boss I've ever had who doesn't yell."

The fact is, I do remember losing my temper twice in my working history. And both times I remember in reflection feeling like a fool. What was wrong with me? Why couldn't I get people to do what I wanted without losing my temper?

Here is a funny example where I did the right thing many years later. I was in a very busy kitchen and asked the dishwasher to clean some oysters. A few minutes later, one of the cooks next to me grabbed me by the shoulder, pointed across the kitchen, and said, "Did you ask him to do that?"

When I looked, I saw Dave the dishwasher pulling a rack of oysters out of the dish machine that was used to wash dishes. So I walked over calmly, put my hand on his shoulder, and said, "Dave, that's not what I had in mind."

Of course, it was not his mistake. It was my mistake because, I had failed to properly communicate to him what I meant when I said *clean some oysters*. The rest of the staff was impressed that I did not blow my top. Instead, I apologized to him for my mistake. I knew he was already feeling dumb and I didn't want to make him feel worse. Dave told me later that as soon as I touched his shoulder he saw his mistake. We got to laugh about that a few times over the years.

My new second-year roommates weren't close friends. They were just looking for a third roommate and I needed a place to stay. One was from Michigan, and the other one was an Army vet. We largely stayed out of each other's way. I had a large bedroom in front of the apartment on the second floor. I tacked up a large tie-dyed sheet on the ceiling and put a bunch of posters on the walls, doing my best to make it look like a bohemian garret. I had a single bed, a small couch, a desk, and a bathroom down the hall. I had little contact with my roommates; they liked to watch TV, but I did not. I frequently felt like I was living in my own private apartment.

I did not have a car but my roommates did, so I got a ride to school with them in the morning. Classes were from eight to two as I recall. Unless you had breakfast cooking duties, then you had to be there at six. School schedules were arranged in such a way that two meals a day were included, breakfast and a hearty dinner-sized lunch, which was made up of more traditional dinner-type entrées. These meals were produced in what was called practical kitchens. These practical kitchens usually focused on one type of cuisine such as French, Italian, international, etc.

If you were not in a practical kitchen, you were in a classroom, learning other aspects of the restaurant business, such as bake shop, meat cutting, facilities planning, menu planning, and design. I remember learning that all kitchen design is based on what kind of food you expect to be cooking. So it all starts with the menu, basic business math, and wine education and appreciation—always very popular. I remember going to a large auditorium for a beer merchandising demonstration where we were shown how to properly pour a draft beer. This demonstration was extremely popular because after the lecture we got to drink a beer.

In the fall of 1970, there were lots of protests happening in New Haven because of the Vietnam War. Bobby Seale, a Black Panther leader, went on trial in downtown New Haven in the courthouse on the northeast corner of the Green across from the Taft Hotel. One weekend, thousands of protesters descended on New Haven to protest the war and to protest this trial.

That Saturday afternoon when I went to work, the kitchen was a beehive of activity. The sous-chef was leaning over one of the large, sixty-quart steam jacket kettles dumping soy sauce into the biggest batch of rice I had ever seen cooked before in my life. I asked him what he was doing.

"I'm making brown rice. We're serving anyone who comes in, the town is full of protesters and the doors are open for anyone who wants some food. We are not ready yet, so get busy. We need those cases of broccoli prepped over there so we can steam them."

"OK, I'm on it!"

I got off my shift at about eight that night. I decided to hang around and watch the demonstrations from a safe distance. A normally calm Green looked like a combat zone. Every corner of the Green was packed full of police in riot gear and behind the police were lines of National Guardsmen with helmets and shields, and behind the National Guardsmen were armored vehicles. I couldn't believe my eyes. I knew this was a big deal so I went to a corner by Battell Chapel to observe the action. From my vantage point on the southwest corner of the Green, I could see a very active, determined, well-organized, and well-equipped group of protesters that were moving from corner to corner in the Green. I watched them go to the northwest corner where they confronted the police and the National Guard. Then several explosions of tear gas canisters and flashes of light, yelling, sirens, and clouds of smoke filled the air. I've never seen anything like it.

These protesters were wearing helmets, bandannas or protective res-
pirators, and protective vests, and they were carrying bottles full of red
paint which they threw at the police who had shields and were holding
shotguns with teargas canister launchers on the ends of the barrels so
they could shoot them into the air a distance of fifty to one hundred
yards. It was mayhem. The protesters would get repelled in one corner,
regroup, and then go to the next corner, and repeat the same futile
exercise. There were people running around with white armbands and
bottles of water to squirt in the eyes of people who had been tear-gassed.
I had some water squirted in my eyes because there were clouds of tear
gas drifting around the Green. I eventually took cover inside the Battell
Chapel.

Graffiti had been sprayed on construction walls around Yale's campus. One of my favorites was, "God needs a wife to restore equality of the
sexes." Another one I remember is, "Coitus Interruptus! Stop the rape
of Vietnam now!" Seemed like everybody had an opinion to express.

So there I was in New Haven, Connecticut, not only getting an
education in the culinary arts but also getting an education in uncivil
disobedience. I knew there were a lot of things worth protesting, but I
didn't want to get that deeply involved. For one thing, I didn't believe it
was within my ability to change the course of the country that was being
run by Lyndon Johnson, Robert McNamara, Dean Rusk, and General
William Westmoreland. It seemed futile at best. I decided that working
on my self-improvement and on the things that I could control would
be a better way to spend my energies and have a positive effect on myself
and those around me. Some might call that a cop-out, so be it.

Sally also made it clear to me that our romantic relationship was in
decline. Obviously, a disappointment, but it was just one more thing
that I had little or no control over. We agreed to remain friends and we
are still friends to this day. But I had to move on. After she graduated

from college, she married and became a mother.

In the spring of 1971, a classmate of mine said he was going to a college mixer. Remember those? I didn't know anyone there. There was a band playing, I was dancing by myself when I noticed an attractive woman also dancing by herself. I was drawn to her because she was tall, and she was wearing a purple leather vest with a very long fringe. I liked the way she made the fringe sway. So, as the music was winding down, I screwed up my courage and went over to her.

Just as the music stopped, I asked, "Would you like to dance?"

She laughed and said, "Don't you think we should wait for the music to start?"

We did. We danced around a bit. This mixer was held in the dining hall. We snuck into the kitchen and I got a couple of raspberry yogurts out of one of the coolers. It was the first time she'd ever tasted yogurt and she loved it. We talked some. Her name was Pamela, she was a student at Southern Connecticut University. Before she left, I got her phone number.

Pamela was a beautiful young woman in her first year of college. She had grown up in Westport, Connecticut. When I told her I was from Ludlow, she thought that was interesting. The name of my high school in Fairfield is Ludlowe. Slightly different spelling. She was intelligent and seemed to know what she was headed for in her education. I decided to pursue her and see what it led to.

A couple of days later I called her up. I went to her room and we went for a nice long walk and got acquainted. A few days later, I called her again and I went to her room. We kissed and hugged some. When it got late, I said, "Well, I have to go back to my apartment." She asked if she could go with me.

"Really?" I said.

"Yeah, really."

We rode bicycles the two or three miles to my apartment. It was pretty late at night, like one am. The whole way she kept saying, "You didn't think I would do this, did you?"

I showed her my room and she asked me if she could spend the night. I said, "Yeah, sure."

On our first night in my single bed together she took off all her clothes except her underpants. She said, "I don't want you to think I'm easy." We had a wonderful, romantic spring together, the kind of blissful time that people write poetry about.

22

Graduation and Leaving Again

Now I was ready to start living my life.

I finished up my second year and graduated in early June 1971. Then I started making plans for the next phase of my life.

I found a job advertised at the school for a position in a small restaurant in Brant Rock, Massachusetts, part of Marshfield, and coincidently not that far from Plymouth. I had sold my motorcycle to pay part of my tuition, so I was now without transportation. However, a friend gave me a ride to the restaurant. The job included room and board so I didn't need transportation.

It was a family-run restaurant serving Italian cuisine, called the Fairview Hotel. The Italian chef was named Pat, and his Greek wife was named Helen. They no longer rented out rooms so that's why I had a place to stay, upstairs in one of the unused hotel rooms. They served dinner six nights a week, so I had a lot of daytime hours to spend by myself exploring the area. Pat, the chef was maniacal about how his tomato sauce was made, and I became a serious student of his and watched him prepare that sauce—slowly simmering it. Patrick was also a penny pincher. On Mondays he would drive around to different supermarkets, looking for products that were on sale like lamb shanks. He'd bring them back to the restaurant and braise them for a dinner special. I learned how to make a really good red garlic sauce for spaghetti. The trick was to heat up some olive oil in a pan with chopped garlic and let the garlic toast to a very light brown before adding the red sauce. The toasting of the garlic heightened the flavor to a level I had not experienced before.

With my earnings, I saved up some money, which was easy because I had no expenses. I used my savings to buy my first adult bicycle for $120, a bright red Raleigh Super Course ten-speed.

Once or twice on my day off, I hitchhiked to see Pamela in Fairfield, Connecticut. Eventually, she came to visit, and the restaurant owners offered her a summer job cleaning and waitressing that included her own room. I think they did this to keep me happy, which, of course, it did. Pamela brought her bicycle and the two of us had a wonderful romantic summer, bike riding, beach-going, and spending time together.

The owners, Patrick and Helen, were getting on in years. I'm pretty sure they were hoping that I was going to take over the operation of the restaurant and they would be able to retire. They never told me this, but when I told them at the end of the summer that I was going to be leaving, Helen became very angry and said she was going to call "that school" and tell them not to send any more fly-by-night job applicants. I felt bad about disappointing them, as they had been very generous to me. But I wasn't ready to settle down. This was not part of my plan.

By the end of August, I had saved up enough money to buy a small Ford Econoline van. My plan was to load up some of my stuff, including my bicycle, and head for the Rocky Mountains. My target was Aspen, a very hot ski town that I had read about in magazines, and friends in high school had mentioned to me.

In mid-September with my van loaded, I drove to Southern Connecticut State University where Pamela had started her second year

THAT'S ME AND MY GIRLFRIEND PAMELA WHEN I
GRADUATED FROM THE CULINARY INSTITUTE OF
AMERICA IN JUNE 1971. LET THE ADVENTURES BEGIN!

of college. I went to bid her farewell. As I was saying goodbye, she looked at me and said, "Aren't you going to ask me to go with you?"

"What? But you're in college."

"I'll drop out," she said.

"Really? OK if that's what you want to do."

So just like that, without any real forethought, I was going to drive across the country with my girlfriend.

First, we had to drive to Fairfield, where we had a very awkward conversation with her father. He was not happy, and I think he said something like, "You're living a kind of life I never thought you would live." We packed up some of her gear, and, just like that, we were on the road together.

Originally, I had said we were going to go to Aspen. But somewhere in the middle of New York, I made one of my many snap decisions. I figured everyone was going to Aspen, making it too popular, and that we should now go to Jackson Hole Wyoming. This ski area had been mentioned to me by my cousin Margaret years earlier. It sounded more exotic and out of the mainstream. It was newer as ski resorts go and just south of Yellowstone and the Grand Tetons. In retrospect, it was not the best decision. Jackson was a much smaller town in 1971. But it was the decision that I made, and I committed to it. I'm pretty sure there would've been many more employment opportunities in Aspen.

Along the way, we stopped to look at Niagara Falls, and after that,

PAMELA LOVED TO FISH. WE BOUGHT A COUPLE OF CHEAP ZEPKO RODS AND REELS, AND LEARNED HOW TO FISH. HERE SHE IS ON A SMALL LAKE SOMEWHERE IN CENTRAL IOWA.

I put my blinders on and we only stopped for gas and to eat and to sleep. After two or three days, we crossed the Mississippi River near Davenport, Iowa, and Pamela asked me if I would pull over at the next rest area. I did as she requested. She got out of the van, stood there with the open door, and said, "I'm not getting back in until you tell me when we're stopping."

"What? Oh, OK tell me. Where do you want to stop?"

"Anywhere. I just don't want to drive straight to Wyoming without seeing anything."

So thanks to her we "discovered" the Amana colonies in central Iowa. We learned a lot of history there, like the fact that this was the most successful commune in the history of the United States, a religious group of Pietists who had immigrated from Germany in the 1830s and settled near Buffalo, New York. Sometime in the 1840s, they decided they needed more land, so they moved further west to east central Iowa. They were completely self-sufficient from the 1840s until the 1930s. As a group, they established seven villages with names like Amana, North Amana, Middle Amana, South Amana, High Amana, and East Amana, and then they bought the town of Homestead because it had a rail line. Amana means "remain true" in their dialect of German.

This was one of my first experiences 'with slices of Americana', the little bits of American history that I had never heard about before. I know now there are many such experiences to be discovered while driving around the blue highways of this beautiful country.

Pamela also wanted to go fishing, so we bought a couple of cheap Zebco rod outfits and some worms and went fishing. It was some time before we got the hang of this new skill, but Pamela was very committed to it. As a result, with time, she became quite accomplished.

Our next stop of note was the Badlands National Park in South Dakota. Driving into the park we saw our first pronghorn antelope.

I remember thinking, wow, I've never seen anything like that in New England. We found out that the national park had no staff after September 30—it was October 1. So there was no one at the entry gate and no one to collect money at the campground. It was after dark by the time we got to the campground. There were no lights anywhere except a small twinkling of what looked like a small town twenty miles or so to the south, that might have been Potato Ridge. It was a little spooky for me, coming from an area of the country where there was always something nearby to an area where there was nothing nearby.

The next day we went to look at Mount Rushmore. I was impressed by the scale of the sculpture, but I thought the patriotic narrative on the loudspeakers was a bit overblown.

We went to Custer State Park for the campground and stopped by a lake to try fishing. It turned out to be a very eventful stop. After not catching any fish, I tried to start the van. I think the carburetor that did not have an air cleaner must have been flooded in some way because all of a sudden there was a strong whooshing sound of a sudden fire. This van had the motor compartment right between the two front seats. I quickly lifted the cover on the motor compartment and flames leaped out! We both opened our doors and fell out of the van. Smoke and flames completely enveloped the front of the van. I freaked out thinking all our stuff was going to burn up. I ran around the back of the van thinking I've got to pull our stuff out. I opened the rear doors and was met face-to-face with a blast of hot air and smoke that forced me to fall back. Ducking down I started pulling our belongings out of the back of the van, not knowing what else to do in a panic.

Another couple that was camped nearby came running down the road and said, "Why don't you throw some water on it?" Everything in my training said you don't throw water on a gas fire but I didn't have any other options. I grabbed a small cooking pot, scooped some water out of

AFTER OUR VAN CAUGHT FIRE BECAUSE OF A FLOODED CARBURETOR,
THESE TWO PEOPLE STAYED CALM ENOUGH TO HELP PUT IT OUT. THEN WE
ALL GOT HIGH TOGETHER AND WERE ABLE TO CHILL OUT.

the lake, and threw it on the fire, it immediately went out! I could hardly believe it.

What the heck were we gonna do now? The sides of the vinyl seats were singed and melted pretty badly, and the roof panel on the inside of the van was singed badly.

After waiting a little while to calm down, and with another bucket of water at the ready, I tried again to start the van with the motor compartment open just in case it caught fire again, and miracle of miracles, it started up and didn't catch on fire. We eventually drove over to the campground next to the other couple who had saved our bacon.

We then set up our smoky van next to their campsite and they invited us to get high with them and try to chill out. That did the trick. Thank God for the kindness of strangers. In my panic, I had assumed that our entire enterprise was going to go up in flames but it was just a minor inconvenience. We never had another engine fire. However, we did have to get the melted spark plug wires replaced and get used to the smoky smell that slowly dissipated.

We decided to visit the Crazy Horse Memorial nearby, something I knew virtually nothing about at the time. It turned out to have a profound and lasting impact on my approach to life. I was overwhelmingly impressed with the fact that this monumental project was led by one man, Korczak Ziolkowski. He was a self-taught sculptor, who had been one of the assistants on Mount Rushmore. He also had a famous sculpture in West Hartford, Connecticut, of Noah Webster that he completed in 1932 after two years of solo labor.

He started working on this Crazy Horse project in 1948 at the behest of Chief Standing Bear who came to him and said "That Mount Rushmore is a nice monument to the white man and we would like a monument like that to the red man." He worked on this monument until he died in 1982.

When I was there in 1971, I spoke with one of the volunteers and offered to sign up to be a volunteer right on the spot. I was so moved by the size and scope of the project. The volunteer very wisely told me that the best way to approach this impulse was to go away from the site and then write a letter requesting to be a volunteer. I wrote a letter when I was in Jackson Hole, but I never sent it. By then, the arc of my life had moved on.

The Ziolkowskis had ten children, five boys and five girls. They built a schoolhouse and hired a teacher, and on the first day of class, Korczak wrote this inspirational quote on the blackboard that I still carry with me:

"If you lose this day loitering it will be the same story tomorrow and the next, days are lost lamenting over days, and delays bring their own delays, Action, there's courage and magic in it."

This stopping point on my journey has had a profound impact

on my approach to my career in the restaurant business and my life in general.

From South Dakota, we went into north central Wyoming and the Bighorn Mountains, where we learned how to fish in a small stream thanks to some fishermen there who explained that the fish were not out in the middle of the stream where we were placing our bait, but right under our feet. They were hiding in the undercut bank, waiting for something good-looking to float by. The fishermen showed us how to set our worms on our hooks so that the hook did not show, and how to let it drift down almost right under our feet and wait for a strike. We caught four nice brook trout and fried them up for breakfast. What a treat. Pamela, of course, was over the moon.

We then went through Cody, Wyoming, into Yellowstone National Park. We did some fishing there as well, the minimum for cutthroat trout was sixteen inches. All the ones we caught were smaller than that so we threw them back. We went to the famous fishing bridge where fishing is no longer allowed and looked at dozens of large German brown trout lounging in the shallow water. There were dozens of fishermen standing on the bridge catching nothing. Those fish were not hungry. I was also told that fish have an optical advantage, if you can see them they've already seen you.

We then visited the Grand Canyon of Yellowstone—Old Faithful. But Pamela poked her ankle with a fishhook that had had some worms on it, and her ankle started to swell. So we headed off to Jackson to find a hospital. This was just the first of her many injuries. She spent two days in the hospital getting antibiotics.

23

Arriving in Jackson Hole

We arrived in Jackson, Wyoming in mid-October of 1971. The summer season was over and the winter season was months away. Half the restaurants in town were closed. After a week of trying, I took a part-time job at the Cattle Baron restaurant, right on the square, across from the well-known elk antler arches. Just across the square, the Million Dollar Cowboy Bar is still there with all those silver dollars embedded in the bar top.

Jackson was a much smaller town in 1971 than it is now. For one thing, the airport north of town was not long enough for jets. But once it was extended, the really big money started to show up and it became the much bigger money destination that it is today.

We were just getting settled in when Pamela decided to go home for Thanksgiving. I wasn't sure she would come back. I think she took a bus to Salt Lake and flew back east from there.

In the meantime, I got myself outfitted for downhill skiing. I bought myself a used pair of 120-cm Rossignol Strato 102, a very inappropriate ski for an intermediate skier—too long and too stiff. I also bought some used ski boots at a size fourteen even though my correct size was thirteen. I bought this ski gear because they were the only ones I could find that I could afford. I then purchased myself a ski pass for the hill in town called Snow King Mountain for sixty-five dollars; 1,600 vertical feet with one double chair lift. The good thing was I could walk to it and during the week there were very few skiers there. The serious skiers all went to Jackson Hole, which was twelve miles outside of town with 4,000 vertical feet. But season passes there cost $400, way out of my budget at the time.

PAMELA PROUDLY DISPLAYED HER CATCH OF THE DAY, WHICH SHE COOKED UP IN A LITTLE FRYING PAN FOR OUR DINNER. I DON'T THINK I'VE EVER SEEN HER LOOK HAPPIER.

So, I was cooking at night at the Cattle Baron about thirty hours a week for three bucks an hour and I was skiing Monday through Friday at Snow King. Pamela eventually decided to come back after the New Year. The nearest airport was Idaho Falls, Idaho, about 100 miles to the west over Jackson Pass. I drove there to pick her up. Fortunately, the roads were clear and I was able to get over Jackson Pass with my front-engine and rear-wheel-drive van.

After Pamela returned, I got her set up for downhill skiing. However, in less than a week she developed a bone spur on her ankle, spent a couple of days in the hospital, and never went downhill skiing again. Thankfully she was still able to cross-country ski.

After living in a mobile home for two months, we moved into a cozy converted motel with two adjoining rooms—one was the bedroom and bathroom, and one was the kitchen and living area. We also got ourselves a kitten and named him Crampon. Pamela eventually got a part-time room cleaning job at one of the motels and the rest of the winter went pretty smoothly.

Long-distance winter travel in Wyoming was a dicey undertaking back then and had to be planned carefully because all the larger population centers were quite a ways away. During one large storm in January 1972, the town was cut off from vehicle traffic for four days, and the supermarkets ran out of milk and eggs within two days. After the roads were cleared enough for car travel, the local radio station would announce when caravans of cars led by state police could meet at the edge of town so people could safely drive out of town in mass without fear of getting stranded.

I skied twice that winter at Jackson Hole. It was a thrill with 4,000 vertical feet and about six miles for an intermediate skier like me to get from top to bottom. I thought I was in pretty good shape after bombing up and down Snow King for several weeks. But after I made three runs, about eighteen miles, at Jackson Hole I was completely spent. Even though I had time for a fourth, I no longer had any energy left in my legs.

THE VIEW OF SNOW KING MOUNTAIN IN THE TOWN OF JACKSON. I DID MOST OF MY SKIING HERE IN THE WINTER OF 1971 AND 1972. I COULD JUST WALK OVER TO THE BASE OF THE MOUNTAIN. IT WAS CONVENIENT AND CHEAP—JUST $62.50 FOR A SEASON PASS.

I did ski over to the top of Corbet's Couloir to look in. It's a narrow slot in the rock face. To ski it you must drop in about six feet and make three or four very quick turns on a forty-five-degree slope before the slot opens up enough to where you could actually ski. I did not ski Corbet's. This couloir is at the eastern end of the Rendezvous Bowl, at the top of the mountain, accessed by a tram that carried sixty skiers in those days. If you stood there at the top for five or ten minutes after getting off the tram you were completely alone on top of this 4,000-

The well-known mountaineer, extreme skier, and amazing banjo player, Bill Briggs.

foot mountain—a completely awesome experience. Rendezvous Bowl is about half a mile wide and pitched about forty degrees. I might be exaggerating, but that's what it looked like to me. Yes, I was intimidated, but I was also determined and fortunately, unlike Corbet's, there were plenty of places to make turns.

I also learned to cross-country ski for the first time in Jackson Hole. Pamela, some friends, and I had some wonderful day trips up in Grand Teton National Park, which has very limited access in the winter.

My most memorable cross-country ski trip was into Taggart Lake at night under a full moon on ten feet of snow. We followed a stream bed from the parking area up to the lake. We could hear the water rushing under the snow and every once in a while, we came to a big funnel-shaped hole in the snow where we could shine a light down ten feet or so to see the water rushing by. I've never seen anything like it in my life. We got to the lake and built a small fire to warm ourselves while taking in the most spectacular view of the Grand Tetons lit by the full moon—as good as it gets.

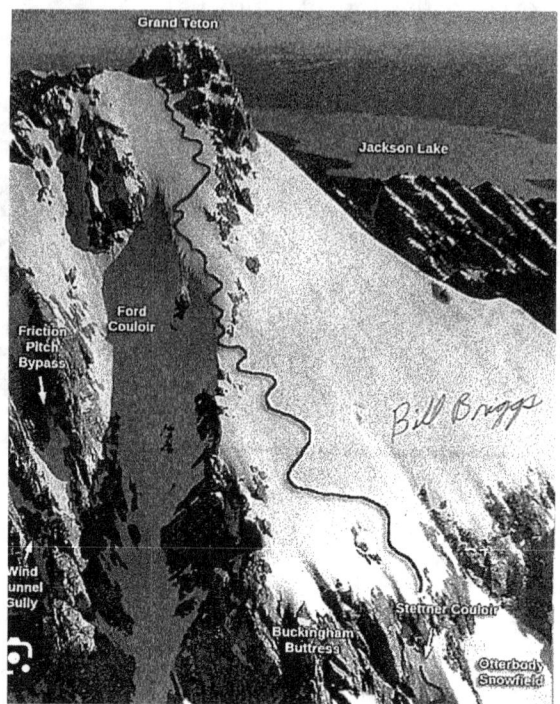

BILL BRIGGS WAS THE VERY FIRST PERSON TO SKI
FROM THE TOP OF THE GRAND TETON, IN JUNE 1971.
A FEW DAYS LATER, A SMALL PLANE FLEW OVER THE
MOUNTAIN TO PHOTOGRAPH HIS TRACKS.

Six nights a week in Jackson the bars closed at two, but on Sunday night all the bars closed at eight. In Wilson, there was a two-room place called the Stagecoach Bar. It was a popular Sunday afternoon drinking spot. I went there a few times.

There was a famous well-known local skier at the time named Bill Briggs, who was also a talented banjo player. I remember watching him play a very spirited tune there. It was getting close to closing time, and he got so wound up that he actually jumped up on top of one of the tables, kicked all the drinks off the table that people didn't grab fast enough, and just kept playing like a madman. Coincidentally, on June 17, 1971, he was also the first person ever to ski a Grand Teton. There was an article about it in the local Teton magazine. His quote when he started down was, "Now make some good tracks." A few days later, somebody flew over the top of the mountain of 13,700 feet in a small plane and took pictures of his tracks near the summit.

The reputation of the Stagecoach was for people to drink as fast as possible until the bar closed at eight, which usually meant quite a few drunk people were misbehaving in one way or another by closing time.

One Sunday when I was there, a guy rode a horse into the bar, which was not easy because the doorway wasn't that high, so the horse and rider had to duck as low as possible to get into the bar. It turned out that the horse did not belong to the rider. The guy who owned the horse was in the bar, needless to say, he was not amused and got quite upset, to put it mildly. There was a bit of a melee. I left as quickly as possible.

On the northeast side of Jackson, there is a national elk refuge. In the winter months, the elk come down from the high country and spend the winter there; they have been doing this for centuries. While they are in the refuge, they are fed hay that was cut in the summertime from those meadows and delivered by horse-drawn sleds managed by the park service. It was possible to go to the elk refuge and buy a ride on one of the horse-drawn sleds and go right into the center of the elk herd.

The year I was there, in the spring, one of the sleds got stuck in some soft ground and when the driver got off the sled to go for a tractor he spooked the entire herd of about 6,000 elk. There was a picture in the Jackson Hole daily paper of the large herd prematurely heading up the side of the mountain on the east side of the refuge. As the snow starts to melt in the spring, you can watch the snow line creep up the mountain sides and the elk go up right behind the melting snow.

24

My Three-Day Solo

On the east side of Jackson, there is a minor mountain called Jackson Peak that is 10,741 feet, it's part of the Gros Ventre Range. In the high mountain valley between Jackson Peak and Table Mountain, 10,263 feet to the east, there is a ski cabin at about 9,500 feet. It is a decent-sized cabin with a large loft, a lower living area, and a steep-pitched roof. I saw a picture online that someone took of this cabin in 1959. As far as I know, it's still there.

On May 3, 1972, I packed some camping gear and Pamela drove me out across the elk refuge to the Curtis Canyon Campground, as high up as we could go until we got to the snow line. It was about 8,000 feet, maybe a little higher. She dropped me off and went back into town.

I planned to hike into the ski cabin, stay there for two nights, and then hike out on the southern side of Jackson Peak into a gulch called Cache Creek, which leads back to town. At this time of year, the snow softens during the day and freezes solid at night. So, when I started out at about 8:00 a.m. it was like walking on a frozen sidewalk. But when I got up between 8,500 feet and 9,000 feet the angle of the snow was facing east and it started to get quite soft. I know now I should've had a pair of snowshoes, but they were not as commonly used then as they are today. Isn't hindsight always 20/20? Pretty soon I was ankle deep and soon post-holing up to mid-shin, then to my knees, and then up to my mid-thigh.

By midday, I was really struggling. I finally got into a spot where there was some shade from some fir trees and the snow was not so soft. I persevered, and I made it to the cabin by early afternoon. The cabin was quite large. I'm guessing maybe twenty feet or twenty-five feet tall at the ridge line. It was not easy to find because I was approaching it from the north, and even in early May the snow still sloped up to the very top of the ridge line obscuring the roof.

But on the south side, because of the angle of the sun's radiation, the snow had all melted away from the entrance. I actually had to walk down to get to the door. On May 3, 1972, there was still ten to fifteen feet of snow on the ground. Thankfully the cabin was well-provisioned with firewood and I was able to make a nice fire in the box stove and heat up some food that I had brought along. Then I tucked into my sleeping bag up in the loft and had a good, warm night's rest.

THE INTERIOR OF THE SKI CABIN THAT I HIKED INTO ON MAY 3, 1972, TO SPEND THREE DAYS BY MYSELF.

JACKSON PEAK, 10,700 FEET, JUST OUTSIDE THE SKI CABIN. I CLIMBED TO
THE SUMMIT AND CAME BACK DOWN BEFORE THE SNOW GOT TOO SOFT.

The next morning, I got up early with a plan to climb to the summit of Jackson Peak before the snow got too soft. This was a 1,200-foot climb on an east-facing slope where the snow would soften up very early. I got a very early start and was on the summit by 9 a.m. I was happy I was able to accomplish this feat. I had the most beautiful view of the entire Jackson Hole Valley and the Tetons Mountains to the west—absolutely spectacular. But by the time I got back to the cabin, the snow was getting quite soft again. I spent the rest of the day trying to make some snowshoes from fir tree branches for my walk out the next day.

I spent a second night in the cabin, cozy and warm, completely alone. I realized it was the first time in my life that I had ever been completely out of touch with the rest of the human race, with no way to get in touch with anyone even if I wanted to. I had no one to talk to but myself. I decided it was a form of silent meditation. I had lots of time to reflect on my thoughts and think about how my life was going and what I wanted to do next. So far I thought things were going pretty well and I was very excited about the future because I knew there were more adventures ahead. I realized then that I was personally responsible for my own happiness. I was less than a year out of culinary school, and I felt like my life was just beginning, I was excited to see what was next.

After two nights in the cabin, I packed up my gear and headed out early trying out my half-assed fir branch snowshoes, which essentially fell apart in less than half a mile. I made it around the south side of Jackson Peak before the snow got too soft for easy walking. I was about 1,200 feet above the valley of Cache Creek.

When I came to the top of a wide-open 1,000-foot snow slope, the snow was quite soft by this time. It looked like a good place to practice glissading or sliding. I put a plastic bag around my lower butt like a big diaper and had an ice axe to use as a break. My plan was to just slide down to the bottom of this 1,000-foot slope and walk back into town.

What I didn't factor in was the shadow that a large spruce tree was casting across the slope about 300 feet below me. This slope was pitched at about forty degrees. I started my descent on the soft snow. Everything

GRAND TETON VALLEY, A.K.A. JACKSON HOLE, FROM THE SUMMIT OF JACKSON PEAK. THE GRAND TETON IS 13,700 FEET ABOVE SEA LEVEL. ON THE FAR RIGHT IS THE FROZEN JACKSON LAKE.

was going fine until I hit the shadow where the snow was still frozen solid! In an instant, it felt like I was going thirty miles an hour and there was nothing at the bottom but a bunch of rocks and scrub trees. Panic set in. I was sure I was going to slide all the way to the bottom of the slope, crashing into the large rocks and brush at the bottom, and being discovered sometime later as a crumpled-up bag of broken bones.

I knew about self-arrest, so as I came out of the shadow, rolled over on my stomach, and did a push-up with my hands and the toes of my boots. I got the purchase I needed. In the softer snow, I came to a stop. I was now about halfway down the slope.

My heart was beating like crazy. Nothing like a really good scare to get your adrenaline flowing. I decided it might be best to walk the rest of the way down. I'd had enough glissading for one day. I walked down to the road in Cache Creek Valley that leads back to the town of Jackson. I arrived back in town in mid-afternoon.

When I got back to our apartment, Pamela wasn't there. I asked one of our neighbors and they said, "Oh, she's in the hospital." I went to find her and see how she was doing. I'm not really sure what the problem was this time but I think it was some kind of anxiety attack because I'd been away for three days. She freaked out about being by herself. Pamela was a beautiful, intelligent woman in many ways, but she had some demons that I was not trained to deal with.

25

Living in a Tipi, Learning About Pottery

Pamela and I lived together for another two months. She decided it would be best for her to go back to college in Connecticut. I agreed with her, and she left sometime in July.

Reginald Laubin and his wife Gladys lived in Moose, Wyoming, a few miles north of Jackson at this time. They had written a book called *The Indian Tipi* and maintained two or three tipis in their yard right across from the entrance to the Grand Teton National Park. I went to visit them and really liked the feeling of being in a tipi, especially when I laid down and looked up at all those poles coming together over my head. It felt primitive and secure. I decided I was going to live in a tipi for the rest of the summer. I bought a tipi cover that I still have from the Blackfoot Canvas Company in Blackfoot, Idaho. They used the same pattern that Reginald Laubin had drawn in his tipi book.

I got a permit from the forest service to cut some lodgepole pine poles and planned to spend the rest of the summer in a tipi on national forest land to save on rent money. There were many primitive campsites in the national forest and federal land all around Jackson. Protocol was you could stay in any one of them for up to two weeks and then you're expected to move.

IN THE SUMMER OF 1972, I SPENT ABOUT TWO MONTHS
LIVING IN A TIPI. THIS WAS MY FIRST SET UP IN
CASH CREEK.

I first set up in Cache Creek, pretty close to town, for two weeks. Then I moved to the other side of the valley up the hill from Wilson near North Fork Creek and stayed there for at least two weeks. I had a tipi mate, Jack, who was staying with me. He was a Mormon from Provo who was working as a summer employee in Jackson. He was a fun guy who taught me the scientific names of many trees. The only one I remember is *Populus tremuloides*, the ubiquitous quaking aspen tree.

North Fork Creek was where we did our bathing and washing up. This creek was coming straight out of a snow field less than a mile up the slope, hence it was extremely cold. One day Jack was helping me wash my hair. He dumped a bucket of stream water on my head to rinse out the soap, the water was so cold I got a headache!

One memorable day we had a very interesting visitor at our North Fork campsite. We were doing our normal lounging around and reading when this small guy walked up wearing blue jeans, a red bandanna, and no shirt. He said, "I just came to look at your tipi." We said, "Oh sure, look around all you want."

He walked around for a few minutes, and I kept looking at him thinking he looked like someone I should recognize. Finally, it dawned on me. I said, "Are you Dick Cavett?" And he said, "Well, yes I am. I'm staying at the dude ranch down the hill and I have an interest in American Indian history." He asked us if we had read the book *Black Elk Speaks*. We had not even heard of it. He said that he had interviewed the author John Neihardt on his show. He said if we were going to live in a tipi we should definitely read *Black Elk Speaks*. I ordered a copy at the local bookstore the next day.

Dick Cavett then told us about one of his favorite pranks when he was having a lawn party at his house out on Long Island. He would slip away, get dressed up in real native loin cloths, and then charge out of the bushes on horseback just like a wild warrior to startle, surprise, and entertain all his guests.

In July 1972, I introduced myself to a woman named Janet Braley, who had a seasonal pottery shop she ran in Jackson in the summertime next to a seasonal glass-blowing shop run by an artist named Greg Zweifel. I believe Janet had an MFA from Scripps College in Claremont, CA, where she studied pottery with a well-known potter named Paul

My tipi mate was Jack, a.k.a. Redhawk. My tipi name was Bear Paw.

Soldner.

I was interested in learning how to throw pots. I asked her if she would give lessons and she said sure, for twenty bucks an hour! That was a lot of money at the time. I told her I had to think about it. I went back a few days later thinking that maybe she could teach me a lot in an hour. When I returned she told me it was a joke. She would give me lessons for five dollars an hour. We made a deal.

I was interested in learning about pottery because of the creation process. I love to make stuff. You start with very humble ingredients—dirt, mud—and create something that wasn't there before. If you master the skill, you can create beautiful, functional things. Plus, pottery making has such a long history in human evolution, going way back to prehistoric times.

Janet had the funkiest pottery kiln I've ever seen. It was a small catenary arch, and her fuel was fuel oil—regular fuel oil. It had two burner ports where she would set some newspapers on fire and turn the petcocks

ONE DAY OUT OF THE BLUE WE HAD A VERY INTERESTING AND UNEXPECTED VISITOR. AFTER HE WALKED AROUND FOR A WHILE, I SAID, "ARE YOUR DICK CAVETT?" HE SAID, "WELL, YES I AM." HE ASKED US IF WE HAD READ BLACK ELK SPEAKS. I BOUGHT A COPY THE NEXT DAY.

on two little copper lines that dropped fuel oil on the newspapers. When she first started it up, it smoked like crazy, but once the draft was established and heat started to rise, it smoked less and she would increase the volume of oil. When the kiln got to cherry red, about 1,600°F, the oil burned without any smoke at all. She had no problem getting that kiln up to cone ten which is 2,381°F, the temperature at which stoneware pottery is substantially vitrified.

I spent the balance of my summer working at the Cattle Baron and spending a lot of time in the pottery shop learning how to throw pots and make slab-built pieces as well. I still have a replica of a Native American storage jar that I made at that time. I used a simple coil technique. I just rolled the clay out in a coil about three-eighths of an inch thick and started to roll it around and around and around, pinching the inside together but leaving the outside to look like the coils. It is glazed on the inside with a beautiful natural glaze that came out of a roadside bank in Carbondale, Colorado, thanks to Janet. It's a beautiful, soft green color.

26

Moving to Laguna Beach

When summer was over, Janet closed up her shop and told me she was going back to her winter teaching job at the Laguna Beach School of Art.

I loved Jackson Hole; it's perhaps the most beautiful place I've ever lived. But even then, the cost of land was $5,000 for twenty-acre parcels and I was still working for three dollars an hour. I didn't see any future for me, at least not in the short term. So, I packed up my stuff and drove to Laguna Beach to become Janet's shop assistant at the art school. I then found a small apartment and I took another job baking pies and doing food prep at a cute, busy restaurant right on the Coast Highway called The Cottage Restaurant.

IN SEPTEMBER 1972, I FOLLOWED MY POTTERY INSTRUCTOR TO THE LAGUNA BEACH SCHOOL OF ART AND GOT A JOB WORKING AT THE BUSY AND BEAUTIFUL COTTAGE RESTAURANT ON THE COAST HIGHWAY IN LAGUNA.

I settled into my new environment—pottery shop, restaurant, and beach—all within half a mile of each other. What's not to like? I let my hair grow. I bought earth shoes. I read more about fasting and I lost more weight. I became quite tan. I became a vegetarian. I sold my van and got around on my bicycle. Living was easy.

In Laguna Beach my days consisted of working in a pottery shop in the morning and working at The Cottage Restaurant in the afternoon and evenings. I spent any extra time I had riding my

IN THE KITCHEN AT THE COTTAGE RESTAURANT, SOME OF MY COWORKERS WITH RANDY, COMMITTED STONER AND SKATEBOARDER, IN THE MIDDLE.

bike around town and working on my tan at the beach.

The pottery shop was part of the Laguna Beach School of Art, a city-run school that included drawing and painting classes. I enjoyed being Janet's shop assistant, so much so that I traded my labor for shop time. My responsibilities included some cleaning up and organizing, and I was required to help load and unload the kilns when there were enough pots to be fired. Then I'd have time to make my own pots and learn how to mix glazes. Janet's mantra was to make utilitarian pieces, cups, mugs, bowls, pitchers, plates, and vases. Most were hand-thrown on the wheel and some slab-built. I still have a few pieces of the pottery I made at that time. I love the act of creation. Much like cooking, making pottery is an act of creation. Start with a few humble ingredients and create something that wasn't there before.

There were many people at the school who I would have to characterize as dilettantes. They made a lot of bad pottery that was never fired. Once unfired pieces got too dry to trim they were deemed useless and were thrown into a corner of the shop. This was my source of clay for all the work I would do there. I had to rehydrate the clay by breaking it up and putting the pieces in buckets of water.

Then I set the slop out in large handfuls on large plaster squares that

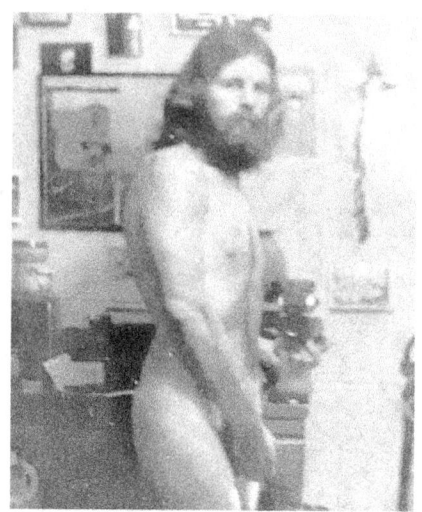

SELF-PORTRAIT I TOOK IN MY
APARTMENT AFTER LIVING IN
LAGUNA FOR ABOUT SIX MONTHS.
I BECAME A VEGETARIAN AND MY
WEIGHT WAS DOWN TO ABOUT 180
POUNDS.

would absorb the moisture from the bottom while the air absorbed the moisture from the top. Eventually, it got to the right consistency where I could knead the clay like one kneads bread to get air bubbles out and bring it to a proper, even consistency. I spent quite a bit of time recycling clay and kneading it into an even consistency that was suitable for pottery making. I loved the act of kneading clay, very similar to kneading bread dough. When it got to the right consistency, I would bag this recycled clay for my personal use. I got some instructions from Janet but mostly I learned by my trial and error on one of the kick wheels.

I loved my time in the pottery shop. It was so different from anything I'd ever done before. I loved the rhythm of it: preparing the clay and making the different shapes one day, letting them dry to what's called leather-hard texture the next. At this stage, they are ready for any necessary trimming, usually a little bit along the bottom to remove excess clay and create a nice foot. Then you let them dry completely.

After the pieces were completely dry, maybe once a week or once every other week, I would help to load up one of the pottery kilns with these dried pieces. Then we'd fire them to a bisque, partially fired, to a temperature of about 1800°. At this stage, the pieces are as shrunk up as they're going to be and are partially vitrified, but not completely.

Following a couple of days, the kiln was opened, and the bisque ware was taken out. At that point, it was ready for glazing, either by dipping or brushing. The pieces were reloaded in the kiln and fired a second time to cone ten, about 2400°. At that level, the clay and the glaze are fully vitrified, meaning the clay particles have melted together enough to create a solid, sturdy usable piece of earthenware pottery.

Back in Massachusetts, I got a job at a little French restaurant called Picot's Place where I worked with my one and only French-trained chef, Jean-Jacques Gauge. We worked with half gallons of heavy cream.

After my morning in the pottery shop, I walked to The Cottage Restaurant to do my paid job of pie baking and helping with prep. People in California were crazy for pie at this time—apple, blueberry, cherry, gooseberry, pumpkin, lemon meringue, chocolate cream, pecan, peach, and on, and on. Just about anything you can imagine. I got quite good at it after so much experience.

Fast forward to 2013 when I was traveling with my wife Alison in Marble Falls, TX. We stopped at a place called the Blue Bonnet Café, which advertised a Pie Happy Hour Monday through Friday from three to five. I thought it was a genius idea. I think they had twenty kinds of pie.

The first wild mushrooms I ever found were right in my parent's backyard in Ludlow. A beautiful little cluster of fresh morel mushrooms—highly praised.

The Cottage was a pretty fun environment for the most part and the people who worked there were talented, hard-working, and fun to be around. There was a very slight, blond dishwasher named Randy. He was always eating stuff that was supposed to be off-limits. He would come over to my station where no one

MY COUSIN, MAUREEN, IN MY POTTERY
SHOP IN LUDLOW, ABOUT 1974 OR '75.

else could see what he was doing while he cut up a nice ripe papaya. As he scooped out the seeds he would look at me with an impish smile and say, "This is the only stuff I eat here." And he would ask a diversionary question like, "What is the only fruit that has its seeds on the outside?" He had that easy-going, So-Cal, laid-back attitude. He also confided in me that he had spent a little time in jail for drug possession because, according to him, he was riding around with a friend while he was quite high and they were pulled over. When the officer asked what he had in his shirt pocket he handed over a little bag of dope. He was a committed stoner. Before he went to jail he ground up some weed in a blender, put it in a balloon, and swallowed it! In jail, he had to watch his toilet carefully. He told me he almost missed it. He loved telling the story and how he asked his cellmate if he wanted to get high in jail.

Randy was also really a happy-go-lucky guy. He was also a serious skateboarder. He would get a ride up into the Laguna Hills and skateboard down two or three miles to the beach. His only protective gear was a pair of thick leather work gloves used to drag on the roadway as he cut his turns.

I invited Randy over to my little one-room apartment to listen to music. He brought along a

A SELF-PORTRAIT, SITTING IN MY LITTLE
SALES ROOM IN MY POTTERY SHOP. I
MADE THE SHIRT THAT I'M WEARING IN
THIS PHOTO THANKS TO MY MOTHER,
WHO TAUGHT ME HOW TO WORK A
SEWING MACHINE.

bag of pot and started to clean it on the back of an album cover, picking out all the seeds and stems very carefully. I remember thinking he looked like a priest, preparing his altar for communion. He then rolled a couple of fat joints, lit one up, and passed it to me. I commented that they were quite generous. Randy said, "No, just normal." We smoked both joints while listening to some LPs on my small stereo. I have never been a big toker, his pot was very strong, and consequently, I got very high.

When the music ended I got up to turn over the records. I was so stoned I could not get the records back on the spindle, I just kept swirling them around and around. Randy found this very amusing and started giggling. Eventually, he got up to assist me. After a while, he said he had to get going which freaked me out. I said, "You can't leave me like this." He just laughed and said, "You'll be fine, don't worry." After I had time to reflect on this experience, I decided I didn't really enjoy feeling that out of control and did not rush to repeat the experience.

THE HAND-CARVED SIGN I
MADE FOR MY POTTERY SHOP.
I STILL HAVE IT WITH ME
HERE IN VERMONT.

At some point, a couple of the people I worked with at The Cottage told me they were doing a particular type of chanting to change their lives in some positive way. "Nam Myoho Renge Kyo" was the chant. They told me the chant originated in Japan, and that it would somehow connect you to the cosmos. They told me that I could chant for anything I wanted, to just repeat the chant over and over thirty to sixty minutes per day, and while chanting, think about whatever it is I want to change in my life.

I had not had a girlfriend in several months, so I started doing this chant thirty minutes a day for about a week, and bingo! Within a week I had two girlfriends. Which I quickly reduced to one. From this experience, I decided the power of chanting comes from making it

A SMALL GAS-FIRED KILLED I MADE
IN LUDLOW SO I COULD FIRE MY OWN
POTTERY.

possible to focus on one thought at a time for an extended period, and then lo and behold as if by magic whatever it is you've been thinking about is more likely to happen. Norman Vincent Peale might call it "the power of positive thinking."

If you think about it, in a normal thirty- to sixty-minute time period, an awful lot of different thoughts can cycle through your mind. But if you're doing the chanting, any kind of chanting, it helps you focus your attention on one thought that you want to be focusing on, and that can change your world.

The chanting I did just made me focus on the idea of having a girlfriend. The result was I started talking to a woman that I already knew. Nothing really profound about that. But the chanting encouraged me to take action. The result was I became very close to a beautiful woman named Diane for the last two months I was in Laguna Beach. Diane was one of the managers at The Cottage Restaurant and we had worked together for a few months by this time. I think she worked at The Cottage for a couple of years and was highly respected by the owners and the other employees. She had previously dated one of the cooks from the restaurant, but that relationship did not last. She was quite attractive, soft-spoken, intelligent, and fun to hang out with. We went out to other restaurants and movies together and soon I started sleeping over at her apartment. It was a beautiful romance. But I was starting to feel a pullback toward the East Coast.

27

Home Sickness

In May of the following year, 1974, Janet, my pottery instructor told me that she was going to do one more season in Jackson Hole, Wyoming. I'd been away from home for almost three years now and I was getting a bit homesick. I had read a book that was originally serialized in *The Whole Earth Catalog* called, *Divine Right's Trip*. The main character, called "the Native," was always waxing about how no one was living where they were born, they were all living somewhere else. This made me think I wanted to go back to the town where I was born and see what was happening there. I would've loved to have lived in Jackson Hole, but the financial reality was it just was not possible. And Southern California was a little too crowded and noisy for me. It was fun for a while, but I was ready to move on.

My beautiful girlfriend Diane wanted me to stay. After I had my new/used pickup truck loaded with all my stuff, I remember her standing at the driver's window looking at me and asking, "Are you sure you won't change your mind?"—begging me to change my mind. But my mind was made up. I had to go. She was a beautiful woman. I'm sure we could've made a nice life together there in Laguna. I had some regrets about it later, but I think it was the right thing for me at that time.

I drove back through Jackson Hole to pick up my tipi and tipi poles.

These polls are twenty-five feet long. This truck has a cap on the back, and I built a rack that came up off the front bumper and attached it back to the front of the cap. So, I was able to lash these polls at the top of the truck. They only hung about five feet off the back.

I decided before I left Laguna that I was going to simplify my eating along the road so I bought a twenty-five-pound box of unsulfured dry apricots—dark, brown, and very firm. Not like the soft orange ones most people sell now. They were very dry and almost leather-hard, I had to suck on them to soften them before I could chew them. That and water was all I ate for the eight days or so it took me to drive across the country. It was a cleanse of sorts, I suppose. After a few days, I noticed a remarkable difference in the quality of my bowel movements. It made me feel like I was sweeping out my intestines with all that fiber, making me feel much cleaner, and perhaps a bit self-righteous.

This was an old 1964 Ford pickup truck with a big bench seat. That's where I slept while I was driving across the country, usually in some kind of truck stop or rest area. I had an incredible bit of luck in Laramie, Wyoming, on a Saturday night when I started hearing a loud whine from my rear wheel. I stopped at a service station and the guy who was working there diagnosed it as bad wheel bearing. He was friends with the owner of a nearby auto parts store and he just happened to have keys to access that store. He was able to replace the bad bearing with a good bearing in about two hours. Oh the kindness of strangers, it's always a pleasant surprise. I have attempted to reciprocate when the occasion has arisen, in other circumstances.

28

Life in Ludlow in 1974

I returned to my hometown with shoulder-length hair, a long beard, and weighing about 180 pounds, about the same as I weighed when I was in seventh grade but taller and much leaner looking. Many family members and friends commented that I looked like Jesus. That look didn't last too long because I was going to have to get a job, so within a week or two I got a normal haircut and shaved off most of my beard except for the mustache.

I reconnected with my old girlfriend Pamela, who was a student at that time at the University of Connecticut in Stores. She had adopted a bluetick coonhound that she was obsessed with. And I would visit her there occasionally, and she would come to Ludlow to visit me. But something kept me from totally committing to that relationship. Oddly enough, after she graduated, for some reason, she became clinically depressed and had problems functioning in the real world. She told me that for three weeks out of the month, she would be fine, and then one week a month a fog that she could see coming would settle over her, making it impossible, or almost impossible to even get out of bed. She couldn't hold a regular job because of that.

I kept in touch with her and she became more and more unpredictable. The last time I met her, she was in some kind of assisted living situation, and some welfare program provided for her basic needs. I felt sorry for her, she was a very beautiful, intelligent woman when I first met her. But something changed, and there was nothing I could do about it.

After returning to Ludlow I pretty quickly got a job at a little French restaurant called Picot's Place out in the country in Wilbraham, about ten miles south of my hometown of Ludlow. The restaurant was owned by a very successful lawyer from Springfield named Ephram Gordon who lived in Wilbraham. He had developed this restaurant and a few shops adjacent to it just because he wanted to.

It really wasn't the best location because it was too far out in the country and it was too upscale for the area. As a result, it was only marginally successful. He had hired several French cooks and waiters to work in this restaurant when he first opened it. By the time I started there, most of them were gone because it wasn't really busy enough to meet their expectations.

Only one of the original chefs was left, his name was Jean-Jacques Gage. Initially, he was quite unfriendly to me because he thought the owner had hired me to replace him. Over time he realized I had no intention of replacing him. I was happy to work there as his sous-chef and learn techniques that he had been trained for when he was a student in France. He had grown up in a suburb of Paris called Argenteuil. When Paris was a smaller city, this town was known for its asparagus production. So many classical French recipes that include asparagus are referred to as "a la Argenteuil." He had been classically trained at a culinary school in Paris, and I wanted to learn from him.

I won him over with my chopped parsley. Every day one of my prep jobs was to chop three bunches of parsley so the chef could sprinkle it wherever he wanted to. So, I spent a lot of time chopping the parsley with a French knife as finely as I could. After a couple of weeks of this, one day he commented that my chopped parsley was the finest he had ever seen. He started to be more friendly to me. And much later on, after I set up my pottery shop in Ludlow, he would come to visit, and he enjoyed making things out of clay. He was very interested in Egyptian mythology. He made an entire chess set in the form of Egyptian gods and goddesses.

The very first wild mushrooms I ever found were in my parents' backyard in Ludlow in 1974. I was out in the backyard, under some pine trees, and I found about a dozen beautiful, morel mushrooms. I had never seen them in the wild before, only in books. I wasn't really sure what they were so I brought them to the restaurant and Jean-Jacques positively identified them. He was very impressed. We cooked them for our staff meal. I didn't realize at the time how rare they are, and how hard they are to find when you're looking for them.

Picot's was the only restaurant I ever worked where we used half-gallon containers of heavy cream to finish almost every sauce. An example would be, steak au poivre. You start by crushing black peppercorns with the bottom of a saucepan and then dredging a filet mignon on both sides with as many crushed peppercorns as possible. Then cooking the steak in a sauté pan in clarified butter to the desired doneness, adding some shallots, red wine, and demi-glace, reduced beef stock, and boiling that down a little bit. Then add a good splash of heavy cream, boiling that until it is nice and thick, and finally, swirl in a spoon of butter. Then put the steak on a plate and the sauce on the steak. It was very spicy and rich, and very popular. Veal scallopini, chicken breasts, and some fish dishes were all finished similarly, with different wines and spices, and perhaps mushrooms or asparagus, but always a nice dose of reduced heavy cream.

I worked at Picot's Place for about a year and a half. My second summer there the chef Jean-Jacques told me that he was going to take a week off and I would be in charge of the kitchen while he was away. This was the first time in my career that I was going to be the person in charge. I remember distinctly the first day I was going to be the chef. I was almost paralyzed by fear of failure. I was standing in the driveway in Ludlow getting ready to go. My stepfather Everett came out of the house and he could see that there was something wrong.

"Hey kid, what's going on?" he asked.

So I told him that this was going to be my first shift where I was in charge of everything in the kitchen and I had some doubts about whether or not I could do it. I felt like I was having some kind of a minor nervous breakdown.

Everett very wisely put his arm around my shoulder and said, "Just take it easy, kid. You'll be fine." That little bit of encouragement made all the difference. I went to work and I didn't have any problems. I was pleased to find out that I had what it took to get the job done.

We even survived a Saturday night power outage. Late in service, at about 8:30, all the electricity went out. But of course, the stoves were still working because they were all gas. The dining room was lit mostly with candles and oil lamps. Guests were waiting for their dinners. We put a few candles around the kitchen and we just kept cooking. It was incredibly hot. The sauté pans that hung off the hood could no longer be touched by hand. They had to be grabbed with the kitchen mitt. I don't think I have ever sweated so much in my life. We got all the dinners cooked and served though.

I went outside after the last meal went out and I took off my double-breasted chef's coat and wrung the sweat out of it, quite a bit of sweat. Like I'd been sprayed down with a garden hose.

1974 was Ludlow's bicentennial. The same year I set up my little pottery shop in Ludlow. It was on a busy street, so I had good visibility, but it was too busy of an intersection. As a result, it was difficult to get in and out of the small parking lot. Consequently, I did not get a lot of drive-in business.

I had to build a kiln and I had to build lots of shelving to hold pots in different stages of production. I hand-carved a sign that I still have here in Vermont. A common nickname for Ludlow is "Jute Town" because the Ludlow Manufacturing Company had created a lot of fabric out of jute that was grown in India. So I named my shop The Jutetown Pottery Shop.

I did a few craft fairs. I went as far away as Danbury, Connecticut, for a three-day craft fair. I met Mary Travers from the well-known singing group, Peter, Paul and Mary, when she came by my booth. But when she realized that I recognized her, she ran away. I sold a few pieces. I traded with other craft people for things they were making, like leather belts and jewelry. I also met a few interesting people who invited me to their houses to socialize and sometimes sleep over. The life of a traveling potter could be quite interesting if you learned to go with the flow.

My friends and Jean-Jacques would come to my shop to make things. My very artistic cousin, Maureen Brennan, now Cotti, was a regular visitor. The most money I made in my shop was from giving lessons for three hours on Wednesday nights, from six to nine. I would typically have three or four students. Some of them were more serious than others. It became a little bit of a social club, where someone would usually bring some wine. Eventually, we had to pass a rule that we wouldn't open the wine till eight thirty. Otherwise nothing would get done. We had a good time socializing, and we did get some pottery made. I have to say it's a lot more fun making pottery with other people in the shop than doing it solo.

29

My First Head Chef Job

After working at Picot's Place for about a year and a half, one of the waiters told me that a friend of his was moving to the area from Minneapolis to open a new corporate restaurant on Boston Road in Springfield and they were looking for a chef. I decided to apply for the job because it was going to pay a lot more than what I was making at Picot's Place. I was hired and it turned out to be a very fortuitous decision in many ways. Number one, it was the first chef job where I was in charge of everything, and expected to have all the answers. I felt like I was ready for this challenge.

I had learned from working at Picot's Place that staff were constantly asking the chef, how do I make this or what goes in that? So I decided I would write up all the basic recipes for soups and salad dressings and put them on the wall so anyone could refer to them. That way, once someone was trained, I could be reasonably assured that there would be some consistency in the products we were serving. This saved me a lot of time as I no longer had to tell people over and over again how to do something. This was a communication technique that I carried with me throughout my career, and it served me well.

This was a big corporate restaurant called T. Butcher Block. It had a huge kitchen and a big staff. It had three walk-in coolers, one just for meat with a meat cutting band saw—I had never used one before—one for produce, and one for everything else. There was a complete prep kitchen with a full complement of stoves, ovens, and a large exhaust hood. There was also a large salad prep station with its own sinks and salad spinners. And, of course, a very large dishwashing station.

It was a mid-western take on the salad bar steakhouse concept that was all the rage in the 1970s with an open display cooking area right behind the salad bar. The restaurant opened with one serious caveat, it was supposed to have two six-foot-long charbroilers. But when we opened, there was only one. The second one was still on order. We had to go through two weeks of very high-volume steak grilling with only half our grilling capacity. I finally told the managers that I wouldn't do another weekend if we didn't take delivery on this second charbroiler. And miracle of miracles, it was delivered two days later.

T. Butcher Block also had a large bar-lounge area staffed by several beautiful young women wearing fishnet leggings and very short black cocktail dresses. So 70s.

The assistant manager was Marty Schupert and after we got to know each other I found out he had grown up in Middlebury, Vermont. This tidbit sparked my memory of riding through Middlebury in 1967 on my way back from the Montreal Expo. I mentioned my drive-by view of Middlebury to Marty and how I had plans to revisit Middlebury at some point in the future.

After four months of working together, Marty announced he was moving back to Middlebury. His mother and all his wife's relatives were still living in the area and they were anxious to get back to their family. He was going to be the manager at a restaurant called Mister Up's Restaurant and Pub. I told him that I was going to come and visit once he was settled in. A few months later, in August of 1975, I did go to visit. Unfortunately, Marty had forgotten about my plans and I didn't get to see him. But I did get a tour of the kitchen; it was incredibly small, a large closet, really. When I talked to Marty about it, he said he was going to get the owner to do a major expansion of the kitchen so that it could become a real restaurant and not just a bar with burgers, fries, and grilled cheese sandwiches.

In January of 1976, Marty called me up again and told me, "I really need a chef up here now." The kitchen had increased dramatically in size and the restaurant was very busy. The guy who was running the kitchen was just not the right guy for the job. All I can say is it didn't take a cattle prod to get me there. After traveling back and forth across the country, seeing the Tetons, the Rocky Mountains, and the Pacific Ocean, and then coming back to my hometown, it was clear to me that as nice as it was, there were better places to settle down.

Even today, when you drive a little bit north of Middlebury, the view to the west of the Adirondack Mountains in New York State is absolutely spectacular, ridge upon ridge of purple mountain majesty. Not quite the Tetons, but the closest thing we have to it on the East Coast.

The really profound thing I learned in my travels was when you move to a new area where no one knows your history you are free to make yourself into whatever you want to be. No one has any preconceived notion of who you are or expectations of what your abilities are. You're free to create or develop whatever attributes or aspects of yourself you think are your most valuable traits, and people will judge you on your current skills and performance. Their opinion of you will not be colored by your past and in my case, my not-so-stellar scholastic history.

I remember explaining this to my mother. I had to move away from my hometown so I would be free of the shackles of my local history and I would be able to become the person I wanted to be, the person I knew I could be. It worked out pretty well.

30

Moving Home to Middlebury

I interviewed for the chef job at Mister Up's in January of 1976. I accepted the job immediately and started making plans to move to Vermont. This is exactly the situation I was looking for.

My honest intention was that I was moving to Vermont to settle down. I was twenty-nine years old and wanted to put down roots and live in one place for a long time. My basic plan was to come to Vermont and figure out how to be a success at my new job. My complete plan was to buy some land, build a house, meet a woman, and start a family.

When I moved to Vermont, I owned a pickup truck, a 1967 Triumph motorcycle, a bicycle, a whitewater capable canoe, some rock climbing and camping gear, downhill and cross-country ski gear, a tipi with lodge-pole pine poles, a pottery wheel, and a big pile of bricks from my kiln in Ludlow that I would rebuild into a new kiln in Vermont. I was excited to get going, to put down roots, and to build a happy life for myself and those I came in contact with. I didn't have the words at the time but I know now I was looking for my road to felicity.

I was excited to get all my gear into one place. To put down roots. To make a home for myself. Earlier in life, when I asked my father why he got married when he did, he said, "I was twenty-nine years old and I figured if I was going to have a family, I better get started." So there I was ready to follow in his footsteps.

Very soon after moving to Middlebury, I was naturally drawn to the Frog Hollow Vermont State Craft Center next to the falls of Otter Creek because of my pottery shop experiences. In 1976, this center consisted of a gallery on the main floor and studio spaces on the lower level, one for pottery and one for drawing and painting. There was also a world-class pipemaker in the building named Andrew Marks.

Probably within the first month or two I went to the pottery studio and introduced myself to the resident potter, Josette Knoll. While I was there in the studio, a friend of hers stumbled in with high-heeled boots, tight jeans, and a leather jacket with a Mary Lynn O'Shea—a very talented local weaver—scarf wrapped around her neck. She reminded me of the Geena Davis character in the 1991 movie, *Thelma and Louise*. Very ostentatious and bordering on the edge of some kind of instability. Near the edge of control, but "interesting." Maybe it was the high heels.

I became friendly with both of these women, very friendly. We did some socializing together. The first thing we did together was an Emmylou Harris (before her hair went white) concert in Burlington. She and Vassar Clements (the father of hillbilly jazz) put on an absolutely fantastic show. A few weeks later, we went to a Paul Taylor Dance Company performance at Middlebury College, much different but also amazing.

I'm sure these women were both well acquainted with many of the other single men in town, and I think they were a little excited to see a fresh unknown treat.

Pretty quickly I was spending overnight time with both of them independently and they started telling me that they were sharing notes about their experiences with me. For a brief period, I had the mistaken impression that I had fallen into some kind of paradise, but of course, pretty quickly feelings started to solidify and I was feeling pressure to commit one way or the other.

That is to say, I felt like I was in heaven for a week or two with two women vying for my attention. Then, almost as quickly, I started feeling like I had fallen into some kind of hell. I decided I had to break off with both of them as that was the only fair thing to do.

I went to say goodbye to Josette the potter first. When I told her I wasn't going to see her romantically anymore she literally threw up. She vomited into her sink.

Then I went to say goodbye to Geena Davis (her real name was Pat). Initially, she called me every bad name she could think of and then somehow she talked me out of it. I actually had my hand on the doorknob of her house on the way out the door, and then...I changed my mind. I didn't want to hurt her feelings. It was one of the worst decisions I ever made, something I wouldn't realize until many years later. It wasn't her fault. It was my fault. I have no one to blame but myself.

I came to Vermont to settle down and start a family, and then I took up with a woman who had one child and did not want to have any more. She had tubal ligation before I met her. I knew about it, and I should've looked at my list of hopes and dreams and just said I'm sorry, something doesn't match up here, I'm going to have to move on. But I didn't do that. It wasn't all bad either. We had many laughs and good times along the way. But I think, now, in hindsight, that decision was doomed from the very beginning. I know now because it ended badly fifteen years later. This is the big mistake I alluded to earlier.

One of the most important lessons I've learned over the years is that you can't go back, you can only go forward. If you've made mistakes, the best you can hope for is that they taught you something and hopefully you don't repeat them. I have a friend who has a poster in his house, that says "I've learned so much from my mistakes I'm going to keep making them."

31

Committing to Pat Samson

So, Pat and I moved in together. At some point, I asked her if her parents were still alive. She said yes. I asked how often do you see them? She said, "I haven't seen them in twenty years, and I don't want to ever see them again as long as I live." Of course, I thought that was strange, but I felt like it wasn't my problem and I didn't have to worry about it. Major red flag. I decided not to question her about it in any detail. It became a problem as our relationship developed. If someone said that to me today, I'd be inclined to say, "I'm really sorry about that, I'll see you later." But I didn't—another big mistake. As Lorenzo, the father, played by Robert De Niro, said to his teenage son in the movie A Bronx Tale, "When you let the little head start telling a big head what to do, that's when you start getting in trouble." Another lesson learned the hard way.

Early in our relationship, I told her about my love of motorcycling, skiing, hiking, overnight camping, and whitewater canoeing. She told me that she would be happy to go along with me on those adventures, except, maybe, downhill skiing. So, we did some motorcycling together. We did a lot of class one, two, and three whitewater canoeing together. We did some hiking and overnight camping together and had fun doing short hikes in the Green Mountains, and cross-country skiing. Pat seemed to be enjoying these activities just as much as I was. Everything seemed to be working out, except, of course, the no-children issue.

After getting settled in my job in Middlebury, I started looking for land to buy. My plan was to buy a parcel of ten acres and build my own house. But in the late summer of 1976, after looking at a lot of swamps and cliffs that were all priced at $1,000 per acre, I was getting a little discouraged. In October, I saw an ad for a ten-acre parcel for $8,000, and I thought, finally, a break in the price. So, I got in touch with the realtor and went to look at the property. I wasn't that interested in the land but right next to it, there was a twenty-five-acre piece for sale for $12,000. So, I thought for a minute. That's another fifteen acres of land for only $4,000. What I found was a beautiful twenty-five-acre piece of land about six miles north of Middlebury.

When I drove out to it, I got out of my truck and ran down the field laughing to myself and waving my arms, "This is it! This is it! This is what I've been looking for. This is where I'm going to put down roots and start building a life for myself. The life I've been dreaming about will be rooted here."

The parcel was a wide long rectangle, about 60 percent meadow and 40 percent pine forest with a small seasonal stream. It had beautiful views to the south of Chipman Hill in Middlebury, and to the east of the Green Mountain National Forest. I drove back to the real estate office and immediately gave them a deposit. I had the whole deal done in less than a week. I started making my house plans. I sited the house near the northern boundary of the meadow that was about a quarter of a mile long.

In the spring I got a foundation established, a water well dug, and a septic system installed. In my spare time from my job, I started building my house. I got the first floor framed up on the foundation walls. I got the walls framed up. I got the second floor installed on top of the walls with stairs from the cellar to the second floor. And then I looked up where the roof rafters were supposed to go and I didn't have a clue how I was going to install them. That's because there was nothing to stand on! So, I hired a couple of professional carpenters and found out that this kind of work is done with staging, so you have something to stand on while you're lifting the roof rafters into place.

I added considerably to my skill set in building that house. What I couldn't teach myself I was able to learn from others who had done it before many times. I love learning, and I really love learning how to build my own shelter. It's a wonderful sense of accomplishment, especially in Vermont, in the middle of a cold winter when you can go into a house that you have seriously participated in building, add some more wood to the fire in the woodstove, and feel cozy and snug in your own home. It was such an unbelievable feeling for me that I had trouble wrapping my head around the reality that I was going to live in my own home—a home I made.

Once the house was finished enough to move into the first night, I decided to sleep on the couch in the living area. In the middle of my first night, I had a nightmare that military-type people came to the door with guns and told me I had to get out, that it wasn't my house, and that I had to move out now. I woke up in a cold sweat. It was such an incredible feeling for me to be in my own home on my own land with all my stuff in one place, I couldn't believe it was true. Or maybe I didn't believe I deserved it. Thankfully, I did get over that feeling pretty quickly and settled in nicely.

My interest in foraging for wild mushrooms continued after moving to Vermont. I was out for a walk along my driveway with my cousin Michael, who was visiting from Ludlow, when we spotted some King Boletes in the pine duff near the drive. These were the first mushrooms I found close to my home. Next were chanterelles that were growing in great profusion around my home in the late 70s and early 80s. Then Hen of the Woods, and then many others.

32

Marriage the First Time

After living with Pat for a few months, one day out of the blue, she asked, "Are you going to marry me or what?"

I thought about it for a little while. It didn't seem unreasonable so I said, "OK, if that'll make you happy, I will marry you."

I know now this was what you call an unconscious decision. Again, I didn't want to hurt her feelings. And I did like her, of course. We had many fun adventures together. But still, there was this lack of children in our future. Her son, my stepson Noah, was great, but it's not quite the same as your own flesh and blood. And there was that black whole of her family history that was lurking in the background. The psychological and emotional baggage that she carried from her childhood would affect our relationship and our ability to be happy in the long term. I don't believe that it was ever properly processed, and as a result, there was always a dark shadow lurking.

But we started planning a wedding for October 1, 1977. We got married at home with about seventy-five or eighty people in attendance. The original plan was to get married out in the meadow by a large cluster of trees that I had named The Ten Brothers, and have the reception in the yard and on the deck that I had built on the south side of the house.

Unfortunately, the weather did not cooperate at all. It rained every day for two weeks before the wedding and I think it might've rained another week after. The ground under the newly planted grass was completely waterlogged. I bought some bales of hay and spread them around on the new grass and borrowed a bunch of folding chairs from somewhere. By the end of the day, the new grass and hay had been all mushed together and just looked like mud. We ended up with a lot of soggy-footed guests on the deck under the temporary shelter made of two-by-fours covered with clear plastic off the side of the house that some friends and I had hastily constructed the day before. By late in the day, our little house was full of muddy feet, lots of muddy feet, and the floor looked more like the muddy yard than a newly finished floor. I would say as a result we put five or more years of wear on that floor in one day.

I made the wedding cake and lots of the food. We also asked people to bring food to share. We had a buffet of food set up on the two large worktables in our kitchen area. We had a band playing, believe it or not, named Downpour, who played on the deck under the temporary plastic roof, hoping they weren't going to get electrocuted. I think most people there had a good time, or at least made the best of it. But it certainly wasn't the sunny country-in-the-meadow wedding that we had envisioned.

Pat and I departed at about five in the afternoon. We planned to honeymoon in Quebec City. Our first night on the road was not well planned, but it worked out great. At about five thirty I made a phone call from a pay phone next to a Howard Johnson's in South Burlington. I called a restaurant in Montgomery, Vermont, in the shadow of Jay Peak called Zack's On The Rocks. Zack answered the phone and said, "I can't take you at six, but I can take you at eight thirty." He also informed us that he now had a liquor license, so we didn't have to bring our own wine. No problem, it was going to take us at least two hours to get there.

We drove up Route 15 to Jeffersonville where we picked up Route 109 that goes up through Belvedere. I remember it was dark and it was raining hard. On Route 109 there are several long, lonely sections of road where there are no houses, no towns, and no lights to be seen of any kind. I began to wonder if we were on the right road or whether were lost. But eventually, we did get to Montgomery Center and the rest of the evening was great.

Zack's was one of the most truly unusual restaurants ever operated in Vermont. A perfectly unique expression of Zack himself. It was located up a steep hill on the Bayley-Hazen Notch Road, a thruway that is not plowed all the way through in the wintertime. There was a beautiful view of Jay Peak from there which is why Zack located his restaurant there. Of course, you could only see the view in the daytime and if it

MY FIRST MARRIAGE, IN OCTOBER 1976. THAT'S MY
STEPFATHER, EVERETT, ON THE LEFT, MY WIFE PAT, AND MY
MOTHER ON THE RIGHT. IT WAS A GOOD DAY, BUT IT
DIDN'T END WELL.

wasn't raining.

We stayed down in the village of Montgomery Center in a small motel next to a raging stream; yes it was still raining. The motel was called Granny Grunts. I remember the room had smoky mirror tiles on the ceiling, perfect for a honeymoon couple. When we got to the restaurant, Zack greeted us at the door dressed in his signature purple caftan with lots of rhinestones and other costume jewelry necklaces. He said, "Come in, come in," and he sat us down in a hurry in The Passion Pit next to the fireplace. And then he disappeared. I kept wondering, who was that guy and where did that guy go? I didn't know until much later that Zack greeted all his guests at the door and that he did all the cooking in the kitchen. He could see guests approaching through the kitchen window. Zack would then run to greet them, and then hurry back into the kitchen to continue cooking for the guests that were in the dining room.

The little restaurant he had built there years before was right out of a fairytale. There were stone walls with steeply pitched roof rafters and a big fireplace on one side of the room. The whole place was lit with candles hanging from the ceiling, which created very low light and made it intentionally romantic. Opposite the fireplace was a bank of small pane windows illuminated by small spotlights that pointed at the wet spruce trees outside. It was really quite a magical experience, one of a kind, just like Zack.

Zack's signature color was purple. The purple caftan was just the start. The menu was also handwritten on brown paper—an old shopping bag—with purple ink and burned around the edges to make it look like it was from another era. There was even purple sugar in the sugar bowl. The most curious item on the menu was the Mushrooms Monkey Center. Because the place was so unusual I thought, does he really have monkey meat on the menu? The waitress laughed and told me no, that

that was Zack's nickname for Montgomery Center.

In later years, Zack became a friend of mine. We had meals together and had fun talking shop and his very long experience in the restaurant business. Like me, he'd graduated from the Culinary Institute of America but in 1954, not 1971.

For a number of years, he had worked at The Tyler Place Family Resort in Swanton, Vermont, on northern Lake Champlain. On his day off he would drive around the countryside, and on one of his drives he discovered a site where he decided to build his restaurant. It was owned by a local farmer and the pasture was full of large rocks. Zack bought the property, and the farmer asked him if he wanted help moving the rocks. "No no," he said, "I love the rocks. Leave them right where they are." Hence the name, Zack's On The Rocks.

Years later when he finally decided to retire, he put the whole property, including his house that he had built for himself and his wife, and a rental house, up for auction. I didn't go to the auction, but I was told that thirty or forty people showed up at the auction. Not one was there to bid on the restaurant. They'd just come to see what was going to happen and to say goodbye to Zack and wish him well. Eventually, the house and rental property were sold. The last time I went by there I didn't see any sign of the restaurant. I assumed it was dismantled.

Pat and I had a pleasant weeklong honeymoon in Quebec City. We had a good time walking down Le Quartier Petit Champlain and driving out to view the Montmorency Falls. We also drove out to Île d'Orléans and bought some hard cider.

We stayed at the landmark Château Frontenac. We had dinner at a restaurant called La Traite du Roy, the treat of the king. All the service staff wore powder blue tuxedos with tails. I remember watching a taxi pull up in the rain, yes, it was still raining, in front of the restaurant to whisk us back to our hotel and thinking, this is so romantic.

But I had to get back to work because it was foliage season in Vermont and Marty the manager of Mister Up's was already upset enough that I had decided to get married when I did and wanted me back at work as soon as possible to be there for the leaf peepers.

33

The Reality of My New Life

So, I settled into my new life in my new house with my new wife and my six-year-old stepson, who was there part-time. Things went pretty well for quite a while. But little by little a trend developed that made me realize my new wife did not really share interest in my hobbies as she told me before we were married.

First, it was the motorcycle. She said, "I won't ride on it anymore, it's too dangerous, I think you should sell it." I needed more work done in the house, so I traded the motorcycle to a carpenter who did the work.

Then it was the canoeing. We had done quite a bit of flat and white-water canoeing around Vermont and had lots of wonderful experiences. Then one day when we were on a gentle part of the New Haven River, something snapped and she told me she had to get out of the canoe right away. I tried talking to her about it and asking her what the problem was. She screamed, "If you don't take me to shore right now I'm going to jump out!" So, I took her to shore, and she never got in a canoe with me again.

Then it was cross-country skiing. We lived on twenty-five acres of land with a big meadow and lots of smaller trails I had made in the trees around the edges. One beautiful winter day, after I prepped all the gear, got everything organized, and the skis waxed, and helped her lace up her boots we headed out. After getting 100 yards from the house, she informed me that she just wasn't into this anymore and she was going back to the house and never went skiing again.

Early in our relationship we did a lot of overnight camping and frequently combined it with hiking to the tops of some of the mountains nearby. Snake Mountain in Addison, which has one of the finest mountaintop views in the state, was a favorite. We would hike up with our camping gear and food, set up our tent, build a fire, cook some

My stepson, Noah, about the age of six. He was a wonderful boy and grew into an even a better man. I'm happy to say we still have a good relationship.

simple food, and spend the night in our cozy little tent. We did several similar trips over the years.

As the years went by, each camping trip required a more comfortable setup.

The last camping trip we did together was at a state park with a big lawn and a beach; we camped out of a van. We had planned this trip for five days. My stepson Noah was with us. After two days of this posh so-called camping, Pat said, "I'm not into this anymore. I'm going home. You guys can stay here if you want." She never went camping again. Ditto with hiking.

I remember telling my ex-brother-in-law that after five years of marriage all we had left in common was an occasional dinner out and a movie, and maybe a roll in the hay. It felt like I had been deceived. My wife told me she liked all that stuff to get me to marry her. I thought she was going to participate in these activities willingly for a long time, and we would have the joy of doing things together. For me, marriage is all about the shared experience.

Half the pleasure of solitude togetherness comes from having someone with you to whom you can say how sweet solitude is. Little by little there were fewer things that we did together, not a recipe for a successful relationship.

34

Running the Boston Marathon

I now went skiing with friends—cross-country and downhill. The same with whitewater canoeing, which naturally progressed to whitewater kayaking. In 1979, one of our neighbors, Randy Ross, told me that he was getting interested in jogging and showed me a copy of Ken Cooper's book called *The New Aerobics*. He and I agreed to follow Ken Cooper's program to achieve a reasonable level of fitness. Five days a week that summer we would meet at the end of our driveway. Initially, we did a walk/run for one mile. Each week we increased our pace a little bit until we got to our goal of a seven-minute mile of jogging. Cooper's goal was to do a seven-minute mile five days a week to maintain a reasonable level of fitness.

After about seven or eight weeks, Randy and I went out and did a six-minute mile. We were shocked at how much we had improved. After that, we started increasing our distance. First, it was three miles, then four, then five, etc. Then one day I went out on my own and did eight miles, something I previously had not believed I was capable of doing. I became mildly addicted to running and started making plans to run a marathon.

I did lots of reading about running and tested myself with a few other friends. I bought a book called *Target 26*. Basically, the program

MY STEPSON, NOAH, ROWING AT ITHACA COLLEGE.

was a hard day, an easy day. It started out with an easy day of two miles, then a hard day of five. It worked up to an easy day of eight miles, and a hard day of fifteen, six days a week. At that level, it gets pretty time-consuming, but I loved it. I love being able to do something that previously I thought was out of my reach.

I was again proving to myself, that the result is directly proportional to the effort in so many things in life. I then read *The Complete Book of Running* by James Fixx. I read *Running & Being* by Dr. George Sheehan who explained in some detail what happens to your body physiologically at different ages and different stages of long-distance running. He explained what it means to hit the wall after about sixteen or eighteen miles, why it happens, and how to deal with it. In my preparation to do a marathon, I did several long runs to test myself and to try to find out where my limits were, so by the time I committed to a marathon I was pretty well conditioned and I knew pretty well what to expect and how to deal with it.

In April 1981, I went with a group of friends to Hopkinton, Massachusetts. We snuck into the back of the pack at the Boston Marathon. My goal, my modest goal, was to finish in under four hours and not feel like I had been run over by a truck. I had been training for about two years. I knew that I had to run much more slowly the whole way, much slower than my shorter six- or seven-minute mile runs in Vermont. Nine minutes per mile equals just under four hours for a marathon of 26.2 miles. The challenge is to run slow enough in the early stages when you're feeling like you could run much faster. Because later in the race, when you run out of all your stored glycogen, it's going to be much harder to maintain your pace.

It just so happens that 1981 was a good year for me to run my one-and-only marathon. There are two John Kelleys, who have won the Boston Marathon—Kelley the Younger and Kelley the Elder. In 1981, Kelley the Elder was running his fiftieth consecutive Boston Marathon that year so there were many people waiting for him to finish at the end of the race. I believe he finished in about four hours and twelve minutes.

THE GROUP I RAN THE BOSTON MARATHON WITH IN 1981. THAT'S MARTY SCHUPERT ON THE LEFT. I FINISHED IN MY GOAL OF THREE HOURS AND 56 MINUTES, AND WAS HAPPY WITH MY RESULT.

I ran by him in Newton in the heartbreak hill section of the race. He was part of a peloton of about fifty runners, and there were crowds cheering him the whole way. When I went by him, I thought, I hope he's wearing earplugs because that deafening cheering sound is following him like a pig in a python.

By the time I got to the finish line in three hours and fifty-six minutes, there were still a lot of people waiting for Kelley the Elder. Coincidentally, they were also cheering for me, because I had followed someone's advice to wear a T-shirt with my name on it. Right to the end, people were yelling, "Yeah, Robert, you can do it!" "Go, Robert!"

Normally that late in the race, the crowd at the finish line would be pretty sparse. It was also one of the hardest sections of the whole race because of the gentle downslope after you go by Fenway Park. This is extremely hard on your quadriceps. My legs were burning and sore for a week afterward. Going down a flight of stairs was a painful reminder. But I was so glad that I did it.

I had set a goal and succeeded and didn't feel like I had been run over by a truck.

After a few days, I resumed my normal three-to-six mile workouts in Vermont and sometime around Labor Day, I was lying in bed thinking this feels really good just lying here. And that was pretty much the end of my long-distance running habit. I did run later in life with my second wife, but never more than three miles. I think it's a healthy habit to maintain a reasonable level of fitness, but I think the addiction to running is just that, an addiction.

35

Buying My First Restaurant

By January 1982, I had been the chef at Mister Up's in Middlebury for almost six years. This was by far the longest job I'd had in my adult life. There had been many discussions with the owner about some form of equity sharing but every time we were ready to have a discussion, there was always some excuse about not being quite ready, or the accountant in Rhode Island not providing the proper paperwork.

Both Marty the manager and I were starting to get antsy. Marty and I were completely running the restaurant while the owner Ron was busy with his construction business and had nothing to do with running the restaurant. Mostly he used it as his personal drinking and dining spot for himself and his friends. Marty and I both wanted to have our own place, or a least a piece of this successful restaurant we were pouring our hearts and souls into. When it looked like this was not going to happen at Mister Up's in 1982 we looked for other options.

Marty went as far as taking his family to the Chapel Hill area of North Carolina on vacation. He found a restaurant for lease. He came back to Vermont and put his house on the market and told Ron he was going to give his notice and move out of state. Initially, Ron said fine, do whatever you want. He was playing hardball. But pretty quickly Ron realized finding a new manager wasn't going to be that easy.

He changed his tune and asked Marty what it was going to take to get him to stay. Marty said 100 percent ownership in less than a month. They got in a room with the lawyers and made a deal happen quickly. Marty then asked me to be his partner, explaining to me that because he had been working there longer than I had, he should own 51 percent and I should own 49 percent. I didn't like the smell of that and I consulted my attorney who said quite succinctly, "You don't want to own 49 percent of anything, because you'll have all your equity tied up in a business that you have no control over." Marty was incredulous, he couldn't believe it. He said, "You mean you'd rather own nothing than 49 percent of Mister Up's?" I had to tell him that that was the advice I had received from my counsel.

I had an ace up my sleeve. My wife was friends with a local accountant, who told us at the very same time in March of 1982 that a restaurant we both admired in South Burlington, Pauline's Kitchen, was going to be up for sale. Pat and I met with Pauline and her ex-husband Sandy on April 2, 1982, and on May 2, we signed a deal to buy the restaurant at 1834 Shelburne Road in South Burlington. It was a small miracle because the prime rate at the time was 18 percent and we really had very little money. We did have a house with some equity in it, and the only reason we were able to buy the restaurant was because Pauline was willing to finance the sale at 12 percent, a gift at that time, with a relatively small down payment of $25,000, which we did not have.

I reached out to family, friends, and fools—$2,000 here, $4,000 there. We put together the $25,000 down payment, signed all the papers, and went to work on May 2, 1982. I'd never owned a business before and to say there was a lot I did not know is an understatement. But my attitude was that no one was born knowing how to do this; if other people could learn how to do it, so could I.

Later, when I talked to a banker about the deal, he said, "You're 100 percent financed? What are you gonna do if this goes wrong or that goes wrong?" I said, "I can't fall back because I have nothing to fall back on." Then I told him, "I'm going to be the Jake LaMotta of restaurateurs." You may remember the 1980 Martin Scorsese film, *Raging Bull*, a biopic about a real fighter named Jake LaMotta. In the film, LaMotta played by Robert De Niro, is getting pummeled by Sugar Ray Robinson. Instead of falling down, he hooks his arms over the ropes, and takes punch after punch, until the referee calls off the fight. When Robinson walks away, LaMotta says, "Hey Ray. I didn't go down, Ray." That was my attitude because I didn't have any other alternative. I could not fail. I had no other alternative. Success was my only option.

I had read somewhere that the best time to start your own business was between the ages of twenty-five and thirty-five, old enough to have some experience but not too old that you were afraid to take chances and maybe rock the boat a little bit. I was thirty-five at the time so I decided that if I was going to have my own business I better get started.

At thirty-five, I had a pretty full tank of gas, and I was really excited about owning my own business, steering my own ship, and doing what I thought was best instead of having to listen to other people tell me what they thought was best. Except for my wife, of course. We decided early on that her domain was the dining room, and my domain was the kitchen. We worked six and a half days a week. On Saturday nights we slept over in the restaurant. We watched *Saturday Night Live* on TV and got up early in the morning to start prepping for Sunday brunch. We took Sunday nights off. I was usually in bed right after *60 Minutes*, at about eight at night, and then back at it by ten on Monday morning. It wasn't easy, but I was so excited to be running my own business for the first three years that I was running mostly on adrenaline and very sporadic paychecks, everything was for the business.

Then one day on our drive to Pauline's from our home in New Haven, we were about halfway to the restaurant, our twenty-six-mile twice-a-day car marathon, and I was very tired and run down. We were not getting a regular paycheck, just taking enough to pay for our absolute basics. I just had so much on my mind all the time. I told Pat I was fed up and I wanted to quit and get a regular job. That way I could get a regular paycheck, some vacation time, and not have so much stuff on my mind.

She said, "What are you talking about?"

I said, "I've had it. Just let me out of the car and I'll walk home and get a regular job and a regular paycheck every other week."

She looked at me with disbelief and said, "Shut up, we're going to work, and don't talk about this anymore."

She was right, I got used to it. I learned how to manage my feelings, how to control what I could control, and not worry about what I couldn't control. I've seen other small business owners go through a similar cycle since then. All excitement in the beginning followed by a feeling of self-doubt and regret about three years in. I've told them all the same thing: Don't give up now, you've done all the hard work, and you've established some momentum. That's why it's been so hard up to this point. Remember this from Issac Newton: "A body in motion tends to stay in motion." So, the effort needed to get something moving is greater than what it takes to keep it moving. The effort needed to keep a body in motion levels off at some point around three years. It becomes manageable. At least that's what happened to me.

36

My First Visit to Europe

Pat had grown up in relative poverty on a small farm in central New York. I think this is why she got much more joy out of spending money and not trying to build up a nest egg. In the spring of 1985, she announced that we had made too much money and to avoid paying taxes on all of it we had to spend some of it on research. What kind of research? She said we're going to France to do research in fine dining and fine wines. I had to admit I liked the idea. I'd never been to France. I wasn't quite sure I would ever go. So, we planned a trip with our neighborhood wine list consultant Tom who was a computer professor at Middlebury College, his wife Diane, and our restaurant manager, Ann Peck. We flew to Paris where we met up with Diane's sister, June, who was living there as a student. She would act as our translator and Paris tour guide. She found us a little apartment to rent, and we had fun exploring the usual sites in Paris for a couple of days.

Then we rented a car and drove to the Champagne region of France, just a little bit north of Paris. I brought along my Michelin travel guide. On our way, I picked our first starred restaurant—The Royal Champagne, a one-star restaurant right along the road we were on. We stopped for lunch. I was over the moon. Me, the farm boy, lunching at a Michelin restaurant!

We had prearranged a wine tour at the champagne cellars of Pol Roger, the favorite champagne of Winston Churchill. He even named one of his racehorses after the champagne. We then visited the Cathedral of Notre-Dame in Reims, the traditional coronation place for many kings of France. I felt like a king just walking into the place. We returned to Paris for a day, and then early the next day we headed to the Burgundy region which is four hours south of where we had a wine tour prearranged. Some of my favorite wines are produced in this area.

After a two-hour tour of a wine cellar in Savigny-lés-Beaune that began at ten thirty that morning and a tasting of several wines—read getting just a little bit tipsy—we were treated to lunch at a fabulous Michelin two-star restaurant, Ermitage de Corton with more wine provided by our host. This establishment had more giant flower arrangements than we had ever seen in a restaurant.

After a three-hour lunch, our host, Herbert asked, "Where are you staying tonight?" We said we didn't have any idea (read now very tipsy). He called his secretary, and she got us a room at the Hôtel le Home in Beaune. Absolutely charming. A beautiful cluster of stone buildings right in the middle of a vineyard. We liked it so much that after we drove to the Mediterranean we stayed there a second time on our way back to Paris.

While in Beaune we also visited the cellars of Joseph Drouhin and the world-famous Hospices de Beaune. We drove around looking for some of the storied vineyards, like Domaine de la Romanée-Conti, Château du Clos de Vougeot, and Gevrey-Chambertin. We were dumbstruck just looking at this hallowed ground where these grapes were grown that produced wines that were respected around the world. I felt like the country mouse who was going to see the queen.

We then drove south toward the Mediterranean and continued to the town of Annecy in the French Alps on the shores of a beautiful lake with the same name. We had a fabulous nighttime tour boat ride and dinner cruise on the lake. The next night we ate at our first three-star restaurant in Talloires, L'Auberge de Père Bise.

This restaurant has to be one of the most beautifully situated in the world, on the shore of a stunning lake with snow-capped mountains towering above. They grew their own crayfish, so of course we had to have the crayfish bisque, a special memory to this day. I feel extremely privileged to have been able to have a meal at such a fine internationally known restaurant. I don't know what I did to deserve it, but I was hell-bent on enjoying the ride.

We then stopped in Grenoble so June could get back to her studies in Paris, and continued south to Cannes and settled for the night in Cap d'Antibes. The next day we had one of the most memorable dining experiences of my entire life. I remember much of it vividly to this day. It was lunch in a three-star restaurant in La Napoule called L' Oasis. The chef was Louis Outhier, one of many three-star chefs of that era who had trained under Fernand Point at La Pyramide in Vienne which was widely regarded as the greatest restaurant in France in the 1950s.

When our little group had lunch at this fabulous restaurant, it was after almost two weeks on the road. After the pre-appetizer, the appetizer, the intermezzo, the main course, and the pallet cleanser, the waiter wheeled over three dessert carts with a total of eighteen choices. Everyone else at the table said they couldn't possibly eat anymore. I looked at them in disbelief and said, "Do you think you're coming back here next week? This is the only chance you will ever get to order dessert at L'Oasis." I browbeat them into ordering one dessert each.

I ordered six desserts, each one served on a twelve-inch wide, Villeroy & Boch China plate! I had a crescent of beautiful desserts surrounding me. I didn't want to eat them all, of course, I just wanted to taste them. Well, it wasn't too long before my friends started poaching some of my choices. It was really unbelievable! The chef even made an appearance at the table and I thanked him as much as I could in my very limited command of the French language and told him my hat was off to him. Everything was just stellar.

The next day, we went to a much more modest restaurant, no stars, right on the Mediterranean. We had two classics, an excellent bouillabaisse and a bourride, two similar, but very different types of seafood stew, sitting right next to the Mediterranean Sea. The quality of the light was mesmerizing. It's little wonder that Vincent van Gogh was drawn there. We drove by St. Tropez, the favorite seaside hangout for people like Brigitte Bardot then skirted Marseille and landed in Avignon.

We stayed just across the river from the famous bridge Pont d'Avignon, of nursery song fame, in the town of Villeneuve-lés-Avignon. We made a day trip to the beautiful hill town of Gordes, just to the east of Avignon. It was absolutely charming, and I remember eating pizza from a wood-fired oven and also having my first bowl of ratatouille provencale.

In Avignon, we saw posters for an Elton John concert in the Roman amphitheater in the city of Orange nearby. We were able to get tickets and I'm glad we did. At the time I have to say I was not the biggest fan of his music but after that show, I was a total convert. What a showman. I didn't realize how many of his songs I already knew. It was a fantastic experience. The show oscillated between ballads and rock 'n' roll songs. It was fabulous, I became a lifelong fan. The song that stuck with me was a duet he sang with Kiki Dee, "Don't Go Breaking My Heart."

The next day we were headed back to Paris, and I realized we were going to drive right by Vienne. I had to see La Pyramide, the storied restaurant of modern French culinary history. They were open for lunch, and we were able to get a table for four. Our restaurant manager Ann had really had it with eating big meals by then and decided to stay in the car. It was another wonderful experience to be in the temple of haute cuisine where so many of the current three-star chefs had trained at the elbow of Ferdinand Point in their youth. Point died in 1955, weighing at least 350 pounds. Reportedly, his last words were, "Butter, more butter."

His wife Mado was still alive in 1985, sitting by the front door with her two dogs, handwriting the menus in a very large script so her customers didn't have to suffer the indignity of pulling out their reading glasses to be able to read the menu. The most memorable thing about the experience there was the fact that the bread was served directly on the tablecloth without any plates. La Pyramid was one of the only Michelin-starred restaurants that was allowed to keep their stars after the death of the chef because of the recognized talent of his wife Mado.

That was the last of our special visits to some of the different landmarks that fell in our path on my very first trip to France in 1985. I've been back a few times since and I've had many wonderful experiences, but the first time is always the sweetest.

37

The French Effect on Pauline's

When we returned to Vermont I was pumped up with new ideas for Pauline's. I wanted to try to take the restaurant to the next level. We spent quite a bit of money on new plates—similar to the ones we had seen in France. Better glassware and better-looking flatware. I did my best to elevate the food we were serving without getting too far ahead of our regular clientele.

In the fall of 1985, I bought my first kilo of black truffles for $350. Today they are $2,600 per kilo or more. They came from an importer named Paul Urbani in the Piedmont region of Italy. They came wrapped in an Italian newspaper, packed inside a nice little strip-woven wooden basket, that was packed inside a snug-fitting Styrofoam box, that was packed inside a cardboard box all taped up very tight. When they were delivered, I put the box unopened in the walk-in cooler.

Within a short period, when I went into the walk-in, I could smell that incredible aroma given off by the black truffles through all those layers of packing. It's quite unforgettable, and there's nothing else quite like it. My favorite description of the aroma of black truffles is from an article in *Geo* magazine. The cover photo was of a man sniffing a large black truffle.

THE FIRST KILOGRAM OF BLACK TRUFFLES THAT I
BOUGHT IN 1984 FROM PAUL URBANI. THEY WERE
THE BEST AND MOST FRAGRANT TRUFFLES I'VE EVER
BOUGHT, A VERY POWERFUL OLFACTORY MEMORY.

"They are reminiscent of a rumpled lover's bed, the smell of musk, they reek of sex." Just think about that for a minute, it's a stink that has an allure like no other. I was thrilled. As far as I know, Pauline's was the first restaurant in the state of Vermont to feature black truffles on the menu. For maximum impact, I would slice these truffles very thin and place Madeira poached slices on a thin slice of steamed potato. They were also used as a garnish for several different menu items. I stacked the slices of truffle and potato on top of each other four high with finely diced truffle dust in a white butter sauce as an appetizer with a few slices of poached leeks around for flavor and visual contrast. I salivate at the memory of it.

It's fairly easy to buy truffles preserved in a jar or a can at specialty shops, but I can tell you from my experience those products are a shadow, a weak shadow of what really good fresh truffles smell and taste like. Of course, these days it's quite common for people to have truffle fries on their menu, which are french fries sprinkled with oil that's had truffles marinated in it. I can tell you, it's not the same. Some of the truffle oil fries I've tasted, especially white truffle oil fries, reek of dirty socks, not sex, not a very alluring aroma.

We organized and promoted many special multi-course wine-tasting dinners every couple of months with specially selected high-end wines. These events were a lot of work, but I felt like they were good for building up the reputation of the restaurant. On special holidays like New Year's Eve, and Valentine's Day we also did very special multi-course menus. We were trying to replicate some of the three-star meals we had had in France. Over time, I came to the conclusion that, even though we told people when they made a reservation that we had these special multi-course menus for these occasions, they would feel somewhat ambushed after they sat down and realized that they were going to have to pay more than they were accustomed to.

I decided these special menus were good for a special-occasion sales boost but not so good for long-term everyday sales. I concluded it was best to offer these special holiday menu choices alongside our regular à la carte menus. They should have a place on the table as well. Learning, learning, learning.

38

We Buy Déjà Vu Café

In the fall of 1986, I noticed an ad in the *Burlington Free Press*: "For sale, the most beautiful restaurant in Vermont." I was intrigued. The restaurant in question was in downtown Burlington at 185 Pearl Street. It was called the Déjà Vu Café and it had an absolutely stunning interior with many beautifully handcrafted features. The Déjà Vu Café had been built over an almost four-year period by a man named Brian Fox who was maniacal about details. It really was the most beautiful restaurant in the state. We had eaten there several times and were always impressed by how beautiful it was and never dreamed we would own such a magnificent space.

The whole building was about 8,000 square feet with cathedral ceilings and two levels of dining. There was an 800-square-foot workroom that was unused at the time. When we looked at it, our first thought was to make this into a special-occasion banquet room separate from the main dining room and that's how we would make the business grow.

So, my wife Pat and I bought the Déjà Vu Café in late 1986 and continued to own and operate Pauline's. We started to work with an architect, Brad Robinowitz, who had trained in Chicago and was very familiar with Prairie School design to rework this new banquet room.

We had been to the Metropolitan Museum in New York City and

seen the Francis W. Little Room which had been taken out of a house designed by Frank Loyd Wright, so that was our model. Lots of oak trim and mirrors on both sides of the room, with Frank Lloyd Wright-type designs etched into them, did a good job of making the room look much larger. We had custom tables made, and very beautiful Prairie School-style chairs. We named it the Frank Lloyd Wright Room.

It was a beautiful room, and we were able to book some private parties in there. But in the final analysis, I don't think it really helped the business to grow. The biggest problem we faced with this restaurant was its location. It was a special-occasion restaurant, but the location was just outside of the normal shopping and dining area of Church Street; not so far away physically, but psychologically I might as well have been on the moon.

I remember talking to a well-known downtown businessman who said I never go there because there's no parking. I reminded him that there was no parking for most of the restaurants on Church Street either. What he said next struck me. He said, "Yeah, but that's different. It's about the perception" I realized he was right, it was all about perception. The perception was we had no dedicated parking area. Location-wise, it was really kind of in no man's land. I learned an important lesson there. It wasn't about me, and my personal skill level. It was location, location, location.

We had some success at Déjà Vu Café, but there was a lot of headwind. We operated the business for almost six years. In the late 80s, a mild recession created problems and then my marriage of fifteen years started to unravel in a meaningful way. After the divorce, I finally sold the restaurant. In 1992, it became Parima—a Thai restaurant.

38.5

Good Times at Déjà Vu, Like Mountain Biking in the Rain

We had several University of Vermont students who worked with us at Déjà Vu Café. In 1988, a group of us decided it would be fun to do some mountain biking together; most of these guys were half my age. We decided to go for a ride in Colchester. It was a cold afternoon in late October. The weather was not perfect, it was overcast, the temperature was hovering around 50, and there was a forecast for light rain. There had been a strong storm a few days before and most of the leaves had blown off the trees. The landscape was barren and unfriendly looking. But the plan for this ride had been made several days in advance, and no one wanted to back out.

The group was made up of five college students and me. Three were employees of mine, who worked at my restaurant. The other two were friends of theirs from UVM. The meetup was behind the Colchester High School where there were several homemade access roads into the forest just off the edge of the school parking lot. These trails are nothing like the bike trails you might find there today. This was in the late 80s.

The group was all together by three. We followed a road into the forest that had several large puddles from the recent rainstorm. The biggest ones spanned the full width of the trail. They were all easily avoided by riding to the edge of the trail. We rode into the forest for a mile or two and bypassed ten or twelve of these puddles on our way in. We came to a small abandoned sandpit that had eroded enough that we were able to ride up and down these not-too-steep sand hills. We all had some fun testing our skills and endurance, mine, was not quite equal to the twenty-somethings.

At about four it started to rain lightly. None of us had rain gear so we decided it was time to head back. As the oldest rider, I was bringing up the rear. We approached the first one of the puddles we had passed on the way in and we all skirted the water by riding to one side or the other. We peddled by three or four of these puddles in the same fashion.

Then I decided that I was going to ride through the next one. It was fun, splashing water and getting a little wet. I was disappointed that no one had witnessed my splashing. So, at the next puddle, as the younger riders were skirting to the outside, I sped up and rode right down the middle, screaming as loud as I could, splashing them and myself. This was even more fun because I surprised the other riders. Most of them were put off by this and started to fall back, but one rider named Isaac picked up on the vibe and caught up with me till we were riding side by side. As we approached the next double puddle, we pedaled furiously, glancing at each other as if to say, "I dare you!" Water went spraying everywhere! What fun, feeling so like a kid, so lost in the moment, the excitement, the pure thrill.

Isaac and I bonded quickly. We were in sync. He got it! He was feeling the same rush I was. We were riding as one, eager to scream through the next water hazard and the next. Puddle after puddle we rode through yelling our war cry, laughing, splashing. After six or eight puddles we were getting pretty wet. By that time, we got to where we could see the school parking lot.

Only one puddle remained between us at the end of the ride—between us and our dry, soon-to-be-warm cars. The last puddle was the biggest, the width of the road, and at least twenty-five feet long. We were ready. We were stoked, high on adrenaline and endorphins, and we were not afraid. Yelling, screaming, laughing, cranking as fast as possible into the mother of all puddles we rode with our hearts as one. This water was black from the thousands of leaves that lay rotting in the bottom of these puddles. It was also cold.

All went well until we were about three-fourths of the way into this small pond. Then without any warning, our front tires simultaneously all but disappeared into two deep potholes. I couldn't believe what I was seeing, I didn't want to believe what I was seeing. In situations like this, your mind involuntarily goes into a brain time warp. When we are scared, the amygdala in our brain becomes more active, it speeds up, which makes our sense of time slow down. As my bike wheel was getting stuck in this large pothole, and I started going over the handlebars, I had time to think about what was about to happen. I thought I'm not really going to land in that cold black water! Please, not now. Isaac was thinking the same thing I was.

But we also knew that the die had been cast and there was nothing we could do to change what was about to happen. We were going face-first into that cold black water and there was nothing we could do to change our fate. Down we went, SPLASH! We both sprung up as fast as we could, dripping black leaves and cold water, and began laughing hysterically, like the children we had become.

39

Divorce, a Very Sad Time

In February 1989, my wife informed me that she wanted to go visit her friend Louisa in Florida. After she told me that she paused, and then she said, "And I don't want you to go." There was another pause. And then she said, "I'm going to take my assistant, Matthew."

Of course, I thought this was a bit odd. We had never traveled separately before, always as a couple. Matthew was her personal assistant, he was also gay, so there was no fear of any romantic hanky-panky. Still, I felt like this was a break or a fracture in the foundation of our relationship. I wasn't really sure how to handle it, but I said, "OK, fine. If that's what you want to do, go have fun." Of course, for Mathew, it was all expenses paid, which was more money drained from the businesses that were not doing especially well at that time.

During our first three years at Déjà Vu Café things went pretty well. But in the late 80s, the economy started to slip into a mild recession and things started to unwind.

About this time, Pat started taking singing lessons from a local singing coach. Along with this new hobby, she developed a new group of friends, which took her focus away from the restaurants somewhat. Initially, I thought this was good because I wanted her to have a life separate from the restaurant business.

But soon she told me she had dreams of becoming a professional singer. I began to realize that perhaps she was getting a little too much fairy dust in her eyes. She told me she was thinking of going for the big time. What does that look like, I asked. I suggested she do some tryouts with the local Lyric Theater group. She told me she thought that was a waste of her time. She wanted to go big, like New York City big, and at her age, late 40s, she could not waste time and energy on local theater.

Then one day without warning, after about thirteen years of marriage, she told me that she had never in her adult life lived by herself and she thought it would be good for her personal growth, and she had decided to give it a try. She informed me after the fact that she had rented a summer camp on Lake Champlain and was going to live there by herself for the summer. She would continue to show up at the restaurants, mostly to have lunch, boss a few people around, and act like a queen in my opinion.

I thought it was odd. What about the two restaurants? I didn't really see the storm clouds on the horizon until a few weeks later when she told me that her singing coach, Bill Read, told her she should start taking lessons in New York City. He told her she was good enough to go to the next level, that maybe she could pursue a singing career there. This was a surprise to me. It's quite a leap to think you can move to New York City in your late 40s and become a professional singer. In fact, it made no sense to me at all. Beware of the fairy dust! To me, it meant you're going to abandon everything you've been building in these two restaurants for the last ten years and trade it for an impossible dream.

Pat continued living her solo life on the lake. We continued to see each other at the restaurants, but less and less. After considering my options I decided that if she didn't come back to our home in New Haven within six weeks of moving out and tell me she was going to stay first and foremost committed to our restaurants and pursue her singing aspirations in a more modest way I was going to tell her that I was done being her husband. This decision was completely self-imposed, and a secret, including from my soon-to-be ex-wife. Near the end of the six weeks, I was really hoping she wouldn't come back. I saw this as my opportunity to move on from a not-very-happy marriage. In my mind, this was my escape hatch. My opportunity to start looking for my own personal felicity.

The six weeks passed. I went to see Pat and told her if this was the way it was going to be, I was done being her husband. She said, "Oh, I don't want to get divorced."

I said, "Neither do I, but I'm not going to go on like this."

She said, "You can't just do this."

I said, "You don't get to make all the decisions. If you want to live a life apart from me, following your passion for singing, so be it. But I'm not going to just keep operating these restaurants while you're off pursuing a singing career, a fantasy dream that I have no faith in."

I don't know what she thought was going to happen, but when I gave her that news, she was very angry. She moved out of the seasonal camp on Lake Champlain into a condominium in Burlington. This move required money. It was late 1989 and the economy was sliding into recession. The businesses were not doing very well. Then she started writing checks for her personal expenses out of the business accounts in addition to her normal paycheck, for fairly large amounts of money at the time. I felt like she was jeopardizing the health of the business and our employees, putting her needs in front of the business and me and everyone else who worked for us. I knew I had to do something, so I decided either she had to go or I was going to go.

This led to an extremely difficult decision that I liken to Michael Corleone in *The Godfather*, where he says, "Either your signature or your brains are going to be on this contract—you decide." I told her she had to leave the business immediately and that she was no longer going to be able to write checks for personal expenses out of the business accounts. I had been to the bank and had her signing privileges removed from the accounts. But if she agreed to go, I would continue to give her a paycheck of $1,800 every two weeks, and she would have some flexibility to pursue her dreams.

I also had to tell her that if she didn't leave voluntarily, then I would leave and she could run the businesses without me, and by the way, several key employees who didn't have trust in her would also leave with me. Imagine, if you can, just how hard this was for me, it was a very uncomfortable conversation. She became very angry, made some threatening remarks, and said this can't be legal. But ultimately, she decided to leave voluntarily so she could pursue her dreams. A few weeks later she moved to Brooklyn Heights and started taking singing lessons somewhere in Manhattan.

I wanted the marriage to be done, wrapped up, and finished ASAP so I could get on with my life. I made two or three overly generous offers for a divorce settlement, which she refused. I think the attitude was if he's willing to pay this much now, he'll pay much more later. This went on for over two years. Then in November of 1991, I was staring bankruptcy in the face. The financial situation at the restaurant was dire. I had to stop the bleeding. So, I stopped sending her money, something I had been advised to do in the beginning. I just couldn't be that hard. But now, faced with insolvency, I had no choice. The divorce was settled in a month.

After the divorce, I lost contact with my stepson Noah for a few years. Obviously, it was reasonable to expect him to support his mother after the divorce. But I'm happy to say that, after a few years, I sent him some old photographs that I had taken when he was going off to first grade, very cute with his backpack and red bandanna, and his missing tooth smile. Since then, Noah and I have been able to maintain a very friendly and mutually beneficial relationship. It pleases me to be able to stay in contact with him. I get a vicarious thrill when I hear stories about his family life with his wife and two beautiful daughters. It gives me great pleasure.

40

Proof of Life after Divorce

During the two-plus years of the divorce process, I spent quite a bit of effort reformatting my life. I did a lot of reading. I knew I had made some mistakes, and I had no one to blame but myself. My goal was to avoid making the same mistakes. I read books with titles like *Uncoupling: How and Why Relationships Fall Apart*. I read Scott Peck's *The Road Less Traveled* and a few other relationship-themed books. In Scott Peck's book, I learned that people build up layers of logic around themselves to explain to the world and themselves why they behave the way they do, like layers of an onion, and it's the job of the analyst to strip away those layers of what I would call pretzel logic, to get back to the core person, the person at the center of your personality.

When I read that I realized that that was what I had been dealing with in my marriage to Pat. More than once, I would be talking to my ex-wife about some issue, and she would say, "You don't understand. Let me explain."

While we were married Pat had gone to a psychiatrist for many years until we got a notice from our Blue Shield Insurance company that said she had used up her lifetime supply of psychiatric help and they were not going to pay for any more sessions—$25,000! My personal reaction was all that money was wasted because as far as I could tell she had not gotten control of her demons. She still was being ruled by her wildly dysfunctional childhood. I can only assume that her analyst was incompetent or just lacked the skills needed to help her.

The most helpful book for me was written in 1988 by Harville Hendrix, called *Getting the Love You Want*. I don't know what it would mean to me now, but back then it was exactly what I needed to hear. I would call it a commonsense guide to romance. I think he started by talking about how most people get into relationships unconsciously. You meet someone you are attracted to, who seems to be attracted to you, and you "fall in love." He uses the Greek example of Eros and Psyche, where they didn't really fall in love with each other, they fell in love with the feeling of being in love.

His book suggests before you go looking for a mate you have to get a clear vision of who you are yourself. What he calls your imago. He has exercises in the book to accomplish this goal once you do some of the exercises and get a clearer vision of who you are and what's important to you.

Next, you make up a list of what kind of traits you're looking for in a partner. You have to be brutally honest. If you want, tall, dark, handsome, and rich, you have to write that down and any other traits you think are important in your ideal mate. Then, when you meet someone, you can mentally compare that person to your list and decide if there are enough matchups that this relationship might be worth pursuing. It's what I would call a conscious relationship instead of an unconscious relationship, which is how I would characterize my first marriage—unconscious.

In an unconscious relationship, you "fall in love" and then a couple of years down the road after the smoke clears you take a good look at your partner and say, "You're not who I thought you were," and they look at you incredulously and say, "What are you talking about? I was never that person." And that was the kind of mismatch that I was involved in in my first marriage. It wasn't my wife's fault, it was my fault. It was a decision that I made unconsciously.

At almost the same time that my divorce became final, I was able to sell Déjà Vu Café, just before I went bankrupt. I lost quite a bit of money on the transaction, $170,000, which I had to transfer to the Pauline's building. My banker wasn't happy because they were then under-secured. *Oh, boo-hoo.* Bankers, they're all your friends when things are going well, until you get in trouble and then they drop you like a hot potato. I got introduced to the workout committee, I call them the knee breakers. Eventually, everyone I owed money to got paid.

I liked being in a relationship. I knew I wanted to be in one in the future and I didn't want to make the same mistakes again. Maybe I'd make some new mistakes but hopefully with a much better outcome.

During this two-year divorce period, I did some casual dating, all done through personal ads in the local weekly paper, *Seven Days*. I didn't find my soulmate using this technique, but I found there were many people just like me, looking to have a relationship with another person in a very normal and honest way.

One of the women I dated had a photograph in her apartment of a group of people that included the psychiatrist that my ex-wife had gone to for so many years. I asked her what the photo was, and she said it was a therapy group that she had gone to that was led by the same guy. I asked her what she thought of the guy, and she said, "To tell you the truth, I thought he was just in it for the money." Which of course verified my opinion of him as well.

I tried out some new hobbies. I took piano lessons from a very nice woman named Jean Tourin. On a whim, I called the artist Cynthia Price whose work I had viewed at a gallery in Middlebury. I went to visit her in her studio in Lincoln. I enjoyed her art and talking to her about art.

We had a lively conversation and she invited me to join her Treehouse Guild drawing group that met twice a month at her home in Lincoln. I was part of this drawing group for almost two years. We did a couple of group shows at Woody's Restaurant in Middlebury.

I didn't know it when I started, but my decision to join this drawing group was going to lead me directly to my road to felicity.

41

Some Enchanted Evening

On December 5, 1992, my artist friend Cynthia was having a gathering at her home to show some of her work that would soon be going to a gallery out of state. I had misunderstood the timing of this gathering and arrived late. By the time I got there, the large room was full of people. As I was embracing Cynthia, I glanced around the room to see who I could recognize. On the other side of the room was a very attractive woman I did not know in a red dress looking directly at me. I made eye contact with her and she did not turn away, she held her gaze. She told me later that she was just curious because she was thinking who is that guy who knows Cynthia that I don't know? They had known each other for over twenty years from their time at Middlebury College.

I turned to Cynthia as we were embracing and said, "Who is that woman in the red dress...and is she single?" She told me her name was Alison Parker and yes, she was very single.

I'm sure many of you know the song, "Some Enchanted Evening" from the movie and stage show *South Pacific*. It goes like this:

"Some enchanted evening you will see a stranger, you will see a stranger, across the crowded room, and somehow you know, you know even then, that you'll see her again and again." La, la, la...

December 5, 1992, was my "some enchanted evening." When I met the woman, I hoped to spend the rest of my life with. Of course, I didn't know it at that time, but that's how it worked out. I gravitated to her. We talked for a few minutes at that party but then she and another couple announced they had another party to go to. She joked about her busy social season here in the hills of Vermont, and then they were gone.

After they left, I was crestfallen. I really needed to speak with that woman more, much more. I had no idea where they were going, somewhere in the nearby town of Starksboro. There was another woman at this party, Liz Ready, who looked at me and said, "I'm going to that other party in Starksboro. Do you want to go with me?" Yes, I would be happy to. Much later she joked with me about how she had taken me to that party, and I had abandoned her. Not completely untrue.

When we got to the Starksboro party I immediately went looking for the woman in the red dress. I caught up with her talking to the now well-known author Chris Bojalian. She was telling him a funny story about a young female college student she had talked to at the college health center where Alison was a nurse. The student had come into the health center because the previous weekend she had had sex with her boyfriend. She said she was sure he was wearing a condom when they started. But when they were finished, they couldn't find the condom anywhere. Alison asked her if she had looked everywhere. She said, "Well, yes." Alison said, "Well, get up on the table and I'll have a look." And there it was still inside her. She was telling this to Chris Bojalian because she knew that he liked these types of amusing stories. At that time, he was also a close neighbor here in Lincoln.

I listened to the story and then got her attention, and we sat down on a couch on one side of the room. I spent the rest of the evening talking with her and trying to find out who she really was and if there was any chance of her matching up to the list I had drawn up for what

I was looking for in a relationship. After I asked some probing pointed questions about the basics I asked her what she did for fun.

She said, "I like to ride bicycles."

I'd heard women say that before. Maybe their idea was to ride to the local coffee shop and get an espresso, and a sweet roll. So, I asked Alison, "What have you done lately on a bicycle?"

She said, "Well, two years ago I rode from Seattle to Atlantic City."

Wow, I thought, you have bike cred! Bicycling is still a major point of contact in our relationship to this day.

A good friend of hers, Carol, was sitting nearby, listening to my very pointed questions. I was trying very hard to listen to Alison's answers and not fall immediately in love with her. Even though it was probably already too late.

After an hour or so Alison left with her two friends Jimmy and Carol. On their way home, Alison turned to her friend Carol, who had been listening, and said, "What do you think of that guy?" And Carol said, "That guy is an asshole, I would stay away from him if I were you!"

I guess I had been just a little too direct with my questions. Carol and I have been able to joke about that comment and get a few laughs for years now.

After that first meeting, I didn't want to seem overly eager or desperate. So, I didn't call Alison the next day, even though I wanted to. I waited until Monday evening. We had a wonderful lengthy conversation during which she said, "Did you say you're at work?" I told her I was but it was not too busy, and would I get called if I was needed.

Alison then told me that she had looked up and memorized my phone number, a very good sign that she had been thinking about me also. Dare I hope this embryonic relationship was getting some traction?

42

Dating and Getting to Know Alison

We made a date to go downhill skiing. We went to Sugarbush. It was a beautiful, sunny day, and I think it's fair to say we were both having a great time. We were very compatible skiing buddies, and we were just laughing and smiling as we were skiing along in the sunshine. While we were skiing downhill I began to have the distinct feeling that my life was going uphill. A sensation that continues to this day.

We made a breakfast date for a couple of days hence at the Squirrel's Nest Restaurant in Bristol. Alison arrived wearing a brown Carhartt barn jacket accented with a red scarf. I was charmed. We had a pleasant breakfast, and I was able to ask her a few more questions while sitting across the table and admiring how beautiful she was.

On parting she pointedly asked, "When will I see you again?" At the time I was working in the kitchen at Pauline's five or six days a week, from ten to ten. I told her that I took a break in the afternoon between two and four. If she wanted to come to the restaurant we could go for a walk. So, she drove the forty-five minutes to Pauline's the next day and she came right through the back door, very assertive, right into the kitchen. I couldn't believe it. Who was this stunning woman coming to the back door of my restaurant specifically to spend time with me?

Things like this had never happened before.

We drove out to Shelburne Point where I knew there were some walking trails. We walked along the shore, playfully chased each other, ran around trees, and occasionally we embraced. I eventually pinned her to a tree and kissed her, and I believe she kissed me back. I don't think either of us wanted this kissing, as pleasurable as it was, to get out of control. So, we chased each other around a bit more, feeling like children, laughing and smiling. What pure joy.

But I had to get back to work. When we got back in her car, she was sitting in the driver's seat. Before she started the engine, she was looking at the steering wheel but talking to me. I was looking directly at her. She said, "I didn't think I would ever meet someone like you." I was feeling the same way. That's when I first felt this relationship was starting to take hold. I was thrilled and excited and still trying to move forward as slowly as possible and not blow it.

AFTER SETTLING IN WITH ALISON, I DECIDED IT WAS TIME TO RETURN TO MOTORCYCLING, SO I BOUGHT THIS LITTLE HONDA SHADOW IN 1995. IT WAS MY FIRST BIKE IN 20 YEARS.

I thought I knew what a good life looked like before I met Alison. But after I met her, I found out what good can be, I'm talking really good! It's been over thirty years now and every day with her has been a gift, a beautiful gift. I had found my felicity, a great shining felicity. Now I had to learn to trust it.

Early on we talked about love a lot. We had both suffered through divorce. So, how do you know when love is real? How do you know it will last? In one of these talks, Alison said, "You haven't been loved by me. I will show you what real love feels and looks like." She was so asser- tive and confident, I was impressed. The fact is she has shown me for more than thirty years now what real love feels like and looks like. And what a beautiful ride it has been. My main job is to be grateful for all my blessings, many of which are associated directly with my relationship with Alison Parker. Lucky, lucky me.

So begins my unbroken chain of earthly delights. Our first trip away

MEETING ALISON PARKER ON DECEMBER 5, 1992, WAS BY FAR THE
BEST THING THAT HAS EVER HAPPENED TO ME. IT'S BEEN OVER 30
YEARS NOW, AND I THANK MY LUCKY STARS EVERY DAY.

together was a ski trip in March 1993 that I had previously planned to Taos, New Mexico. When we arrived in Albuquerque it was 73°. We stayed with a friend of mine for a couple of days in Santa Fe. We also skied one day in Taos, under a beautiful, bright spring blue sky; it was 50°.

We spent the rest of our week exploring places like Bandelier National Monument, the Ghost Ranch, and the Abiquiu home where Georgia O'Keeffe spent the later years of her life. We then went to Taos Pueblo and Canyon de Chelly. We had a truly unforgettable experience at an abandoned hot spring right on the bank of the Rio Grande Gorge just north of Taos. We were the only people there, and we spent most of the day laying naked in the hot spring right on the edge of the river as one or two rafting trips floated by checking out the local wildlife, i.e., two naked people in the hot spring.

Thanks to my friend Patrick, we got to spend a night in an Earthship near Taos. This is a passive solar home built into the ground of mostly recycled materials. It had massive walls built of old car tires packed full of adobe clay. A bank of windows on the south side made a whole structure into a large solar heat sink. Sleeping close to the floor at night with the door slightly ajar we had the unique experience of feeling the cool night air coming through the door balanced by the collected solar heat radiating from the floor and the walls.

43

Moving In with Alison, Molly, and Oakley

In April 1993, I moved into Alison's house in Lincoln with her two children, Molly, fifteen, and Oakley, twelve. They tolerated my intrusion pretty well. I did my best to impress on them that I was there to be their mother's new partner in life and not in any way try to become another father figure. They already had a father who was devoted to them. They spent half their time with their father, who lived just a mile up the road. I am happy to say that we are all very good friends to this day.

During this time, Alison was working as a registered nurse at the Middlebury College Health Center. It was a full-time job of mostly days that she enjoyed very much. She liked being able to spend enough time with each patient to treat the whole person, not just their symptoms.

We settled into our domestic life together, quite easily, like two peas in a pod.

Not before long, we started planning our future life together. I couldn't have been happier. It was so good I of course wondered if it was real and if it was going to last. During this time Alison gave me a card that said "The irony is, if you want to find Out, you have to go In."

Every morning, I got to wake up with this beautiful woman in bed next to me. She would roll over and smile and tell me she loved me. I really began to feel like I was in paradise or very close to it. I couldn't imagine being happier, such a beautiful gift. I dared to think, this is what the road to felicity feels like.

So where do we go from there? A side benefit of moving in with Alison was it became possible for me to adopt her twenty or so Lincoln friends who became good friends of mine over the years. Many of them I had known casually but thanks to my relationship with her we all became much closer.

As noted earlier I had sold my downtown Burlington restaurant, Déjà Vu Café. This simplified my business life, and I was able to re-concentrate my efforts on my original restaurant Pauline's. In 1993, I went forward with an idea I had wanted to do for some time. I made a deal with a contractor to build an addition on the north side of Pauline's, that would add twenty-five-plus additional seats. At the same time, I contracted some improvements in the kitchen, such as building a bigger, walk-in cooler into the hillside behind the restaurant, to thereby create a larger prep kitchen. These improvements worked out very successfully.

The staff and the customers were jazzed and excited to see these enhancements. And now we had the space to do more creative menu items. The net result was that the sales increased by over 30 percent the next year. In 1994, sales increased another 20 percent on top of that. Anyone who has run a small business like this can tell you it's very difficult to achieve that kind of growth. It was a valuable lesson for me to learn—to realize that if you want positive change, you have to plan carefully and make that change happen. It was exciting to find out that it was actually possible. Obviously, I was happy about the outcome, and I know the employees were also. They were as proud of our success as I was, and I hope I was able to make them feel confident in their contribution. I felt empowered to do more. I gained confidence to do more.

44

Proposing Marriage

In March 1994, Alison and I vacationed in Tortola, British Virgin Islands. It was my first trip to the Caribbean. I decided ahead of time that I would propose marriage to her there. We rented a little car and went to a different beach every day. From where we stayed in Cane Garden Bay, we could see St. Thomas at night. It looked like the spaceship from *Close Encounters of the Third Kind*, a giant, floating mountain of shimmering light.

Every day on Tortola, I thought, okay, today is the day I'm going to ask her. I was apprehensive because I had never proposed marriage to anyone before. As a result, I let the days slip by one by one.

On our last night at Stanley's Welcome Villas, after drinking a couple of frozen piña coladas, I screwed up my nerve and bubbled out my question. "Alison, would you ever want to get married again?" A terrible way to ask; I'm still embarrassed when I think about it.

After a moment she said, "What? Is that a proposal? Are you asking me to marry you? Is that your proposal of marriage? Really?" After she realized how dumb I felt she forgave me and said, "If that's what you're asking...Yes, of course, I will marry you, on one condition...Take me to Greece on our honeymoon."

Deal!

Her first marriage was at home in a borrowed dress and she went back to work at her job the next day. This time around she wanted a traditional affair. A real wedding gown, a rehearsal dinner, a ceremony in the church in Lincoln with 100+ guests, a reception with live music and a big wedding cake...and a real honeymoon in Greece. We decided on June 17, 1995, so there would be plenty of time to savor the journey.

I PROPOSED MARRIAGE TO ALISON IN TORTOLA, BRITISH VIRGIN ISLANDS, IN 1994. WE WERE MARRIED ON JUNE 17, 1995, AND WE HAD A SPECTACULAR HONEYMOON IN THE GREEK ISLANDS.

And that's how it went down. We had over a year to plan. We went to a couple of bridal showers, and Alison finally found the perfect gown. Alison's sisters and daughter were her attendants. I had my brother Douglas as my best man.

Early on the wedding day, my brother and I drove to Pauline's to pick up the cake I had made so I could set it up at the reception site before the wedding. It was a large multi-layered cake that needed some assembly. When we got to the site at ten that morning, I was surprised to find that all the doors were locked. It took me some time to locate a small, unlocked window that I was barely able to squeeze through. After setting the cake in place, we realized we were way behind schedule, and I might be late for my own wedding! We had to drive like the proverbial bats out of hell. It was a minor miracle that we didn't get stopped for speeding. We made it to the church just in the nick of time.

At the ceremony, I read an E.E. Cummings poem to Alison.

"i thank you God for this most amazing
Day; for the leaping greenly spirits of trees
and a blue true dream of sky; and for everything
which is natural which is infinite which is yes

(i who have died am alive again today,
and this is the sun's birthday; this is the birth
day of life and of love and wings: and of the gay
great happening illimitably earth)

how should tasting touching hearing seeing
breathing any—lifted from the no
of all nothing—human merely being
doubt unimaginable You?

(now the ears of my ears awake and
now the eyes of my eyes are opened)"

We were married in the church in Lincoln by Paster David Wood. We
were chauffeured to the reception by my friend David and his wife Jane
in his 1936 touring car to Kingsland Bay State Park on the shores of Lake
Champlain. The weather was perfect, sunny, and warm. Everything was
perfect, the food, the music, the guests. Alison's father Gerry became
quite emotional as he wished us well on the journey we were about to
start, it was very touching and heartfelt.

At the end of the festivities another friend, Mitch Fletcher and his
wife Kim whisked us away in their 30' Lyman cabin cruiser, taking us
about five miles down the lake to the Basin Harbor Club for our first
married night together. Pure bliss...moving farther along the road to
felicity.

MEETING ALISON PARKER ON DECEMBER 5, 1992, WAS BY FAR THE
BEST THING THAT HAS EVER HAPPENED TO ME. IT'S BEEN OVER 30
YEARS NOW, AND I THANK MY LUCKY STARS EVERY DAY.

The Shape of You

I wake from my nighttime dreams
I drift into my waking dream
The dream of you so close to me
Next to me in our soft marital bed

Lying on your side before waking
I imagine the spine of the green mountains
I roll over to touch your summits
Mountains runs the length of your body

Touching your hip with my hand
I feel the summit of Mount Mansfield
Sliding south, over your rib cage
I imagine the summit of Camels Hump

I journey farther south
I caress the summit of Mount Ellen
Then your shoulder, Mount Abraham
Our sacred mountain, watching over us

You roll over, smile at me
I am thrilled to be with you in this way
You roll your body alongside mine
So intimate, your arm on my chest

You smile, tell me you love me
So intimate, your head on my shoulder
I reciprocate, wrapped in your love
This buoys me for the rest of the day

45

The Beginning of My Best Life,
My Felicity Becomes Real

The honeymoon was beyond all expectations. We spent two weeks traveling around Greece. Two or three days in Athens, taking in all the normal sites like the Acropolis and Erechtheion, dining at several street-side restaurants, eating things like hummus, baba ganoush, tzatziki, several different types of kebabs, and lots of fish, including octopus.

I had to pinch myself, the farm boy honeymooning in Athens, Greece. Like living in a dream, a dream that has come true. I have to credit Alison with all this good fortune. Meeting her and having her fall in love with me and me with her was all a dream come true, almost good to believe. As good as it gets.

We took a high-speed hydrofoil boat, The Flying Dolphin, from the port of Piraeus to the island of Hydra, a popular weekend getaway for people from Athens. It's a small island off the Peloponnese Peninsula. There are no cars there. When you get to the dock, if you want help, there are some porters with small donkeys who offer to carry your bags for you to your hotel. We had a blissful time there for three days, swimming and walking from one small village to the next.

Our favorite snack was Greek yogurt with Greek honey. This was before Greek yogurt was known so widely in this country. Both the yogurt and honey were very thick. An oversized martini glass filled with Greek yogurt drizzled with Greek honey looked more like vanilla ice cream with caramel sauce and tasted really, really good.

Our favorite meal at the end of the day was a classic Greek salad with bread and a half-liter can of Heineken. The Greek salads were fantastic, I had been told about them before, but I had never actually seen one. There is no lettuce, just a bowl of tomatoes, cucumbers, onions, peppers, briny kalamata olives, and a slice of feta cheese on top sprinkled with oregano in a mild dressing of olive oil and lemon juice or red wine vinegar. We spent many evenings eating these quintessential salads with half a loaf of white bread and a big cold can of Heineken while watching the sun sinking into the western Mediterranean. It was fantastic, a memory to last a lifetime.

We went back to Athens and flew to the very popular resort island of Mykonos. Just the drive from the airport to our B&B was enough for us to know that this popular island was too crowded for us, especially after coming from an island that had no cars. There were cars and motorbikes whizzing by in every direction. In the evening, we went into the downtown, which is quite small with many narrow streets that were crowded enough that we were forced to just shuffle along with the crowd.

The next day at breakfast I mentioned this to one of the B&B owners. They said, "Oh, I was downtown last night. It wasn't so bad. It gets much more crowded than that."

We didn't need to hear anymore. We stayed there two nights, but really only one day. We did go to the two well-known clothing-optional beaches, Paradise and Super Paradise. There was too much activity there for our liking. It was, and probably still is, a very popular destination for a younger generation. It's popular with lots of Europeans and Scandinavians and Russian tourists these days I've been told.

From Mykonos, we took a ferry to Naxos, a much larger Island with a lot fewer people. We planned to stay there two days and then go to Santorini, but there was a ferry strike, because, we were told, the government was putting pressure on the ferry companies to pay some of their taxes and their pushback was to call a three-day ferry strike. We couldn't go anywhere off the island so we rented a car and had a wonderful time driving all over the island. Naxos is quite large and provided us with a few very nice, unexpected experiences. The island was big enough, we were told, to grow all the potatoes for the entire country of Greece.

One of the interesting things we read in a guidebook to Greece was it is the responsibility of the person who is approaching someone who's stationary to be the first one to extend a greeting. So, if you're walking down a small street and someone is sitting on their front stoop it is your responsibility to say hello, yasas, in Greek. If you don't extend the greeting, they won't extend a greeting. And then you're likely to think these people aren't very friendly, and they're likely to think tourists aren't very friendly. It's extremely helpful to know about local customs.

We drove to the far side of the island which took all day, because the roads are very narrow and twisty. We passed many of the small white villages in the hills. We had a very interesting interaction in one of these towns. The towns are so small you have to park on the edge of town and walk in. There are no drivable roads in the village. These towns are populated mostly by very old people and very young people. The working-age people are off somewhere, working.

We stopped at the village of Keramoti high in the hills about halfway between Naxos Town and Apollonas. The first people we saw were a group of four youngsters who were eight or nine years old. We wanted to practice our Greek which was very limited, and they were excited to practice their English. So, we said hello in Greek, "Yasas," and they said, "Hello," in English. We told them we wanted to buy some honey, "mele"

in Greek. They took us to the home of an older couple who were napping when we arrived.

One of the things we had read about Greek hospitality was that
when someone comes to your home you don't know, and you're concerned that they might be some kind of god in disguise, you always offer
some kind of a small gift just to be sure you can stay on their good side.
This older couple offered us blueberries.

When we told them we wanted mele they pulled a wash tub out
from under their daybed, which had several tins of wild mountain thyme
honey in them. We bought one. I think it weighed about one kg. We still
have a small portion of it in a jar in our cupboard, every once in a while
I take the lid off just to smell it. The olfactory memory is very powerful.
If I close my eyes, it brings me right back to those halcyon honeymoon
days in a little white village in the hills of Naxos.

We stayed overnight in Apollonas, at the time a very small, kind
of half-built resort town on the northeast side of the island. At dinner
in one of the seaside tavernas, we struck up a conversation with three
Americans, who happened to be three of the four French horn players
from the New York Philharmonic. They had been on tour and were
doing a little side trip before they went back to New York. We had a fascinating discussion with them about the importance of a mouthpiece on
a wind instrument. One of these players had his mouthpiece in his shirt
pocket, he said, "I never go anywhere without it, it's not important."

We drove around the island for four or five days, going to different beaches and white villages—charming, charming, charming. The
weather was perfect, warm, and sunny, the people were friendly, and of
course, our love for each other was deepening day by day in the most
beautiful way.

When the ferries started to run again, it was time for us to head
home. We went back to Athens by ferry and spent our last honeymoon

night in Athens, looking at the lighted Acropolis from our hotel room window. Then we flew home to Vermont.

It was a perfectly idyllic honeymoon, still a wonderful memory to this day.

46

Married Life on the Lake

On returning to Lincoln, we had two beautiful summer months stretching out in front of us. We made plans with two other families to rent a summer camp on Thompson's Point in Charlotte, Vermont, and so began our annual summer love affair with the lake, the beautiful Lake Champlain with the equally beautiful Adirondack Mountains to the west to frame one beautiful sunset after another. It's only thirty-five minutes from Lincoln, but a completely different world. I have to say we fell in love with each other, and we also fell in love with summer on the lake.

We rented something on the lake every summer until the fall of 2006 when we finally bought our own camp on Long Point in Ferrisburgh, Vermont. Our first season started on July 4th weekend of 2007. We had two other couples celebrating with us. We ate dinner, got in our motorboat, and went south to Basin Harbor Club to watch some fireworks. By the time we returned in the dark, our camp was completely engulfed in flames and it burned to the ground. We were devastated, we had just set up for the summer with all our favorite summer clothes. Everything was gone.

After some crying and cursing, I was forced to conclude that the best things in life are not things, a very bitter pill to swallow, but I saw no other way forward. Two different inspectors with dogs came to examine the remains and were not able to determine the cause. Over the winter the camp was rebuilt by our friend Dan Berry who did an excellent job, so our first real season on Long Point was in 2008.

Alison's childhood name had been "Sunny" so I decided to name our camp Sunnyside Cottage. We now traditionally start setting up at camp in mid-June and stay there until late September or early October. It's a wonderful tradition that we are still in love with to this day. We have many friends that visit in the warm months.

Two good friends of ours, Peter and Maja bought the camp right next door. Peter and I are rowing buddies. Every morning when conditions are right, no wind or rain, we spend an hour or more rowing on the lake. It's a wonderful low-impact exercise that for me is also a form of meditation. To be out on the lake, a mile or more from shore, stroking along sometimes with my eyes closed, is so relaxing and peaceful.

We have friends that have places much farther away, Maine or Cape Cod, and they only get to spend a few weeks there at most because they are so distant. These places are beautiful destinations, but it takes so long to get there and it's hard to balance the enjoyment with the effort. Our cottage on the lake is a perfect solution for us.

47

1997: Going to Ghana, A Complete Recalibration of My Worldview

In the mid-90s, things were going very well at Pauline's. I was happy with the progress of the business and the people who were working with me. They seemed to be pleased also. In 1996, I decided I would like to do something significant to mark my fiftieth birthday. I decided climbing Mount Kilimanjaro in Africa would be a good mile post.

When I mentioned this to Alison, she said, "Oh, if you want to go to Africa, we should have my friends Mark and Shelley over for dinner because they lived in Nairobi for two years, and they know about Africa."

So, we had Mark and Shelley over for dinner and I told them about my plan. They said if you want to go to Africa you should come with us, we're going in February and March 1997. They continued, "We're taking a group of high school students and some adults to Ghana, West Africa; we're going to be there for a month. We'll study drumming and dance for two weeks with a drumming master named Godwin Agbeli in the village of Kopayia, a small village with no running water or electricity. Then we will be traveling around the country for another two weeks with a Canadian expat naturalist named Malcome Stark. We will visit Mole National Park, which also has one of the world's first canopy walks. We will visit some of the many old slave castles on the coast and we will visit the large central city of Kumasi, the seat of the Ashanti, one the most powerful tribes in the country."

I had never been to a developing country before. I was intrigued and so was Alison. So, we committed to the trip. Normally when I went on vacation from Pauline's for a week or at most two, I would get other employees to cover my schedule, and when I returned, I would resume my schedule. But because we were going to go away for a month, I decided to make a schedule that did not have my name on it.

When we returned from this life-changing trip, I asked the staff how it was going, and they said it was going great. So, I said we'll just leave it like this for now. I'll spend my time catching up on deferred maintenance of the building and the gardens.

Except for marrying Alison Parker, going to Ghana was the single most life-changing experience I've ever had. What I learned:

1. Ghana is hot. The southern coast is on the Gulf of Guinea about five degrees north of the equator. I had never been this close to the equator, it's amazing. The sun comes up every day at six and it sets at six every day.

2. Ghana has a well-defined political boundary, but it also has many, much older, tribal boundaries. The official language is English because England was the last colonial power but there are at least sixty-eight Indigenous tribal languages that are still spoken regularly. These tribes have a well-defined social order, some are perceived as strong and some are seen as weak.

3. I had the mistaken idea that during slave times Europeans went to Africa and rounded up Africans and forced them onto ships so they could be sold into slavery. I found out that Europeans went to Africa and made deals with the strong tribes like the

Ashanti, who rounded up people from the weaker tribes and sold them to the Europeans.

4. I found out England outlawed slavery in 1806, sixty years before it was outlawed in the United States. When the English told the Ashanti they could no longer sell slaves they were not happy about this change. They tried to rebel. The English had to go to Ghana with a military force large enough that they could march inland to the city of Kumasi and lay siege to the city to force the Ashanti to stop selling slaves. The Ashanti had a lot of gold and their most sacred item in 1806 was a golden stool, so sacred that not even the king was allowed to sit on it. The English demanded that they give up their golden stool as an act of contrition to prove they would stop selling slaves. Instead, the Ashanti made a fake stool, gave it to the English, and kept the real one hidden for over seventy years.

5. In the rural areas most people are extremely poor, but they also seem to be happy because they have their families with them nearby and have enough to eat.

6. Education for people in rural areas is difficult because of the pressure to help with farming, etc. We have helped many students over the years with their educational expenses, believing it's the only way to rise above the poverty level. We've had some successes and some failures.

7. By far the biggest change for me personally was going to Ghana created some distance between my physical self and my restaurant's stoves—stoves that I had been so closely tethered to for so many years.

So, when an opportunity presented itself to me instead of saying, I'm too busy to think about that, I could actually see the silver lining in the opportunity, and I was able to take advantage of it and I have to say it radically altered my business life. If I had not gone to Ghana and created that space between myself and my stoves so that I could see a larger view of the world and realize a good opportunity when it was staring at right at me, I may not have moved forward. To have the room and courage to take advantage of this opportunity has made all the difference in my current lifetime success.

48

Buying Leunig's Bistro

After returning from Ghana, I started thinking about formulating an exit strategy from the restaurant business. Perhaps I could get some of my long-term employees to start buying into Pauline's and slowly buy me out of it. I talked to my accountant about this, and she suggested I talk to a business broker. I went to see my friend, Bill Kiendl from VT Commercial.

He said, "Well, yes, you could do that. Or you could buy another business and create an opportunity for growth for some of those long-term employees that way."

I looked at him and said, "What are you talking about? I didn't come here looking to buy another restaurant."

He said, "But just listen. I happen to know where perhaps the best restaurant location in the state might be for sale."

I was intrigued.

He said, "It's Leunig's Bistro on the corner of Church and College Street."

I knew the restaurant well and I knew the location was second to none. I also knew that despite its reputation, it was not exactly top-notch, it was just always busy. Then he showed me some drawings that the current owner had done to put a sidewalk addition on the south side

THE FIRST RESTAURANT I EVER OWNED, TAKEN ABOUT 1995 ON
SHELBURNE ROAD IN SOUTH BURLINGTON, VERMONT. I RAN THIS
RESTAURANT SUCCESSFULLY FOR 26 YEARS.

where traditionally there were just seasonal seats in the summer. When I saw those drawings, I compared them to what had happened at Pauline's when I put an addition on the side of that building. I got excited. I saw the possibility for growth and the possibility to create growth opportunities for my good employees who were looking for advancement challenges.

It was very easy for me to get excited about a project like this. But of course, I wanted to make sure I was seeing things clearly and not viewing everything through rose-colored glasses. I decided the best way to do that was to ask other people what they thought. I asked people to try and talk me out of it if they thought it was a bad idea. That didn't happen. Many people said they thought it looked like a great opportunity.

So, I then decided I needed to raise some money. I started asking people if they would support this idea by loaning me money and promising them a good return on their investment and a generous dining discount.

I eventually convinced ten people to loan me $10,000 each. I did not have this kind of cash lying around; this became my down payment, enabling me to buy the business. But it also gave me the confidence that I was not the only one who thought it was a good idea.

I bought the business in August 1997. I talked to my contractor friend, Scott Gardner, about starting the College Street addition. He said, "Don't you want to wait and see how it's going to go?" I said, "No. I know how it's going to go. We have to get this addition built as soon as possible." It was finished the first week in December 1997 and sales increased 40 percent over the next twelve months, far exceeding my expectations.

The key to any successful business, and restaurants in particular, is to have the right people in the right positions and to be able to incentivize them properly so that they do their best work. Then the guests, I do

My most successful restaurant, Leunig's Bistro on the corner of Church and College Street in downtown Burlington. It's perhaps the best restaurant location in the state.

not like to call them customers, have a good experience and hopefully tell all their friends how wonderful the dining experience at Leunig's or Pauline's is, and how they plan to return soon. It's a classic win-win situation.

Occasionally, I would stand by the door with the host as people were leaving. I would ask them how everything was. If they said everything was great, I would say, please tell all your friends. This always made them laugh but planted the seed. It's called asking for a referral, a very important aspect of getting the positive word out. Conventional wisdom says if people have a good experience they tell two people about it. If they have a bad experience they will tell ten people. So, the idea is to get more of your satisfied customers spreading the good word.

I believe one of my most valuable management tools was a weekly management meeting. At Leunig's, this was every Thursday afternoon from 2:30 to 3:30. There were six of us who met every week. I had a young bar manager named Seth who worked at Leunig's for a year or two and then moved to Connecticut for a corporate job. Sometime later he sent me a postcard telling me that he used to think those management meetings at Leunig's were a colossal waste of his time. But now, he was working in a large organization where very little of that kind of interdepartmental communication was taking place, resulting in a lot of incomplete communication and confusion. He was now quite appreciative of the management meetings he had attended at Leunig's, confirming for me that I was on the right track.

I'm fond of saying, buying Leunig's Bistro has paid for all my sins. As a business, it has been successful on my wildest expectations. Over the sixteen years I owned and operated the business, the sales increased 500 percent—you can't ask for more than that.

49

Cubbers, Snap's, Bristol Bakery, and The Bobcat Café and Brewery

In 1998, Drew Smith and I became partners in the local pizza shop in Bristol called Cubbers, which is very popular to this day with families and local students. One day in 2001, the two of us were standing in the front window of Cubbers looking out at the street and he commented, "There's nowhere in town where a friend and I can go for a burger and a beer," i.e., a medium-priced adult restaurant. I chewed on that thought for a while and then later in 2001, the building right across the street at 5 Main Street was put up for sale.

I got very excited about building a medium-priced adult restaurant in that location. Again, it's very easy for me to get excited about ideas like this. I wanted to make sure it was a good idea. I wanted to know if there would be buy-in from the community. I literally picked numbers out of the air. I said to myself, I want at least twelve people to loan me $5,000 each, not as an equity stake in the business but just as a personal loan to prove to me that I wasn't the only person who thought this was a good idea. I figured if I couldn't convince twelve people to make me a small loan maybe it wasn't a good idea. I wrote up a hit list of people I knew and started making calls.

Initially, the response was very lukewarm. So, I made up a small package that I would call a business plan that consisted of four pages of not-very-detailed information. When I started calling people a second time, I got more enthusiasm. One by one people started to commit. Then something very unusual happened. People I didn't know started calling me up saying, "I heard you're doing this thing on Main Street, I want to know about it, send me the packet." In a month or so, I had thirty-two commitments, a total of $160,000 of unsecured money guaranteed by nothing but my good name and my signature. Wow, I was not the only person who thought this was a good idea, so I went to work.

Another interesting thing about this style of raising money was that most of these checks came from couples, which meant that there were about sixty people in the community who could serve as my marketing group. And that they did. They told their friends about it, and the place was completely packed from day one.

I bought the building with another partner and I built The Bobcat Café and Brewery with the help of Gary Rutherford, Ted Inghram, and others. We opened on April 3, 2002. It has a beautiful twenty-one-foot-long, nine-foot-high 100-year-old bar that was originally built in Albany, New York by Leo Spalt and company. It's one of the most beautiful antique bars anywhere. It was found for me

THIS RESTAURANT I BUILT FROM SCRATCH—THE BOBCAT CAFÉ AT 5 MAIN STREET IN BRISTOL, VERMONT. IT'S A WONDERFUL NEIGHBORHOOD GATHERING SPOT WITH ONE OF THE MOST BEAUTIFUL 100-YEAR-OLD BARS ANYWHERE.

by Mark Lavoie, a local musician who told me about it.

Along the way, I also became a partner in the Bristol Bakery with Kevin Harper for a period of time. And then I became a partner with Sheri Rockwood in Snap's Restaurant. Eventually, I sold my interests in all these restaurants and they continue operating successfully, which of course pleases me.

The town of Bristol, population of about 4,000, is unique in many ways as small towns in Vermont go. It's built on an old alluvial plain nestled up against the western slope of the Green Mountains. It has a nice flat grid of streets full of neighborhoods where adults and children can walk or ride bicycles to friends' homes and to school. It has the high school and the elementary school in the same town. It has a large multi-use town green adjacent to the beautiful clock tower on Holly Hall adjacent to Main Street, with one concentrated, well-defined block of two-story buildings. I like to think of the Bobcat as part of this idyllic small-town picture. The Bobcat continues to be very successful. It is a wonderful gathering place, a "third place," distinct from home and work where people gather to stay connected to the community.

Honestly, I'm quite proud of it because I think it, along with the other businesses in this concentrated little village, makes Bristol a great place to live, work, and play. The Bobcat is one of the major threads in the tapestry of Bristol that make it one of the best small towns in Vermont.

50

Retirement

*"Let us live our own brief lives mining that
which joy alone can give."*

—Friedrich Schiller

In May of 2013, I sold Leunig's Bistro to the manager, Bob Conlon, and the chef Donnell Collins. This marked my official retirement from the restaurant business. I was sixty-eight years old and ready to move on to the next phase of my felicity.

Alison and I decided to celebrate my retirement by going to France. We had been to Paris before and we wanted to see some new places, so we had lunch with Karen Kane who runs a travel consulting company called Paris by Design. We told her we had seen lots of the major sites in Paris and we wanted to see some of the less explored or new to us areas. She made us a beautiful itinerary of several different neighborhoods that we had not been to before.

One of my favorites was a Saturday afternoon when she directed us to Marche Aligre, a large flea market square in the twelfth arrondissement of Paris. An area that according to Karen is not visited by many English

In 2013 I sold my last restaurant, and we had a wonderful
European holiday, including dancing on the edge of the
Seine River in Paris with Notre Dame in the background.

speakers. Karen told us, "This is as French as Paris gets." And, coincidentally, her favorite cheese shop in all of Paris is just off the square. It's one
of those cheese stores that when you walk in your senses are immediately
and completely flooded with the powerful olfactory sensation of cheese,
like you're inside a big wheel of the most wonderful cheese ever.

Thanks to Karen Kane we went to the Canal Saint-Martin, walked
over some of the arched walkways, and watched canal boats go through
locks. We had lunch at the charming Chez Prune next to the canal. We
just loved it, we loved it all.

After a week in Paris, we went to the Loire River Valley and did a
weeklong bicycle adventure following the river. Day after wonderful day.

We are in the habit of buying small mascots and traveling with them
on our adventures. We have Bob the Bobcat. We also have a Buffalo
named Bill. We have an all-white Fluffy of Tintin fame. And on this trip,
our mascot was the little French cartoon character, Oui Oui (Yes, Yes),

fun, fun, fun. French children know this character well and every time they spotted him in our bike bag they would smile and say "Oui Oui!"

We traveled to Brussels, Belgium, the mecca for beer drinkers. We visited two friends of ours from a previous bike trip in Southeast Asia. We visited a beer guild hall and looked in a store in Brussels that stocked 1,050 different kinds of Belgian beer—very impressive. I developed a taste for sour lambic beers while in Belgium. These unique beers are fermented in open vats that rely on whatever wild yeast and bacteria are in the air at the time. In my mind, this is how beer was made before brewers knew what made beer *beer*. Cantillon, a wonderful 100 percent lambic sour beer is sometimes available in the US.

We went to visit the beautiful cathedral in Ghent, then to the canal city of Bruges, and out to Wenduine for a look at the North Sea. In Bruges, we took a canal boat tour and climbed up into the beautiful clock tower to get a close-up look at the clockworks and bell-ringing machinery that looked like a giant music box mechanism—fascinating.

We rode bicycles along the canal into the Netherlands and had lunch inside a giant windmill. The wooden gears and works inside this windmill were truly impressive.

Our traveling adventures continue to this day. So much to see, so much to learn.

So, there you have it, my life in a nutshell. When Winston Churchill was quite old, he was invited back to his prep school, Harrow, to give a lecture. (Of special interest to me is the fact that Winston Churchill maintained a poor academic record throughout his schooling. Even so, in 1953 he was awarded a Nobel Prize in Literature.) After getting to the lectern, he stood there for quite a while, so long people began to wonder if he was going to say anything at all. Finally, he said, "Never give in, never give in, never, never, never."

After starting, from what I consider to be humble beginnings, struggling with my early education, and experiencing several failures along the way, despite myself, or in spite of myself, I have been able to create a very enjoyable life for myself, my personal felicity. Obviously, I don't expect to be winning a Nobel Prize, or any other kind of special notoriety. But I do believe that as Winston said, if you do not give in, and you keep trying, your chances for success, however, you might define success, increases greatly.

My message is simple: If I can do it, anybody can do it. I'm really serious about that.

When I graduated from high school, my class rank was 107 out of 210 students. It doesn't get any more average than that. I'm a very average guy. The only thing that really saved me was my willingness to work. It has been said that 80 percent of success is just showing up. I learned to set achievable goals for myself and then found out that achieving those goals wasn't really so difficult. Once one goal is achieved, you look around and decide what is the next goal and then you head off in that direction.

Yes, I had failures but I prefer to call them "learners." I like to say I had winners and learners. My learners—i.e. failures—gave me some of the most valuable information that I was able to apply to my eventual successes. I do not think I'm happy because I'm successful. I think I've been successful because I have been happy.

A quote from Joseph Conrad, "All one's work might have been better done; but this is a sort of reflection a worker must put aside courageously if he doesn't mean every one of his conceptions to remain forever a private vision, an evanescent reverie."

Oh, of course, my decision to marry Alison Parker thirty years ago has been the number one contributor to my incredible felicity. The more consciously and thoughtfully I behave, the happier my life becomes.

I'm happy with my life, I'm happy with the people I have surrounded myself with. I believe the good people who worked with me in my businesses were generally happier and felt better about the work they were doing because they knew I was pleased with their commitment to our shared success. They did their best work and our guests benefited by having a heightened dining experience, which naturally leads to more rewards in the future. The classic win-win. That is why all my businesses continued to grow and prosper every year I owned them. I was pleased to be able to share the benefits with my workmates. If the guests are happy, and the staff is happy, it is easy for me to be happy also.

I'm happy with my place in the world and I'm completely comfortable in my own mind and body. As far as I know, it doesn't get any better than that. So, my job is to be grateful, to be thankful, and to enjoy the ride.

I would like to refer you to a book by Rolf Dobelli called, *The Art of the Good Life*. This book provides very helpful outlines for deciding how to make decisions that will improve the quality of your life, what I would call conscious living versus unconscious living. I moved to Middlebury, Vermont, in 1976 specifically to settle down and create a good life for myself. I had traveled around the country some and I had a good idea of where I wanted to live, where I would be able to pursue all manner of interesting activities that would add to the quality of my life. So far so good.

I would also like to refer you to some of my favorite quotations:

"My predominant feeling is one of gratitude. I have loved and I have been loved; I have been given much, and I have given something in return... Above all, I have been a sentient being, a thinking animal, on this beautiful planet, and that in itself has been an enormous privilege and adventure." —**Oliver Sacks**

Some quotes from **Winston Churchill**:

"Some see private enterprise as a predatory target to be shot, others as a cow to be milked, but few are those who see it as a sturdy horse pulling the wagon."

"Success is the ability to go from failure to failure without losing enthusiasm."

"Every day you make progress. Every step may be fruitful. Yet there will stretch out before you an ever-lengthening, ever-ascending, ever-improving path. You know you will never get to the end of the journey. But this, so far from discouraging, only adds to the joy and glory of the climb."

"A pessimist sees the difficulty in every opportunity, an optimist sees the opportunity in every difficulty."

My message is simple: If I can find Felicity, you can too.

Acknowledgements

First and foremost, my wonderful wife, Alison Parker, for her unwavering support. Luella Bryant, my friend and well-established writer, and a former professor of writing. Bill Schubart, a truly extraordinary local writer and successful entrepreneur. Jay Perini for recommending me to Claudia Cooper, a former Middlebury College professor who really helped me get this project rolling. John Elder, also a retired Middlebury College professor and longtime friend. Ruth Farmer, a local writer who helped me get started. And another memoir writer here in Lincoln, Jackie Tuxill, gave me lots of encouragement. Special thanks to my wonderful Canadian friend, Christopher Neil, for helping me so much with editing an early draft of my manuscript. Thank you all for your support and encouragement. I couldn't have done it without you.

About the Author

A graduate of the Culinary Institute of America who enjoyed a 40-year odyssey as a restauranteur, Robert Fuller grew up in rural New England where some farmers still used horses and their own hands to do the work. His grandfather, a fourth-generation dairy man, milked his cows and drove around in a covered delivery wagon, ladling milk into his customers' containers. With the oscillating sound of a horse-drawn sickle bar cutter deep in the folds of his mind, he tells the story of how he overcame early failures to create a happy life for himself—his felicity.

**For more about Robert or to contact him, visit
RobertFullerAuthor.com**